G000320371

Stéphane Reynaud's

365

good reasons
to sit down
to eat

For *mes p'tits* and for Isa who I love,
We'll eat four times a day this year to forget all of the meals we haven't eaten together.

A big thank you to Marie-Pierre, we'll do 600 next time, pure pleasure!
'A photo without Marie-Pierre is like a *choucroute* without beer, there's still the sausages but it doesn't last!'

A big thank you to José ... and to Nino, we're coming to drag you away from your drawing board!
'An illustration without Jojo is like a third Thursday in November without *bojo*, no use at all!'

A big thank you to Jacky, always there for precious advice, you're too good!
'A book without Jacky is like a meal without friends, not possible!'

A big thank you to Rose, maximum respect!
A big thank you to Emmanuel, I came especially from Montreuil to see you and finish my book!
A big thank you to Flo, mauururu roa hoa!
A big thank you to Aurélie, the Unknown Woman of email!
A big thank you to Élodie, I really like these knives, this *cocotte* is superb ... Ah, you think we have to give them back?

Thanks to all those who, like me, love to live, life is good!
Thanks to all those who, like me, love to laugh, laughing is good!
Thanks to all those who, like me, love brie, brie is good!

Stéphane

Stéphane Reynaud's

365

good reasons
to sit down
to eat

Photographs by Marie-Pierre Morel
Illustrated by José Reis de Matos

MURDOCH BOOKS

Stéphane Reynaud's

365

good reasons to sit down to eat

We're hungry, what are we eating? What is there to eat?

Ah yes, these are the little phrases which everyday life is made of, ringing out from morning time over the buttered toast and returning constantly like a well-oiled refrain. The brain-teaser of mealtime, the riddle of dinner, the terror of the blank saucepan, the solitary struggle with the lunchbox, all that is in the past. It's high time we got in tune with Mother Nature to finally resolve these questions angst-free.

This year, the market is your gift; produce comes, then goes.

Oysters play hide and seek with the tides, old-fashioned vegetables take a dip in simmering stewing pots. It's time for *pot-au-feus* that warm the insides and redden the outsides – « boiled meats and vegetables, it should be reimbursed by *la Sécurité Sociale* ». Messages are written on the steamed-up kitchen windows, it's night-time. The pig has given the best of itself: it is savoured and there'll be a few weeks' wait while the sausages are made. The snow shows its face, the cheeses melt, the wine is warmed; it's the Chinese New Year with its colours and aromas, cooking comes from everywhere. We'll love each other on 14th February, « *on a star or on a pillow, we'll love each other till we scorch our skin …* » but I digress, let's get back to our saucepans …

And then spring returns, the leaves wake up, everything turns green, the baby vegetables thumb their noses at winter curves, we eat healthy, summer's coming.

The asparagus stands erect like an army at attention, the cattle hear the Easter bells chime, they toll for them. The strawberries look cheery, their perfume inundates the end of the meal, the windows are open. It's sunny, everything's growing as if on seasonal steroids, it's a time of abundance, *youpi*! Tables go outside, the first barbecue coals are lit, the sardines are as rigid as an overconfident magistrate, the mackerel don their striped suits again, shiny like a jar of hair cream, the kebab skewers are sharpened, the better to impale imprudent prawns. The coals become redder, the meat as well, skirts are shorter and shorter.

It's a time for big gatherings around the table, baptisms, communions, Nanna's birthday, one-dish meals, paella for a change, *olé*, the cherries join in. A pyramid of melons, like a giant's billiard game, lingers on the caravan table. The smell of sunscreen hovers in the air, the fish jump off the beach to invade the kitchen, they run into a horde of vegetables ready to melt at the sight of olive oil, the garlic is there, the thyme, the rosemary.

It's back-to-school time: you cut your hair, buy some trainers, a few mushrooms, pack the bag, the chestnuts emerge from their burrs, you sharpen your pencils, apples make a comeback, it's pie time, you catch up with your friends, it's card-swapping time. The pumpkin steps out, and for once we're proud of it: it's made into gratins, soups, it's all used up. The turtleneck comes back from the dry-cleaner's, it's time to stew and simmer, the kitchen windows steam up again, the cast-iron of the *cocottes* scrapes across the stovetop, the kitchen's in a sweat.

The lights in the streets have a festive air, glamour products gleam in the shop windows, the truffles rub shoulders with the lobsters, the scampi flirt with the foie gras, the scallops alongside stay quiet and it's just as well. Believe me, when they decide to open their big traps, the whole of Brittany bursts into song … They play hard-to-get by hiding in the sand, making them all the more desirable, and when they finally yield, you don't let go. The fir tree is dressed for winter. A classy tone prevails in the kitchen, the chef's hat is out, the chickens have blue feet … Champagne!

Stéphane

January

the greengrocer
Beetroot
Mâche
Jerusalem artichokes
Leeks
Swedes
Parsnips
Potatoes
Turnips
Celeriac
Cabbages: green, white
  and red
Orange and purple
  carrots
Radishes
Witlof
Oranges
Pineapples

the fishmonger
Line-caught bass
Oysters
Mussels
Cod

the butcher-deli
Sirloin
Beef short-ribs
Stewing beef
Oxtail
Marrow bones
Roasting veal
Roasting pork
Bresse hen
Ham on the bone
Prosciutto
Speck
Duck breast
Spicy chorizo

the cheese-seller
Comté
Aged Beaufort
Roquefort

the grocer
Bottarga
Foie gras

February

the greengrocer
Jerusalem artichokes
Purple potatoes
Leeks
Swedes
Parsnips
Potatoes
Celeriacs
Chinese cabbages
Orange and purple
  carrots
Oranges
Pineapples
Bananas
Fresh ginger

the fishmonger
Clams
Scallops
Lobsters

the butcher-deli
Beef steak
Roasting beef

Pork belly
Pork tenderloin
Lamb shoulder
Air-dried duck breast
Prosciutto
Speck
Diot sausages
Toulouse sausages
Pork spare-ribs, brined
Pork neck-blade, brined
Morteau sausages

the cheese-seller
Comté
Raw-milk raclette
Tomme de Savoie
Reblochon fermier
Beaufort
Emmental
Cancoillotte

the grocer
Buckwheat pasta

March

the greengrocer
Green cabbages
Potatoes
Snow peas
Green beans
Peas
Broad beans
Baby turnips
Radishes
Savoy cabbages
Mushrooms
Dutch carrots

the fishmonger
Pike
Monkfish
Cuttlefish
Mussels
Razor clams
Wild brown trout

the butcher-deli
Lamb leg
Lamb shoulder
Roasting beef
Calf liver
Free-range chicken
Veal
Andouillettes
Calves' feet
Prosciutto
Speck
Chorizo
Air-dried duck breast

the cheese-seller
Sainte-Maure
Goat's cheese

the grocer
Puy lentils
Cannelloni
Flageolet beans
Tinned snails

008 054 100

280 326 370

July

the greengrocer
Eggplants
Zucchini
Tomatoes of all colours
Cucumbers
Capsicums
Celery
Fennel
Bulb spring onions
Spinach
Chives
Lettuce
Herbs and spices
Rocket leaves
Apricots
Peaches
Nectarines
Apples

the fishmonger
Zander
Sea bass
Whiting
Cod
Rock fish
Mullet

Velvet crab
Bream
Cuttlefish
Octopus
Small prawns

the butcher-deli
Duck breast
Pork tenderloins
Chicken
Pancetta

the cheese-seller
Buffalo mozzarella
Ricotta
Goat's cheese
Parmesan cheese

the grocer
Lasagne sheets

August

the greengrocer
Eggplants
Zucchini
Green beans
Radishes
Tomatoes and cucumbers
Cauliflower
Celery
Asparagus
Broad beans
Fennel
Rocket leaves
Beetroot leaves
Herbs and spices
Apricots
Purple figs
Redcurrants

the fishmonger
Bream and small sole
Prawns
Cod
Razor clams and octopus
Cockles and mussels
Dog cockles and clams
Cooked whelks

Spider crabs and edible
  crabs
Sardines in oil
Anchovies in oil

the butcher-deli
Roasting beef
Lamb leg
Morteau sausages
Cooked roast veal
Beef paleron
Pancetta
Duckling

the cheese-seller
Parmesan cheese
Mozzarella cheese

the grocer
Lasagne sheets

September

the greengrocer
Capsicums
Zucchini
Eggplants
Celery
Red onions
Potatoes
Green beans
Tomatoes
Corn
Lettuces
Baby spinach leaves
Herbs and spices
Chanterelle mushrooms
Cep mushrooms
Oyster mushrooms
Purple figs
Green figs
Conference pears

the fishmonger
School prawns
Salt cod
Bream

the butcher-deli
Chicken
Hamburger steaks
Veal escalope
Duck breast
Speck
Ham on the bone
Prosciutto

the cheese-seller
Comté cheese
Raclette cheese

the grocer
Short-grain rice
Lasagne sheets
Sweetened chestnut
  purée
Chestnuts

April

the greengrocer
Frisée lettuce
Tomatoes
Eggplants
Fennel
Celery
Snow peas
Green beans
Bulb spring onions
Peas
Green and white
   asparagus
Broad beans
Carrots
Baby spinach leaves
Radishes
Raspberries
Strawberries

the fishmonger
Salmon
Smoked haddock
Red mullet
Mussels

Prawns
Pike

the butcher-deli
Lamb leg
Lamb shoulder
Free-range chicken
Veal rump
Veal sweetbreads
Rack of veal
Prosciutto
Speck

the cheese-seller
Goat's cheese

the grocer
Polenta
Arborio rice
Confit gizzards

May

the greengrocer
Red and green
   capsicums
Purple artichokes
Tomatoes
Bulb spring onions
Peas, broad peas
and snow peas
Baby turnips
Green asparagus
Baby spinach and rocket
Fennel
Cucumbers
Raspberries
Strawberries
Rockmelon
Rhubarb

the fishmonger
Mussels
Prawns and scampi
Squid and cuttlefish
Clams and razor clams
Whiting

Pollock
John dory
Salmon

the butcher-deli
Rib steak
Rack and saddle
of lamb
Rabbit
Calves' feet
Veal breast
Duck breast
Roasting veal
Spicy chorizo

the cheese-seller
Pecorino cheese
Parmesan cheese
Mascarpone
Saint-Marcellin

the grocer
Camargue black rice
Haricot beans

June

the greengrocer
Zucchini
Red, green and yellow
   capsicums
Bulb spring onions
Tomatoes
Cucumbers
Eggplants
Broad beans
Snow peas
Peas
Green beans
Green asparagus
Rocket leaves
Mung bean shoots
Alfalfa sprouts
Herbs and spices
Cherries
Rhubarb
Strawberries
Raspberries
Bilberries or blueberries

the fishmonger
Mackerel and sardines
Smoked salmon
Tuna
Anchovy fillets
Small squid and
   cuttlefish
Rascasse

the butcher-deli
Beef steak
Veal escalope
Chicken
Rabbit
Duck
Minced beef
Bacon lardons
Pork neck
Pork spare-ribs
Lamb leg

the grocer
Arborio rice
Semolina

146

190

236

414

460

504

the greengrocer
Pumpkins
Carrots
Celery
Leeks
Onions
Cep mushrooms
Mushrooms
Herbs and spices
Reinette apples
Dried fruit and nuts
Bananas
Dried figs

the fishmonger
Cockles
Albacore tuna loin
Bream

the butcher-deli
Boar
Venison
Pheasant
Chicken
Lamb shoulder
Stewing beef

Beef cheeks
Shin of veal
Smoked pork shoulder
Rack of pork
Veal roast
Fattened duck
Spicy chorizo
Smoked pork belly
Air-dried duck breast

the cheese-seller
Parmesan cheese

the grocer
Snails
Arborio rice
Tomato paste
Sweetened chestnut
   purée

the greengrocer
Hokkaido pumpkins
Beetroot
Cauliflower
Potatoes
Apples
Tomatoes
Celery
Dill
Carrots
Mushrooms
Turnips
Fennel

the fishmonger
Skate
Salmon
Small cuttlefish

the butcher-deli
Chicken
Veal kidneys
Veal head
Roasting beef
Pork chops
Roasting pork

Guinea fowl
Pigeon
Boudin noir
Pork spare-ribs
Pork knuckle
Toulouse sausages
Morteau sausages
Duck confit
Minced beef
Lamb knuckle
Prosciutto
Beef blanket tripe
Lamb neck

the cheese-seller
Comté cheese

the grocer
Juniper berries
Puy lentils
Tarbais beans

the greengrocer
Fennel
Carrots
Leeks
Potatoes
Truffles
Apples
Celery
Green mangoes
Mung bean shoots
Oranges
Grapefruit

the fishmonger
Bass
Lobster
Scampi
Scallops
John dory
Rascasse
Sea urchins
Conger eel
Rock fish
Weevers

the butcher-deli
Chicken
Foie gras
Chicken breast fillets
Rump beef steak
Hanger steak
Boudin blanc
Duck fat
Toulouse sausages
Speck

the cheese-seller
Parmesan cheese

the grocer
Spelt
Dried kidney beans
Chestnut honey
Cinnamon

October

November

December

January

the greengrocer

BEETROOT (BEETS)

MÂCHE (LAMB'S LETTUCE)

JERUSALEM ARTICHOKES

LEEKS

SWEDES (RUTABAGA)

PARSNIPS

POTATOES

TURNIPS

CELERIAC

CABBAGES: GREEN, WHITE AND RED

ORANGE AND PURPLE CARROTS

RADISHES

WITLOF (CHICORY/BELGIAN ENDIVE)

ORANGES

PINEAPPLES

the fishmonger

LINE-CAUGHT BASS

OYSTERS

MUSSELS

COD

the butcher-deli

SIRLOIN

BEEF SHORT-RIBS

STEWING BEEF

OXTAIL

MARROW BONES

ROASTING VEAL

ROASTING PORK

BRESSE HEN

HAM ON THE BONE

PROSCIUTTO

SPECK

DUCK BREAST

SPICY CHORIZO

the cheese-seller

COMTÉ

AGED BEAUFORT

ROQUEFORT

the grocer

BOTTARGA (CURED FISH ROE)

FOIE GRAS

01 New Year's Day	02 Basil	03 Geneviève
DETOX SOUP	CABBAGE-SOY SALAD	CARROT AND ORANGE PURÉE
08 Lucien	09 Alix	10 Guillaume
FRENCH EPIPHANY PASTRY	FRIED EGGS WITH BACON	WITLOF WITH BLACK OLIVES
15 Rémi	16 Marcel	17 Roseline
CABBAGE SOUP	LEEKS WITH A HERB VINAIGRETTE	LEMON CELERIAC MASH
22 Vincent	23 Bernard	24 François
CLASSIC POT-AU-FEU	JERUSALEM ARTICHOKE AND FOIE GRAS	HOT-POT OF OLD-FASHIONED VEGETABLES
29 Gildas	30 Martine	31 Marcelle
SALAD OF MÂCHE, BEETROOT AND APPLE	BEETROOT CARPACCIO	ROAST PINEAPPLE WITH HONEY

04
Odilon

POACHED HEN WITH VEGETABLES

05
Édouard

SEA BASS WITH PARSNIPS

06
Mélaine

OYSTERS WITH RICE VINEGAR

07
Raymond

PINEAPPLE CARPACCIO

11
Hortense

MAXI RUM BABA

12
Tatiana

PARSNIPS WITH CHORIZO

13
Yvette

CABBAGE STUFFED WITH PORK

14
Nina

MUSSELS IN WHITE WINE

18
Prisca

OYSTERS WITH BROWN BUTTER

19
Marius

WITLOF WITH HAM

20
Sébastien

WITLOF WITH ROQUEFORT AND WALNUTS

21
Agnès

ARDÈCHE POTATO CAKE

25
Paul

COD WITH WITLOF

26
Paule

SIRLOIN WITH ROOT VEGETABLES

27
Angèle

POT ROAST VEAL

28
Thomas

CHOCOLATE FONDANT CAKE

01 02 03 04

MARIE & LÉON

New Year's Day and pommes sautées

difficult awakening this 1st January in the Vachecrot household; the evening of 31st having kept its promises. Léon wakes up painfully, with no idea of time or place. He barely recognises the worn old lounge opposite the TV, which, this morning, serves as his bed. A nice cosy blanket has nevertheless saved him from an almost certain bout of flu, a generous gesture of his dear wife Marie. In short, his snores have disturbed nobody but the population of his dreams, his breath, fit to unblock the stuffiest nose, has spared woman and child. Léon has overindulged — what to do?

The first solution consists of doing as little as possible, avoiding any movement that could set off a certain headache and closing the shutters in order to forget that you're lolling in bed like an old sea cow worn out by a winter swell. Turn off your mobile phone, the best wishes for the new year can wait a few hours (above all, you'll avoid the smart comments of your companions from the night before, who are only too happy to remind you about your midnight strip-tease!). Best to empty a full glass of aspirin and begin the new year on 2nd January. An easy way out that will pave the way for some ... how shall we put this ... mild familial tension ... « *Marie, stop sulking!* »

The second solution consists in violently confronting reality. Darling son Kevin will be delighted to serve as a reminder, with his cheerful morning mood, that all excess is automatically punishable by a painful aftermath. Head and stomach sing in unison, « *I'm sick, completely sick ...* » It is therefore time for action. Shower: hot, cold — you turn the taps, you scald yourself, you freeze, you clean, you scour, you try to put on a good show. Detox breakfast to restore the intestinal flora, and *voilà*, as if by magic, you come back to life. The indigestible vapours of the night before disappear and there you are ready for lunch *chez* Aunty Marinette's. Tougher sorts will opt for the *Cyclotouriste* cocktail of the 1960s: a lukewarm beer, a sugar and off you go again ... P.S. Don't turn your mobile phone back on, Léon, your kind-hearted friends have already tried to call you for ... you know what!

01 jan

Detox soup

Serves 6

JOGGING TIME 30 MINUTES
PREPARATION TIME 15 MINUTES
COOKING TIME 45 MINUTES

2 aspirin
1 jog
4 onions
3 leeks, white part only
1 bunch of celery*
3 tablespoons olive oil
salt and pepper
snipped chives

At 1 pm, you're finding it hard to wake up, your eyes are puffed up like helium balloons, your mouth is as fresh as a sewerage outlet on a night of heavy rain, your head is ringing like a Tibetan gong and your feet are still majestically enrobed in your socks. The 31st got the better of you, it's up to you to get the better of the 1st. Two aspirins taken on the go, mouth hosed down Kärcher-style, followed up with a jog and a good sweat. Back at the house: you peel and finely slice the onions, slice the leeks and celery, you gently sauté everything in olive oil, then you add 1.5 litres (52 fl oz) water, cook for 45 minutes, season, top with the chives. A good shower in the meantime, and a day to clean yourself out with soup and raw celery.

✱ SERVING SUGGESTION: *Set aside a little raw celery, it's good to chew after all!*

02
january

CABBAGE-SOY SALAD

02 jan

Cabbage-soy salad*

Serves 6

PREPARATION TIME 15 MINUTES

½ white cabbage
½ red cabbage
1 French shallot (eschalot)
100 ml (3½ fl oz) olive oil
2 tablespoons soy sauce
1 tablespoon tomato paste (concentrated purée)
1 tablespoon tomato sauce (ketchup)
1 bunch of tarragon
salt and pepper

Finely shred the cabbages. Peel and finely chop the shallot. Combine the olive oil with the soy sauce, tomato paste and tomato sauce. Strip the leaves from the tarragon and mix everything together, season.

✱HOW CAN I RUIN THIS RECIPE? *To ruin this recipe, I can only imagine cutting the cabbage into very thick strips and leaving the French shallot whole.*

03 jan

Carrot and orange purée

Serves 6

PREPARATION TIME 15 MINUTES
COOKING TIME 30 MINUTES

*800 g (1 lb 12 oz) carrots**
2 oranges
125 g (4½ oz) butter
fleur de sel and pepper

Peel the carrots and slice them into rounds. Zest and juice the oranges. Boil the carrots with the zest for 30 minutes, then drain. Add the butter and juice, purée everything together and season.

✱VARIATION: *Carrots are friends of cumin and star anise, so you could easily add one or both of these.*

04 jan

Poached hen with vegetables

Serves 6

PREPARATION TIME 20 MINUTES
COOKING TIME 1 HOUR

3 carrots
3 purple carrots
3 parsnips
3 leeks
6 turnips
1 onion studded with 3 cloves
*1 boiling hen (Bresse is the best!)**
1 celery stalk
1 bouquet garni
fleur de sel and pepper

Peel all of the vegetables. Stuff the hen with the celery stalk. Place the hen in a large flameproof casserole dish, surround it with vegetables and add the bouquet garni. Cover completely with water and simmer very gently for 1 hour, uncovered. Season with the *fleur de sel* and pepper. Serve with cornichons and strong mustard. The broth should be served in small glasses on the side.

✱WHAT MAKES A BRESSE HEN SPECIAL? *The poule de Bresse is one classy bird, the sort that makes eyes at you, its legs, a lovely light blue, freshly plucked, its well-presented crest a bold red. Fussed over like diamonds, it comes adorned with jewellery: a ring bearing the name of its protector ... oops, producer, a tricolour seal for vanity's sake, an identifying seal around the neck, it has to be just right.*

05
january

SEA BASS WITH PARSNIPS

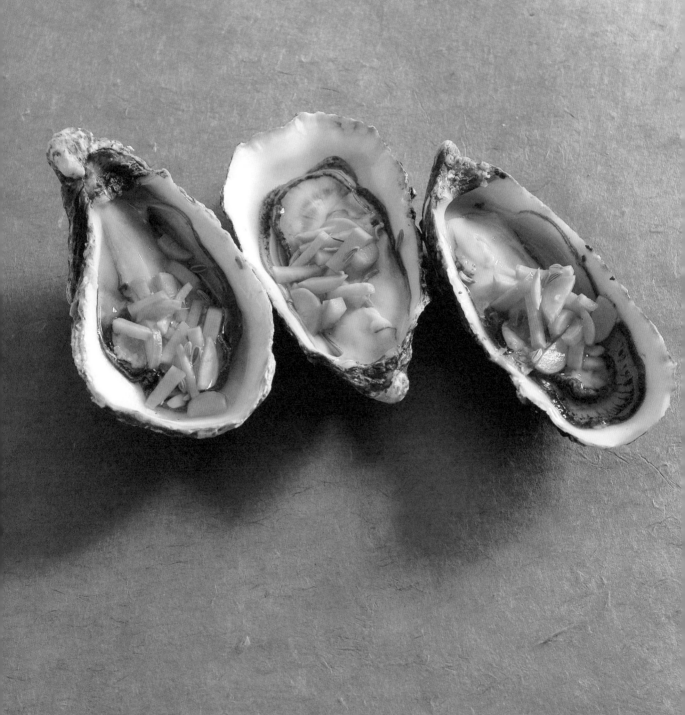

05 jan

Sea bass with parsnips

Serves 6

PREPARATION TIME 15 MINUTES
COOKING TIME 30 MINUTES

6 thick fillets of line-caught sea bass* or other
  firm-fleshed white fish
1 lemon
½ bunch of flat-leaf (Italian) parsley
1 French shallot (eschalot)
800 g (1 lb 12 oz) parsnips
2 onions
200 ml (7 fl oz) pouring (whipping) cream
1 dash ground nutmeg
salt and pepper
olive oil

*WHY LINE-CAUGHT BASS? *It is important to use line-caught bass, as it has a subtle taste and firm texture, rather than farmed bass that has a blander taste and softer texture.*

**WHAT'S GREMOLATA? *Originally from Italy, gremolata is a mixture of parsley, garlic and citrus zest that is used as a seasoning on dishes such as osso buco. The basic recipe can be varied by adding parmesan cheese, shallot instead of garlic, pine nuts ...*

***How DO YOU KNOW WHEN IT'S COOKED PROPERLY? *The fish is cooked when the fillets just start to come apart.*

Using a (clean!) pair of tweezers, remove the bones from the bass. Zest and juice the lemon. Chop the flat-leaf parsley, peel and slice the shallot, combine with the lemon zest to make a gremolata**. Peel and slice the parsnips and onions and cook together in a saucepan filled with water for 30 minutes with the lemon juice. Drain, add the cream and the nutmeg, purée and season. Pan-fry the bass in olive oil (cooking time will depend on the thickness of the fish***). Serve it all with the parsnip purée and scatter over the gremolata.

06 jan

Oysters with rice vinegar

Serves 6

PREPARATION TIME 30 MINUTES

1 bunch of radishes
50 ml (1½ fl oz) sake
200 ml (7 fl oz) rice vinegar
1 squeeze of wasabi from a tube
36 pousse-en-claire or Sydney rock oysters

For this recipe, it's always important to have a few extra oysters, a drop of chilled white and a comrade to lead the charge with. Scrape the radishes and cut into thin sticks. Heat the sake and flambé it*, combine with the rice vinegar. Add the radish sticks and wasabi. Start opening the oysters, empty the liquid from the first two, eat the third one, have a break for refreshments (accidents happen so quickly), repeat until you've gone through the whole stock (I mean the oysters, not the wine!). Serve the oysters with a spoonful of the rice vinegar with radishes.

*WHY FLAMBÉ THE SAKE? *You want the taste of the sake without the alcohol!*

07 jan

Pineapple carpaccio

Serves 6

PREPARATION TIME 15 MINUTES

1 pineapple
100 ml (3½ fl oz) white rum
50 g (1¾ oz/¼ cup) sugar
1 vanilla bean
1 lime

*How DO YOU PEEL THE PINEAPPLE EASILY AND REMOVE THE EYES? *Use a bread-knife to remove the skin, then the point of a vegetable peeler to remove the eyes.*

Using a serrated knife, peel the pineapple and remove the eyes*. Cut the pineapple into slices, as thin as possible. Combine the white rum and sugar in a saucepan, split the vanilla bean in two, scrape out the seeds and add them to the rum, heat and flambé. Zest and juice the lime, add them to the rum. Arrange the pineapple carpaccio on a plate. Pour over the rum with lime.

08 jan

French Epiphany pastry

Serves 6

PREPARATION TIME 35 MINUTES
CHILLING TIME 30 MINUTES
COOKING TIME 25 MINUTES

100 g (3½ oz/1 cup) ground almonds
100 g (3½ oz) sugar
100 g (3½ oz) butter, melted
2 eggs + 1 egg yolk, lightly beaten
bitter almond extract
2 sheets store-bought butter puff pastry, each cut into a round
1 tablespoon icing (confectioners') sugar
1 fève (lucky charm to hide in the cake)

Combine the ground almonds with the sugar, butter and 2 eggs. Add a few drops of bitter almond extract. Place the almond cream in the centre of one pastry round. Moisten the edges with the beaten egg yolk using a pastry brush. Cover with the second pastry round. Press the edge so that the two pieces of pastry are sealed together well. Make a rosette pattern using a knife, starting from the centre, and brush with the egg yolk. Chill for 30 minutes*. Preheat the oven to 180°C (350½F/Gas 4), bake for 20 minutes, take it out of the oven and sprinkle with icing sugar. Bake for a further 5 minutes. You've just realised that you forgot to put in the *fève*, no need to panic: in the third drawer down in the kitchen, at the back on the left-hand side, find the *fève* from 4 years ago, clean it well (frangipane tends to stick), put it carefully into the edge of the galette, the littlest one won't notice a thing!

✳ WHY CHILL IT BEFORE PUTTING IT INTO THE OVEN? *So that the pastry solidifies a little and the flaky layers rise well.*

09
january

FRIED EGGS WITH BACON

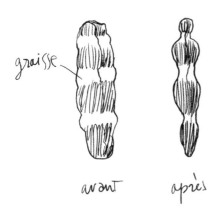

graisse

avant   après

09 jan
Fried eggs with bacon
Serves 6
PREPARATION TIME 10 MINUTES
COOKING TIME 10 MINUTES
200 g (7 oz) speck, cut into lardons
1 white onion
12 eggs
salt and pepper
a dash of wine vinegar

❋WHY BOIL
THE LARDONS?
*Boiling the pieces
of speck will remove
some of their fat,
making them more
digestible.*

Boil the *lardons* for 5 minutes and drain*. Peel and slice the onion. In a non-stick frying pan, sauté the *lardons* over a gentle heat with the sliced onion. Gently break the eggs into a bowl and slip them into the pan without adding any fat. Cook for 5 minutes. Season, then add a dash of wine vinegar.

10 jan
Witlof with black olives
Serves 6
PREPARATION TIME 20 MINUTES
6 good-looking witlofs (chicory/Belgian endives)
2 French shallots (eschalots)
1 bulb spring onion (scallion)
50 g (1¾ oz) pitted black olives
2 tablespoons crème fraîche
2 tablespoons olive oil
1 tablespoon balsamic vinegar
salt and pepper

❋WHY REMOVE
THE CORE? *The core
of the witlof is the
bitterest part, so it
needs to be removed,
especially for a salad.*

Cut the witlofs into quarters lengthways, remove the cores*. Slice the witlofs finely, again lengthways. Peel and slice the shallots, slice the spring onion, including its stem, and roughly chop the olives. Combine the crème fraîche with the olive oil and balsamic vinegar, season. Mix everything together, serve well chilled.

11 jan
Maxi rum baba
Serves 6
PREPARATION TIME 20 MINUTES
RISING TIME 2 HOURS
COOKING TIME 30 MINUTES
For the baba:
200 ml (7 fl oz) full-cream (whole) milk
25 g (1 oz) fresh yeast
8 eggs
25 g (1 oz) honey
250 g (9 oz/1⅔ cups) plain (all-purpose) flour
100 g (3½ oz) butter, melted
For the syrup:
200 ml (7 fl oz) rum
300 g (10½ oz/1⅓ cups) sugar
For the cream filling:
300 ml (10½ fl oz) pouring (whipping) cream
150 g (5½ oz) sugar
100 g (3½ oz/½ cup) glacé fruit, chopped
Equipment:
savarin (ring) mould or tin

For the baba, preheat the oven to 180°C (350°F/Gas 4). Heat the milk to lukewarm*, add the yeast. In a separate bowl, beat the eggs and honey with a fork, add the flour, butter and milk mixture and stir until smooth. Butter and flour the savarin mould. Pour the mixture into the mould, leave to rise for 2 hours at room temperature, covered. The mixture should double in size. Bake in the oven for 30 minutes. Remove the baba from the oven, turn it out from the mould and place it on a wire rack set over a mixing bowl.
Make a syrup by combining 200 ml (7 fl oz) water and the rum and sugar. Heat until the sugar dissolves completely. Pour over the baba. Recover the excess that falls into the bowl and repeat this process.
For the cream filling, whip the cream with the sugar into a chantilly. Place the baba on a plate, fill the middle with the chantilly and scatter over the glacé fruit.

❋WHY DOES THE
MILK NEED TO BE
LUKEWARM? *The
milk needs to be
lukewarm to allow
the yeast to grow.*

12
january

PARSNIPS WITH CHORIZO

13 jan — Cabbage stuffed with pork

Serves 6
PREPARATION TIME 20 MINUTES
COOKING TIME 30 MINUTES

1 savoy cabbage
3 French shallots (eschalots)
600 g (1 lb 5 oz) roast pork
4 eggs
½ teaspoon ground nutmeg
150 ml (5 fl oz) pouring (whipping) cream
salt and pepper
2 onions
250 g (9 oz) speck
250 ml (9 fl oz/1 cup) white wine

Preheat the oven to 160°C (315°F/Gas 2–3). Separate the leaves of the cabbage and select the 12 best ones. Remove the central rib from each. Bring some salted water to the boil, immerse the leaves for 7 minutes, then rinse them immediately in iced water. Peel the shallots and slice them. Process the roasted pork with the shallots, eggs, nutmeg and six of the cabbage leaves to create a homogenous mixture. Add the cream and season. Divide the mixture into six equal portions. Fill each remaining cabbage leaf with this mixture like a *pétanque* ball* and arrange them in a gratin dish. Peel and slice the onions, chop the speck into small strips, scatter the onions and speck around the stuffed cabbage leaves, pour over the wine. Cook in the oven for 20 minutes, basting the cabbage rolls regularly.

✳ HOW WILL THE CABBAGE LEAVES HOLD FIRM? *Roll the leaves nice and tightly around the stuffing so they hold firm during cooking.*

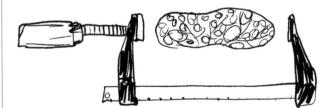

12 jan — Parsnips with chorizo

Serves 6
PREPARATION TIME 15 MINUTES
COOKING TIME 20 MINUTES

6 parsnips
200 g (7 oz) spicy chorizo
2 onions
100 ml (3½ fl oz) olive oil

Peel the parsnips, cut them into chips. Peel and slice the chorizo into chips. Peel and slice the onions. In a non-stick frying pan, gently sauté the parsnips with the onions in the olive oil over a gentle heat for 15 minutes. Add the chorizo and cook for a further 5 minutes. There's no need to season*.

✳ SEASONING NOT NEEDED? *The chorizo is already salty enough, so there's no need to add salt (plus it makes my cardiologist happy).*

14 jan — Mussels in white wine

Serves 6
PREPARATION TIME 10 MINUTES
COOKING TIME 10 MINUTES

3 French shallots (eschalots)
6 garlic cloves
1 bunch of flat-leaf (Italian) parsley
300 ml (10½ fl oz) white wine
100 g (3½ oz) butter, cubed
3 kg (6 lb 12 oz) mussels, cleaned

Peel and finely chop the shallots and garlic. Roughly chop the parsley. Pour the white wine into a large saucepan. Bring to the boil, add the shallots and garlic, and allow to reduce by half. Add the butter, then the mussels. Cook for 5–10 minutes, stirring gently. When all the mussels have opened*, add the parsley, then serve in the cooking pot.

✳ COOKING TIME FOR MUSSELS: *Once the mussels open, they are cooked. Discard any mussels that haven't opened.*

16 jan

Leeks with a herb vinaigrette

Serves 6

PREPARATION TIME 15 MINUTES
COOKING TIME 30 MINUTES

6 leeks
1 carrot
1 tablespoon semi-dried tomatoes in oil
1 bunch of flat-leaf (Italian) parsley, leaves picked
1 French shallot (eschalot)
100 ml (3½ fl oz) olive oil
fleur de sel and pepper
Equipment:
steamer

Trim the end and the green part of the le[...]
Next, cut each leek in half and clean u[...]
running water. Arrange in a steaming b[...]
and cook for 30 minutes. Peel and cho[...]
carrot into very small cubes, finely cho[...]
semi-dried tomatoes, parsley and sha[...]
Combine the chopped ingredients and [...]
over the olive oil. Serve the leeks lukew[...]
coated with the herb sauce, season with [...]
de sel and pepper.

✹Why not keep
the green part
of the leek? *The
green part is too
strong-tasting and
tough to be eaten in
a salad. It is used
in soups and in a
bouquet garni.*

15 jan

Cabbage soup

Serves 6

PREPARATION TIME 15 MINUTES
COOKING TIME 45 MINUTES

3 potatoes
1 savoy cabbage
1 end-piece of prosciutto* or
*   1 thick slice of cooked smoked bacon*
olive oil
150 g (5½ oz) lightly salted butter
salt and pepper

✹The end-piece
of prosciutto:
*A leftover piece of
prosciutto (from
either end) will give
a smoky and slightly
rancid note to the
soup (in France,
this is considered
a good thing!).*

Peel the potatoes, cut them into cubes.
Separate the leaves of the cabbage, set aside two
good green-coloured leaves and roughly chop
the rest. Place in a saucepan with the end-piece
of prosciutto and cover with water. Bring to
the boil and cook for 45 minutes. Slice the
two cabbage leaves that you set aside and sauté
them briefly in olive oil then set aside. Remove
the piece of prosciutto. Purée the soup with
the butter. Season. Serve with the sautéed
cabbage scattered over the soup.

17 jan

Lemon celeriac mash

Serves 6

PREPARATION TIME 20 MINUTES
COOKING TIME 30 MINUTES

800 g (1 lb 12 oz) celeriac
2 lemons
50 g (1¾ oz) fresh ginger
200 ml (7 fl oz) pouring (whipping) cream
salt and pepper

✹Why plunge
the celeriac
cubes into
iced water? *The
vegetable is plunged
into iced water so
that it doesn't oxidise.*

Peel the celeriac, cut it into large cubes[...]
plunge into iced water*. Peel and cho[...]
ginger. Zest and juice the lemons. Pu[...]
celeriac, ginger and lemon zest in a sauc[...]
cover with water. Bring to the boil and [...]
for 30 minutes. Drain the celeriac, le[...]
and ginger. Purée everything with the cr[...]
season and add the lemon juice.

MARIE & LÉON

want some oysters? there you go

*I*n the beginning, Marie Vachecrot, a very ordinary cook married to Léon, a lover of fine food, would wait impatiently for the return of the peak of the oyster season each year. She has a consuming passion, as it were, for this mollusc. When the oyster beds spill their contents onto the market stalls, Marie smiles, she's reached the Grail.

Pacific *belles creuses* (from the open sea or beds), full-bodied *fines*, voluptuous *spéciales*, expansive *pousses* ... all so fleshy as to make you forget the very existence of a steak. The *bouzigues* from the Étang de Thau, with their very thick shell, are subtlety itself. The *belons* are both flat and generously proportioned (it takes all kinds!) and have a pronounced flavour, it's the ocean on a plate.

Léon, handy with a knife, takes care of opening the shellfish, this is men's work, and Kevin sets the table. As for Marie, she patiently waits for her man to gulp down the three dozen bought that morning. *Eh oui*, Marie's interest is in the shell, the flesh is for Léon.

The next day is craft day for Marie — just watch her make an ashtray, a saltshaker or a soap holder, a doll to stand on the *buffet normand*. Art's on the menu and the Mizous next door are quite jealous.

And that is how Marie, destined for the anonymity of her kitchen, became the Marie (in her home) who went down in history.

18 jan

Oysters with brown butter

Serves 6

PREPARATION TIME 15 MINUTES
COOKING TIME 5 MINUTES

12 spéciales or extra fleshy oysters
100 g (3½ oz) butter

Open the oysters, discard the first water* and gently detach them from the shell, then drain them in a colander, over a bowl, to collect the second water. Heat the butter in a non-stick frying pan over medium heat until it is nut brown — *noisette***. Add the oyster water to the butter to stop it cooking further. Reduce, add the oysters to the pan and sear for 2–3 minutes. Spear with toothpicks and serve.

* WHAT IS THE OYSTERS' FIRST AND SECOND WATER? *The first water of the oysters is sea water, plain and simple. The second water (also sea water) is what has filled the middle of the oyster and is loaded with iodine.*

** THE BUTTER IS NOISETTE *when it takes on a lovely golden colour with an aroma that is ... nutty!*

20 jan

Witlof with Roquefort and walnuts

Serves 6

PREPARATION TIME 10 MINUTES

6 witlofs (chicory/Belgian endive)

50 g (1¾ oz) sultanas

50 g (1¾ oz) air-dried duck breast

150 g (5½ oz) Roquefort cheese

2 tablespoons cider vinegar

4 tablespoons olive oil

2 tablespoons canola oil

50 g (1¾ oz) whole walnut kernels

salt and pepper

✳ WHY SOAK THE SULTANAS IN THE LUKEWARM WATER? *15 minutes in lukewarm water will plump the sultanas up again.*

Cut the witlofs into quarters lengthways and remove the core. Slice finely. Soak the sultanas in lukewarm water*. Slice the duck, crumble the Roquefort. Combine the cider vinegar with the oils, mix all the ingredients together, season with the coarsely ground black pepper and the salt.

19 jan

Witlof with ham

Serves 6

PREPARATION TIME 20 MINUTES

COOKING TIME 40 MINUTES

For the witlof:

6 witlofs (chicory/Belgian endive)

40 g (1½ oz) butter, cubed

1 tablespoon sugar

6 slices ham off the bone

6 slices prosciutto

150 g (5½ oz) aged Beaufort cheese, cubed

For the béchamel sauce:

40 g (1½ oz) butter

40 g (1½ oz) plain (all-purpose) flour

salt and pepper

500 ml (17 fl oz/2 cups) full-cream (whole) milk

200 ml (7 fl oz) pouring (whipping) cream

½ teaspoon ground nutmeg

✳ WHY COOL THEM ON A RACK? *The water will drain out of them that way.*

✳✳ IS THE WOODEN SPATULA NECESSARY? *For the béchamel sauce, the wooden spatula lets you get into the corners to stop the flour from sticking, without damaging the enamel of the saucepan.*

Preheat the oven to 200°C (400°F/Gas 6). Cut the witlofs in half and arrange them side by side in a gratin dish. Dot with the butter, sprinkle with sugar and fill the dish with water. Bake for 20 minutes, turning them regularly. Place on a wire rack* and allow to cool to lukewarm. Roll the witlof halves in the slices of leg ham and prosciutto. Arrange them once again in a gratin dish and dot with the Beaufort. Reduce the oven temperature to 160°C (315°F/Gas 2–3). To make the béchamel, melt the butter in a saucepan, add the flour, stir over gentle heat for 5 minutes using a wooden spatula**, season. Add the milk, cream and nutmeg, cook for a further 5 minutes, stirring. Pour the béchamel over the witlof then bake in the oven for 20 minutes.

21 jan

Ardèche potato cake

Serves 6

PREPARATION TIME 20 MINUTES

COOKING TIME 15 MINUTES

800 g (1 lb 12 oz) large baking potatoes

4 eggs, lightly beaten

3 onions

1 bunch of chives

salt and pepper

olive oil

Equipment:

grater

✳ HOW DO YOU TURN IT OVER? *It's ideal to have two pans and to turn the potato cake over into the clean pan, otherwise, just use spatulas to flip it over.*

Peel the potatoes, then grate them on the fine side of the grater (the potatoes will thus become a mush). Mix with the eggs. Peel and slice the onions, snip the chives into short lengths, combine with the rest of the mixture and season. Pour a layer of olive oil into a non-stick frying pan. Heat, pour the potato mixture into the pan and cook over a gentle heat for 7–8 minutes. Carefully turn the potato cake over*, cook for a further 7–8 minutes. Serve with a frisée lettuce salad.

MARIE & LÉON

there's heat in the kitchen

oday is *pot-au-feu* day in the Vachecrot household. Where there's *pot-au-feu*, there's a crowd around the table, as this one-pot of beef and vegetables is something to be shared.

It all starts at the market where the butcher, with his stallholder's cheekiness, shouts to anyone who'll listen that since it's boiled meat and vegetables, the *pot-au-feu* should be reimbursed by *la Sécurité Sociale* ... « *You see Marie, I'm telling you, eating well is like going to the doctor, except it's better!* »

An oxtail, some short-ribs, some stewing beef, a bit of bacon, some marrow bones ... « *Good fat doesn't hurt you, plus with all that we're going to drink, it won't be putting up a fight!* » And with the meat, some good vegetables, roots, « *You see Marie, it's a sly one this vegetable, it waits for winter and the frozen soil to give us its best!* »

Back at the house, the saucepans are dancing bare-headed, all a simmer. The windows are steamed up, the evening promises to be a delicious one and we can even read on one of the window panes, written with an index finger: « *I love your pot-au-feu Mum ... Kevin.* »

22 jan

Classic pot-au-feu

Serves 6

PREPARATION TIME 45 MINUTES
COOKING TIME 2 HOURS 35 MINUTES

3 leeks
2 celery stalks
½ savoy cabbage
3 swedes (rutabaga)
6 carrots
3 parsnips
6 jerusalem artichokes
600 g (1 lb 5 oz) beef short-ribs
400 g (14 oz) stewing beef
1 oxtail
1 bouquet garni
3 marrow bones
coarse sea salt (Guérande is best!)
cornichons

Peel all of the vegetables and cut them in half. Place the different meats in a saucepan, cover with water, bring to the boil. Skim the liquid, add the leeks, celery, cabbage and bouquet garni. Cook on a low heat at a bare simmer for 2 hours. Next, add the swedes, carrots and parsnips*. Cook for a further 15 minutes, then finish with the jerusalem artichokes and marrow bones for 20 more minutes. Serve the meat and vegetables on a dish with a little coarse salt, the cornichons and the broth on the side.

✲WHY COOK THE VEGETABLES SEPARATELY? *Each vegetable has a different cooking time. Cooking them separately lets you control the cooking.*

23 jan

Jerusalem artichoke and foie gras

Serves 6

PREPARATION TIME 15 MINUTES
COOKING TIME 15 MINUTES

400 g (14 oz) jerusalem artichokes
100 ml (3½ fl oz) balsamic vinegar
3 tablespoons walnut oil
50 g (1¾ oz/⅓ cup) roughly crushed hazelnuts
6 slices of semi-cooked foie gras
50 g (1¾ oz/⅓ cup) whole almonds

Peel the jerusalem artichokes and cut them into small batons. Boil the balsamic vinegar until it has reduced by half (it should have a syrupy consistency). Cook the jerusalem artichokes in a frying pan over a gentle heat with the walnut oil (they should be quite soft). Allow them to brown with the crushed hazelnuts* and add a tablespoon of the balsamic syrup. Allow to cool. Serve a slice of foie gras with a generous spoonful of the jerusalem artichoke mixture, add the almonds.

✱ HOW DO YOU CRUSH THE HAZELNUTS? *Crush the hazelnuts in a solid container with a high rim using a rolling pin: use it like a pestle.*

24 jan

Hot-pot of old-fashioned vegetables

Serves 6

PREPARATION TIME 20 MINUTES
COOKING TIME 20 MINUTES

3 parsnips
3 swedes (rutabaga)
6 jerusalem artichokes
2 carrots
3 French shallots (eschalots)
50 g (1¾ oz) lightly salted butter
1 tablespoon olive oil
6 garlic cloves, peeled
1 teaspoon dried thyme
150 ml (5 fl oz) white Port
3 marrow bones
salt and pepper

Peel all of the vegetables, cut them into small batons. Cut the shallots in half lengthways. In a large, flameproof casserole, melt the butter with the olive oil. Add all of the vegetables, garlic cloves and shallots, sprinkle with the thyme, sauté for 5 minutes until brown, moisten with the Port. Cover, simmer over low heat for 10 minutes. Meanwhile, cook the marrow bones* in boiling water for 15 minutes, scrape out the marrow, place it on the vegetables, season. Serve from the cooking dish.

✱ COOKING BONES WITHOUT LOSING THE MARROW? *Careful: when cooking the marrow, you have to be vigilant checking each bone using a pointed knife (it should go through the marrow easily).*

25 jan

Cod with witlof

Serves 6

PREPARATION TIME 15 MINUTES
COOKING TIME 15 MINUTES

2 lemons
2 oranges
1 tablespoon soft brown sugar
3 witlofs (chicory/Belgian endives)
6 thick cod or blue-eye trevalla fillets
1 tablespoon herbes de Provence
  (Provençal herb mix)
120 g (4¼ oz) butter
salt and pepper
Equipment:
baking paper

Preheat the oven to 180°C (350°F/Gas 4). Zest and juice the lemons and oranges. Mix together and add the brown sugar*. Trim the ends of the witlofs and slice finely. Combine the witlof with the citrus juice and zest. Cut the baking paper to make six parcels. Place a mound of witlof on the paper and top with a piece of cod, add a pinch of *herbes de Provence*, some orange and lemon juice and 1 tablespoon butter. Season. Seal the parcel so that it is airtight. Repeat to make six parcels. Bake for 15 minutes. Serve the parcels on the plate.

✱ WHY SOFT BROWN SUGAR? *It will give more of a real sugarcane taste.*

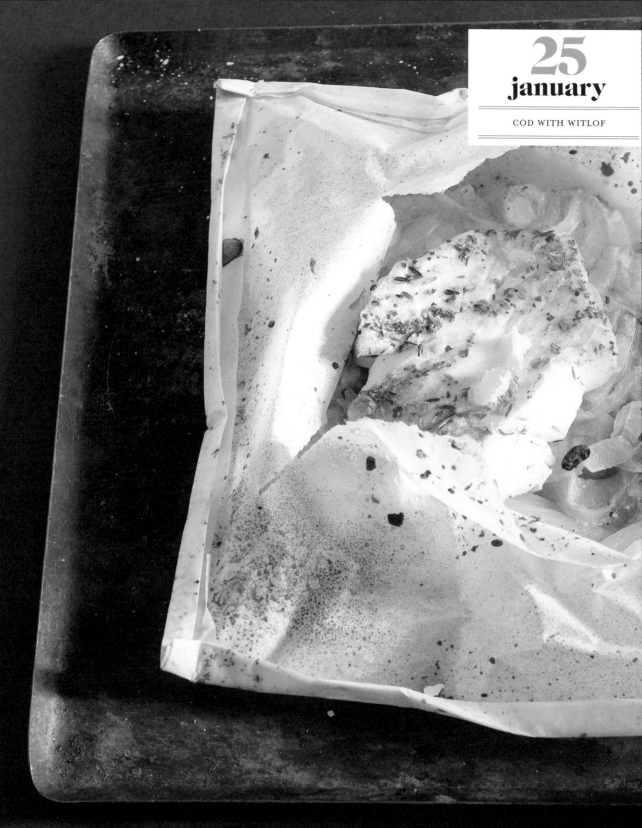

26 jan

Sirloin with root vegetables

Serves 6

PREPARATION TIME 20 MINUTES
COOKING TIME 30 MINUTES

3 parsnips
3 carrots
3 swedes (rutabaga)
80 g (2¾ oz) butter
1 tablespoon sunflower oil
2 x 600 g (1 lb 5 oz) sirloin steaks
3 French shallots (eschalots)
250 ml (9 fl oz/1 cup) white wine
salt and pepper
Equipment:
cast-iron frying pan

Peel the vegetables, cut them into wedges, and cook for 15 minutes in boiling salted water. Drain. In a cast-iron frying pan*, melt 30 g (1 oz) butter and add the oil. When this mixture is very hot, sear the meat to caramelise it well and add the shallots. Cook for 3–5 minutes on each side according to the desired level of doneness. Remove the sirloins from the pan, cover with foil. Deglaze with the white wine, scraping up *les sucs*** well. Reduce, then whisk in the remaining butter, reheat the vegetables in this *jus*, season and serve immediately.

*WHY CAST-IRON? *It distributes heat very well, which is better for searing the meat.*

**LES SUCS? *The small bits of meat that stick to the bottom of the pan during cooking.*

27 jan

Pot roast veal

Serves 6

PREPARATION TIME 20 MINUTES
COOKING TIME 45 MINUTES

6 carrots
6 young leeks
1 kg (2 lb 4 oz) veal roast
2 tablespoons olive oil
juice of 1 orange
125 ml (4 fl oz/½ cup) white wine
12 garlic cloves, peeled
1 tablespoon cumin seeds
salt and pepper

Peel the carrots and cut them into small batons. Trim the green part of the leeks. In a flameproof casserole dish, sauté the veal roast in olive oil to brown it on all sides. Add the carrot, leek, orange juice, white wine, garlic cloves and cumin, cover and cook over a gentle heat for 45 minutes. Add a little water if necessary (the base of the pot should always be wet*). Season.

*WHY ADD WATER TO THE BOTTOM OF THE CASSEROLE? *This stops the roast and vegetables from sticking to the bottom of the dish.*

28 jan

Chocolate fondant cake

Serves 6

PREPARATION TIME 15 MINUTES
COOKING TIME 15 MINUTES

250 g (9 oz) good-quality dark chocolate
250 g (9 oz) butter
4 eggs, separated
100 g (3½ oz) sugar
100 g (3½ oz/1 cup) ground almonds
1 tablespoon cornflour (cornstarch)

Preheat the oven to 160°C (315°F/Gas 2–3). Melt the chocolate with the butter in a double-boiler. Whip the egg whites to stiff peaks. Whisk the yolks with the sugar until they become pale and frothy. Add the chocolate mixture, ground almonds and cornflour. Gently fold in the egg whites using a spatula*. Butter and flour a tin. Pour in the chocolate mixture, cook in the oven for 10–15 minutes (the texture of the cake depends on the cooking time**).

*THE SPATULA: *A flat, soft spoon, perfect for gently incorporating whipped egg whites.*

**TIPS FOR THE TEXTURE OF FONDANT CAKE: *The fondant cake should stay very soft in the middle. Served warm, it is best eaten with a spoon. Served cold, you can cut the cake into slices (the chocolate and butter will have solidified).*

29 jan

Salad of mâche, beetroot and apple

Serves 6

PREPARATION TIME 15 MINUTES

2 cooked beetroot (beets)
1 granny smith apple
juice of 1 lemon
100 ml (3½ fl oz) wine vinegar
6 eggs
1 tablespoon Savora (honey mustard) sauce
1 tablespoon cider vinegar
100 ml (3½ fl oz) olive oil
250 g (9 oz) mâche (lamb's lettuce)

Peel the beetroot and apple and cut them into thin matchsticks. Combine the apple with the lemon juice. Boil some water in a saucepan, add the wine vinegar. Break the eggs into individual ramekins. When the water is simmering, slip each egg into the saucepan and keep simmering for 1 minute. When the whites have set, take out the eggs using a slotted spoon and keep them in some lukewarm water*. Combine the mustard, cider vinegar and olive oil. Dress the mâche lettuce with this vinaigrette. Place the egg in the middle, scatter over the matchsticks of beetroot and apple.

✱WHY DIP IN LUKEWARM WATER? *The lukewarm water will retain the egg's temperature without continuing to cook and harden the yolk.*

30 jan

Beetroot carpaccio

Serves 6

PREPARATION TIME 15 MINUTES
MARINATING TIME 1 HOUR

2 raw beetroot (beets)
juice of 2 lemons
100 ml (3½ fl oz) olive oil
salt and pepper
50 g (1¾ oz) bottarga (cured fish roe)
50 g (1¾ oz) Comté cheese
a few leaves of flat-leaf (Italian) parsley
a few leaves of tarragon

Peel the beetroot and slice very thinly. Place the slices of beetroot in a dish, pour over the lemon juice and olive oil and season. Marinate for 1 hour. Slice thin slivers of bottarga and Comté*. Arrange the slices of beetroot on a plate, scatter over the slivers of bottarga and Comté, add a few leaves of parsley and tarragon. Serve at room temperature.

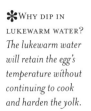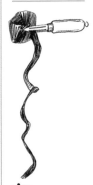

✱FOR REALLY THIN SLICES: *Use a vegetable peeler.*

31 jan

Roast pineapple with honey

Serves 6

PREPARATION TIME 15 MINUTES
COOKING TIME 30 MINUTES

1 large pineapple
1 vanilla bean
50 g (1¾ oz) butter
3 tablespoons honey
150 ml (5 fl oz) brown rum

Preheat the oven to 160°C (315°F/Gas 2–3). Peel the pineapple using a serrated knife, remove the eyes. Pierce holes in the pineapple through the middle lengthways*. Split the vanilla bean in half, insert each half into the pineapple. Place the pineapple in a gratin dish. Add the butter, honey and rum, then bake in the oven for 30 minutes, turning and basting the pineapple regularly. Serve warm.

✱How? *With a carving fork, for example.*

February

01 — Ella
CLAMS WITH HERB BUTTER

02 — Théophane
BEEF WITH ONIONS

03 — Blaise
QUICHE WITH PROSCIUTTO

08 — Jacqueline
CARAMEL PORK

09 — Apolline
CHINESE VEGETABLE STIR-FRY

10 — Arnaud
VIETNAMESE SPRING ROLLS

15 — Claude
BANANA SPLIT UP AND DOWN

16 — Julienne
TRUFFLE CANAPÉ

17 — Alexis
LAMB WITH CHILLI AND COCONUT MILK

22 — Isabelle
OLD-FASHIONED VEGETABLE SOUP

23 — Lazare
INDIVIDUAL RACLETTES

24 — Modeste
POTATO SALAD WITH TOMME CHEESE

29 — Auguste
PORK POT-AU-FEU

30 — Saint-Glinglin
LOBSTER WITH HERB BUTTER

01

04
Véronique
SAUSAGES EN PAPILLOTE

05
Agathe
PINEAPPLE CRUMBLE

06
Gaston
CREAM OF JERUSALEM
ARTICHOKE SOUP

07
Eugénie
CARROTS IN COLOUR

11
Héloïse
NOODLE SOUP

12
Félix
FROSTED ORANGES

13
Béatrice
FRIED RICE

14
Valentin
VODKA-GINGER COCKTAIL

18
Bernadette
SCALLOP STEW

19
Gabin
PURPLE POTATO MASH

20
Aimée
GINGER CRÈME BRÛLÉE

21
Damien
SLOW-COOKED PORK BELLY

25
Roméo
TARTIFLETTE

26
Nestor
BUCKWHEAT PASTA GRATIN

27
Honorine
FONDUE

28
Romain
WALNUT TART

02 03 04 05

01
february

CLAMS WITH HERB BUTTER

01 feb
Clams with herb butter
Serves 6

PREPARATION TIME 10 MINUTES
COOKING TIME 5 MINUTES

36 clams (vongole)
1 French shallot (eschalot)
1 garlic clove
100 g (3½ oz) lightly salted butter
1 bunch of flat-leaf (Italian) parsley
3 slices dry baguette

Preheat the griller (broiler) to hot. Open the clams*. Peel the shallot and garlic, process them with the butter and parsley along with the bread. Top each clam with a teaspoon of the herb butter and grill for 3–4 minutes (the herb butter should start to become brown and crusty). Serve very hot.

✻TIPS FOR OPENING THE CLAMS: *Opening clams is a hazardous activity. You need a pointed knife, a spare hand is advisable, some bandages within reach of the good hand just in case, and a glass of alcohol for l'émotion. You just have to delicately insert the point of the knife into the side of the clam, slide it round, argh ... and voilà, done!*

02 feb
Beef with onions
Serves 6

PREPARATION TIME 10 MINUTES
COOKING TIME 10 MINUTES

4 onions
4 garlic cloves
800 g (1 lb 12 oz) beef steak
2 tablespoons sunflower oil
1 tablespoon Savora (honey mustard) sauce
1 tablespoon soy sauce
1 tablespoon sesame seeds
4 sprigs of coriander (cilantro), leaves picked and torn
Equipment:
wok

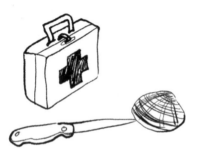

✻STIR-FRYING IN THE WOK: *Sear the vegetables on high heat so they stay crisp.*

✻✻DEGLAZE: *Add a liquid to detach the bits that stick to the base of the pan.*

Peel the onions and garlic, slice finely. Slice the meat. Heat the oil in a wok and stir-fry* the onions and garlic to caramelise them. Add the meat, sear it quickly, then deglaze** with the honey-mustard and soy sauces. Add the sesame seeds and coriander.

03 feb
Quiche with prosciutto
Serves 6

PREPARATION TIME 15 MINUTES
COOKING TIME 25 MINUTES

4 eggs
1 dash ground nutmeg
*200 ml (7 fl oz) pouring (whipping) cream**
200 ml (7 fl oz) full-cream (whole) milk
100 g (3½ oz) Comté cheese, grated
8 slices prosciutto
1 sheet store-bought shortcrust pastry

Preheat the oven to 180°C (350°F/Gas 4). Beat the eggs with the nutmeg, combine with the cream*, milk and cheese. Cut the prosciutto slices in half lengthways and roll them up. Lay the shortcrust pastry in a round tart tin, keeping the baking paper backing. Arrange the prosciutto rolls side by side. Cover with the cream mixture, bake for 25 minutes.

✻WHY POURING CREAM? *Pouring (whipping) cream is a heavy liquid cream that stands up well to cooking.*

MARIE & LÉON

taste buds and tasty parcels

*J*n the beginning, Marie Vachecrot, a very ordinary cook married to Léon, a lover of fine food, spent her time eating little chocolate sweets wrapped in silver paper called papillotes. Sweet by sweet, Marie had a tendency to *montgolfier* (a verb used mainly in and around Annonay, based on the Montgolfiere balloon, and meaning: « *Good Lord you eat a lot of papillotes, if you keep that up you'll get mistaken for a hot air balloon!* ».

Léon, not too keen to see his wife fly up and away, lost no time in dropping a few small remarks on the astronomical quantities of *papillotes* that passed her way every day. Irritated by all the sarcastic comments, Marie retorted by making a 100 per cent porky papillote, with sausage, red wine and onion ... and rushed to serve it to her husband: «*There, you eat papillotes too, so you can keep your comments to yourself!* » Léon is unable to contain his emotion in the face of so much deliciousness. He closes his eyes and, filled with benevolence towards his sweet Marie, buys a larger bed!

And that is how Marie, destined for the anonymity of her kitchen, became the Marie that went down in history.

04 feb

Sausages cooked en papillote

Serves 6

PREPARATION TIME 10 MINUTES
COOKING TIME 20 MINUTES

4 onions
2 sausages
300 ml (10½ fl oz) red wine
100 g (3½ oz) butter
2 sprigs of rosemary
2 sprigs of thyme

✷Cut the butter into small pieces and scatter it over: *The butter is scattered over the dish so that it lends its creaminess to the whole dish.*

Preheat the oven to 160°C (315°F/Gas 2–3). Peel and slice the onions. Cut the sausages into 1 cm (½ inch) thick slices. Make two *papillote* (parcels) from foil, lay out the onion slices, then the sausage slices, divide the red wine between the two parcels, as well as the butter✷. Place a sprig each of rosemary and thyme in each parcel, seal them tightly. Bake in the oven for 20 minutes.

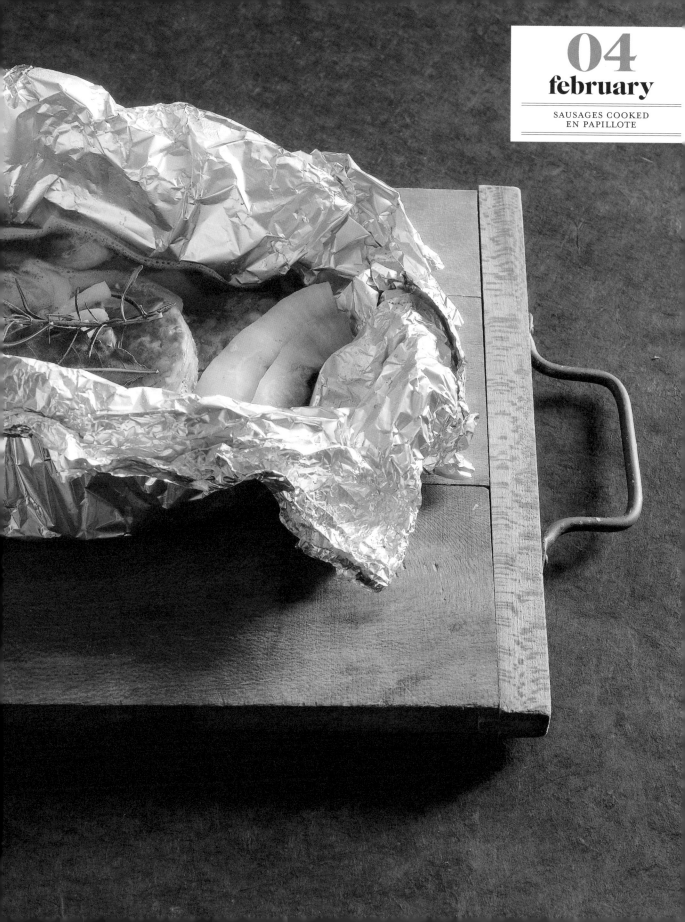

05 feb

Pineapple crumble

Serves 6
PREPARATION TIME 20 MINUTES
COOKING TIME 20 MINUTES

1 large pineapple
150 g (5½ oz) butter
100 ml (3½ fl oz) rum
100 g (3½ oz/⅔ cup) plain (all-purpose) flour
100 g (3½ oz) desiccated coconut
100 g (3½ oz) soft brown sugar

Preheat the oven to 180°C (350°F/Gas 4). Peel the pineapple*. Remove the eyes and cut into quarters lengthways. Remove the core. Cut the rest of the pineapple into 1 cm (½ inch) cubes. Melt 50 g (1¾ oz) of the butter in a frying pan, add the pineapple cubes, brown, and flambé with the rum**. In a separate saucepan melt the remaining butter, add the flour, coconut and brown sugar, combine. Place the pineapple in a gratin dish, scatter over the crumble mixture, bake for 15 minutes.

*PEELING A PINEAPPLE: *Trim both ends, remove the skin with a bread knife, remove the eyes with the point of a vegetable peeler.*

**TO FLAMBÉ: *Pour the rum into the pan with the pineapple cubes, heat, strike a match ... watch out for your fringe!*

06 feb

Cream of jerusalem artichoke soup

Serves 6
PREPARATION TIME 20 MINUTES
COOKING TIME 20 MINUTES

1 kg (2 lb 4 oz) jerusalem artichokes
200 ml (7 fl oz) pouring (whipping) cream
salt and pepper
1 sprig of rosemary
30 g (1 oz) butter, melted
30 g (1 oz) plain (all-purpose) flour
1 tablespoon sugar
30 g (1 oz/¼ cup) roughly chopped walnuts

Preheat the oven to 160°C (315°F/Gas 2–3). Peel the jerusalem artichokes, cover with water, bring to the boil and cook for 20 minutes. Purée, add the cream and season. Meanwhile, strip the rosemary leaves and chop them finely. Combine the melted butter, flour, sugar, walnuts and rosemary. Scatter this crumbly dough over a sheet of baking paper and bake for 15 minutes. Serve the cream of jerusalem artichoke soup in bowls, scattered with pieces of the walnut-rosemary crumble. Get ready for the concert*.

*THE CONCERT: *The jerusalem artichoke is a fun-loving vegetable that will continue to amuse after the meal, if you see ... if you sense what I mean!*

07 feb

Carrots in colour

Serves 6
PREPARATION TIME 10 MINUTES
COOKING TIME 15 MINUTES

4 orange carrots
4 purple carrots
3 bulb spring onions (scallions)
1 orange
2 tablespoons cider vinegar
80 ml (2½ fl oz/⅓ cup) olive oil
salt and pepper

Peel the carrots, cut into *sifflets**. Cook in a saucepan of boiling water for 15 minutes, refresh immediately**. Slice the spring onions, zest and juice the orange, combine and then add the vinegar and oil. Dress the carrots with this vinaigrette and then season.

*CUT INTO SIFFLETS: *Slice the carrots on the diagonal like the reed on a saxophone.*

**WHY REFRESH THE CARROTS? *This lets you stop the cooking process straight away, so you get exactly the texture you want.*

10 feb

Vietnamese spring rolls

Serves 6

PREPARATION TIME 45 MINUTES
COOKING TIME 30 MINUTES

20 rice-paper wrappers
vegetable oil
For the base:
2 carrots
100 g (3½ oz) dried wood-ear mushrooms
200 g (7 oz) rice vermicelli
3 bulb spring onions (scallions)
1 bunch of coriander (cilantro)
1 tablespoon sugar
For the filling — choose 1 or more:
pork tenderloin fillet
small prawns (shrimp)
air-dried duck breast
chicken breast fillet
anything that comes into your head (that you can eat!)
salt and pepper
For the sauce:
2 tablespoons fish sauce
1 tablespoon sugar
juice of 1 lemon
1 garlic clove, finely chopped
1 small chilli (optional)

08 feb

Caramel pork

Serves 6

PREPARATION TIME 15 MINUTES
COOKING TIME 20 MINUTES

4 onions
2 pork tenderloins
sunflower oil
1 tablespoon soy sauce
1 tablespoon honey
100 g (3½ oz/⅔ cup) cashew nuts
1 bunch of coriander (cilantro), leaves picked and torn
Equipment:
wok

✳STIR-FRYING IN A WOK: *Sear the vegetables over a high heat so they stay crisp.*

Peel and slice the onions. Cut the pork into small cubes. Stir-fry the sliced onions with a little sunflower oil in a wok* over high heat. Next, add the cubes of pork, cook for 10 minutes, add the soy sauce and honey, cook for a further 5 minutes, then finish with the cashew nuts and coriander.

✳WHY TURN OFF THE HEAT JUST WHEN YOU PUT THE VERMICELLI IN? *The water mustn't boil any more, otherwise the vermicelli will overcook.*

✳✳WHY PUT IT ON A DAMP CLOTH? *The cloth needs to be damp so the rice-paper wrapper doesn't stick to it.*

✳✳✳A TIP FOR ROLLING? *The rice-paper shouldn't be too wet, and roll it up quickly.*

✳✳✳✳ HOW TO BEST ENJOY THE ROLLS: *Make a salad with lots of different herbs, slip them into a lettuce leaf and, why yes, some home-made apéritif would be lovely, thank you!*

For the base, peel the carrots, grate them fairly coarsely. Rehydrate the wood-ear mushrooms by soaking them in hot water for 10 minutes. Plunge the vermicelli into a saucepan of boiling water, turn off the heat*, leave for 5 minutes then rinse it in cold water. Slice the spring onions and mushrooms, strip the leaves from the coriander and chop them, snip the vermicelli into 10 cm (4 inch) lengths with scissors, combine everything with the sugar. Prepare the filling by chopping up the item(s) of your choosing, combine with the base mixture, season. Dip a rice-paper wrapper in hot water, holding it by an edge, and turn it over: it should be translucent. Place it on a damp cloth**. Place a spoonful of filling (allow 1 tablespoon per roll) at the edge of the rice-paper wrapper, fold in the sides then roll up***. Repeat with the remaining wrappers and filling. Deep-fry in batches for 7–8 minutes, or until crisp.

For the sauce, combine the fish sauce, sugar, lemon juice, garlic and, for the more daring souls, a small chopped chilli. Serve the spring rolls with the dipping sauce and a salad**** made up of mint, basil and coriander (cilantro) leaves.

09 feb

Chinese vegetable stir-fry

Serves 6

PREPARATION TIME 20 MINUTES
COOKING TIME 5 MINUTES

6 carrots
50 g (1¾ oz) fresh ginger
½ Chinese cabbage (wong bok)
1 leek
4 bulb spring onions (scallions)
4 garlic cloves
1 tablespoon sunflower oil
1 tablespoon soy sauce

✳WHY ONLY AT THE LAST MINUTE? *The soy sauce should only be used as a seasoning, not a cooking liquid for the vegetables.*

Peel the carrots and ginger, cut them into thin sticks. Finely slice the Chinese cabbage, leek and spring onions. Peel and chop the garlic. Heat the oil in a wok, sauté the garlic then add all of the vegetables, sauté for 3–4 minutes. The vegetables should stay crunchy. Just before serving*, season with the soy sauce.

11 feb

Noodle soup

Serves 6
PREPARATION TIME 20 MINUTES
COOKING TIME 10 MINUTES

1 carrot
1 bunch of chives
500 g (1 lb 2 oz) roasting beef
50 g (1¾ oz) butter
4 onions
sunflower oil
1 tablespoon soy sauce
1 tablespoon Savora (honey mustard) sauce
100 g (3½ oz) rice vermicelli
2 tablespoons salted peanuts

Peel the carrot, cut into thin sticks. Snip the chives into 1 cm (½ inch) lengths. Sear the beef in the butter over a high heat just to colour it (it musn't cook*). Peel and slice the onions, sauté in a saucepan over high heat with a little oil: they should be well-browned. Moisten** with 500 ml (17 fl oz/2 cups) water, add the soy sauce and the Savora sauce. Boil for 2 minutes, then add the rice vermicelli, turn off the heat. Finely slice the beef, arrange in a soup bowl with the carrot sticks, chives and peanuts. Swish some kitchen scissors through the vermicelli a few times, pour this soup over the dish of beef. Serve immediately.

✱WHY NOT COMPLETELY COOK THE BEEF AT THIS POINT? *The beef has to stay rare, the soup will finish the cooking.*

✱✱MOISTEN WITH WATER: *Add water to the ingredients that are already cooking.*

12 feb

Frosted oranges

Serves 6
PREPARATION TIME 20 MINUTES
FREEZING TIME 2 HOURS

8 oranges
100 g (3½ oz) sugar
100 ml (3½ fl oz) Cointreau
1 egg white

✱EMPTY OUT THE ORANGES: *Remove everything inside the oranges.*

✱✱WHY PUT THE EMPTIED ORANGES IN THE FREEZER? *So that they freeze, which will later keep the orange ice cold.*

✱✱✱ WHAT'S THE EGG WHITE FOR? *To emulsify the oranges and give them a creamier texture.*

Cut the tops off six of the oranges. Using a sharp knife, empty out the oranges*, then squeeze in your hand to get out the juice. Add the sugar and Cointreau. Place the emptied oranges in the freezer**. Zest the other 2 oranges, then remove the skin and pith and cut out the segments. Combine the juice, sugar and Cointreau mixture with the chopped zest and the orange segments. Freeze in an ice-cube tray. Process the Cointreau-orange ice cubes with an egg-white*** and fill the emptied oranges with this mixture.

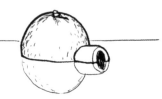

13 feb

Fried rice

Serves 6
PREPARATION TIME 10 MINUTES
COOKING TIME 10 MINUTES

3 eggs
2 onions
6 chives
sunflower oil
100 g (3½ oz/⅔ cup) frozen peas
6 slices speck, chopped
*500 g (1 lb 2 oz/2½ cups) cooked rice***
salt and pepper

✱HOW LONG SHOULD THE EGGS BE COOKED? *The omelette should be well done, leave it for about 5 minutes.*

✱✱TYPE OF RICE: *Standard long-grain or basmati, according to taste.*

Break the eggs, beat them until just combined. Cook the omelette* in a non-stick frying pan, then slice it into thin strips. Peel and slice the onions and snip the chives into 1 cm (½ inch) lengths. Sauté the onions in a little oil with the peas, speck and rice for 5 minutes, add the chives and the chopped omelette and season.

MARIE & LÉON

ah, the joys of Valentine's Day

The restaurants are all booked out with tables for two, the florists are smiling, Champagne sales are up five-fold (a half-bottle just in case, a bottle for a firm date, a magnum to forget). In short, it's all happening. Two aspirins as a preventative measure, you don't want a headache today of all days, an appointment with Johana, the beautician, « Next! » ... You rush around, do yourself up like a freshly gift-wrapped package. You're beautiful, you're ready, you picture yourself on a bearskin rug in front of an open fire, perfect for stoking the embers, it appeals like a yen for Béziers in the middle of summer. It's Valentine's Day and it will be good. Marie knows her Léon will make love to her just like the first time (actually, best not, since she gave him the nickname Buzz Lightyear!). Marie knows she doesn't live just for Valentine's Day, Marie knows truffles can be eaten whenever and wherever one wants, so Léon, you'd better be prepared.

❋ WHAT GLASS TO SERVE IT IN? *Serve in highball glasses.*

14 feb

Vodka-ginger cocktail
Serves 6

PREPARATION TIME 15 MINUTES
COOKING TIME 30 MINUTES
CHILLING TIME 1 HOUR

vodka
200 g (7 oz) fresh ginger
1 litre (35 fl oz/4 cups) water
300 g (10½ oz/firmly packed 1⅓ cups) soft brown sugar

Place the vodka in the freezer. Peel the ginger, chop into small cubes. Place them in a saucepan, cover with water, add the sugar and cook over a low heat for 30 minutes. Purée this mixture and chill for 1 hour. Serve the ginger syrup with crushed ice and vodka* (serve it with the caramel and whipped cream, if you get my drift!).

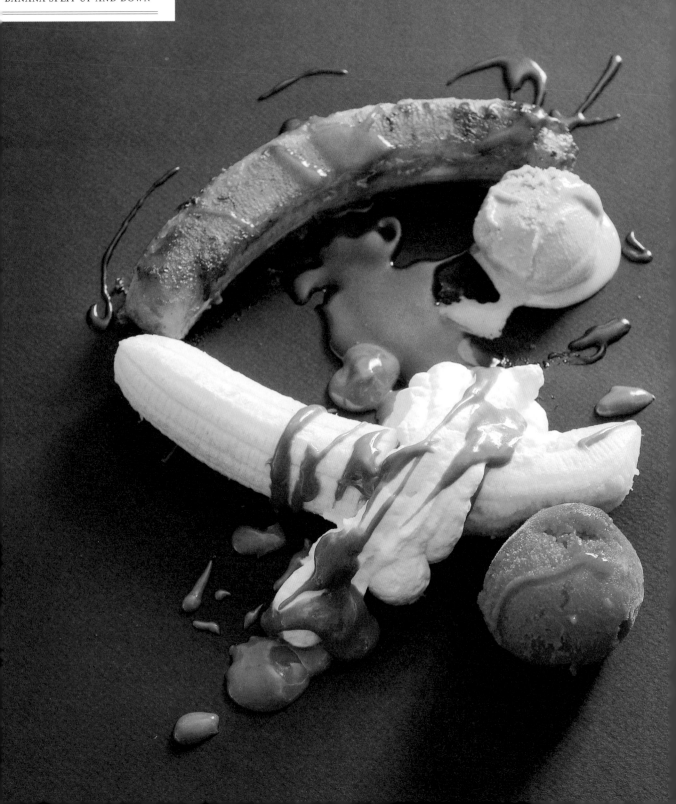

15
february

BANANA SPLIT UP AND DOWN

15 feb

Banana split up and down

Serves 2

PREPARATION TIME 15 MINUTES
COOKING TIME 10 MINUTES

2 bananas
50 g (1¾ oz) butter
100 g (3½ oz) sugar
3 tablespoons rum
150 ml (5 fl oz) pouring (whipping) cream
whipped cream
sorbet and ice cream

❋X-RATED
VERSION: *Dessert
is finished ... and
there's some caramel,
whipped cream and
one fiancé left over.
Delicately spread
the body part of
your choice with
caramel, top with
whipped cream, eat
straight from the
animal. Swap roles.
Just as well it's not
tartiflette night
(see page 90), the
result would be much
less glamorous.*

Peel the bananas. Gently cook the butter with 50 g (1¾ oz) of the sugar in a frying pan, cook one of the bananas for 5 minutes: it should be caramelised. Flambé with the rum. In another saucepan, make a caramel with the remaining sugar, add the pouring cream, cook for 2 minutes to get a creamy caramel. Arrange the bananas on a dish, add ice cream and sorbet, whipped cream and a little caramel sauce (keep some for the end of the evening, you never know, if all goes well*...).

16 feb

Truffle canapé

Serves 2

PREPARATION TIME 2 KISSES
COOKING TIME 2 MORE KISSES

1 old baguette
olive oil
1 fresh truffle*
fleur de sel *and* pepper

❋WHERE DO
YOU BUY A FRESH
TRUFFLE? *Fresh
truffles are bought
from a professional
(a fine food store).
Beware of imitators,
such as Chinese truffles
and unripe truffles ...*

You love him/her, you've broken the piggy bank to invest in the black diamond and you were right. No more cheap jewellery dressed up in a blingy box, hello to some real *savoir-vivre*, refined, elegant, chic and so simple. This year, we're eating the diamond. Cut a few thin slices of baguette, drizzle over some oil, place under the grill (broiler) for 2–3 minutes, uncork the Champagne, finely slice the truffle, place a few slivers on the croûtons, a little *fleur de sel*, pepper and ... come what may!

17 feb

Lamb with chilli and coconut milk

Serves 6 (2 this evening, the rest in the freezer!)

PREPARATION TIME 30 MINUTES
COOKING TIME 1 HOUR

800 g (1 lb 12 oz) boneless lamb shoulder
1 tomato
4 garlic cloves
2 onions
1 green chilli
80 ml (2½ fl oz/⅓ cup) olive oil
1 tablespoon plain (all-purpose) flour
15 g (½ oz) chicken stock (bouillon) powder
300 ml (10½ fl oz) coconut milk
1 teaspoon ground ginger
1 tablespoon curry powder
Equipment:
flameproof earthernware or casserole dish

❋TRIM THE LAMB:
*Use a knife to remove
excess fat from the
lamb.*

❋❋PEEL THE
TOMATOES: *Make a
cross-shaped incision
in the base of the
tomatoes, immerse
them for 12 seconds
in boiling water, then
remove the skins.*

❋❋❋ WHAT'S
THE FLOUR FOR?
*The flour will serve
to bind the cooking
sauce.*

❋❋❋❋
WHY ADD THE
CHILLI AT THE LAST
MINUTE? *Since the
chilli is very stong
and pure, we avoid
overwhelming the
dish with its power
through prolonged
cooking. It is added
last so that if the
prospect of a mouth
like Mick Jagger
scares you, it's easy
to remove the chilli
from your plate.*

Trim the lamb* and cut it into large pieces. Peel** and dice the tomato. Peel the garlic and onions, chop them roughly. Finely chop the chilli. Pour 2 tablespoons of the olive oil into the dish, sauté the lamb for 5 minutes to brown. Remove the lamb, drain the fat. Add the remaining olive oil, sauté the onions, garlic, add the lamb, then the flour***, cook for 2–3 minutes, stirring well. Next add the tomato, chicken stock powder, coconut milk and the ginger and curry powders. Simmer for 45 minutes, add the chilli 5 minutes before serving****.

MARIE & LÉON

Saint-Jacques, pray for us

In the beginning, Marie Vachecrot, a very ordinary cook married to Léon, a lover of fine food, spent her time inhaling the iodine-rich spray of Brittany and massacring the treasures caught by Léon with the greatest of ease. Exasperated by so little culinary proficiency, Léon, weighed down with 5 kilograms of *coquilles Saint-Jacques* (scallops) loses his temper with his wife and lets fly: « *Don't ruin the* Saint-Jacques, empotée *(clumsy oaf)!* »

Marie, determined to show she has made a real effort with her cooking, buys cabbage, bacon and makes her dear Léon the *Saint-Jacques en potée* (scallop stew) he so wanted, a quality dish acclaimed by hordes of gourmets.

And that is how Marie, destined for the anonymity of her kitchen, became the Marie who went down in history.

✱ How do you remove the roe? *You just need to detach it from the white part by removing the membrane that surrounds it.*

18 feb

Scallop stew

Serves 6
PREPARATION TIME 20 MINUTES
COOKING TIME 20 MINUTES

18 good-looking scallops
2 carrots
1 Chinese cabbage (wong bok)
3 onions
100 g (3½ oz) bacon slices
olive oil
125 ml (4 fl oz/½ cup) white wine
200 ml (7 fl oz) pouring (whipping) cream
salt and pepper

Prepare the scallops by removing the roe* and dicing it. Peel the carrots and finely dice. Slice the cabbage and peel and slice the onions. Thinly slice the bacon. In a large saucepan sauté the carrots with the bacon, onions and roe in the olive oil, then add the cabbage and white wine. Cover and simmer for 10 minutes. In a separate frying pan, fry the scallops quickly (a few seconds each side) in olive oil, then add them to the stew. Add the cream, cook uncovered for 5 minutes. Season. Scallops are always a hit on Valentine's Day and the cabbage provides some laughs, ho ho! *Pardon.*

19 feb

Purple potato mash

Serves 6

PREPARATION TIME 30 MINUTES
COOKING TIME 55 MINUTES

1 kg (2 lb 4 oz) purple potatoes
300 ml (10½ fl oz) pouring (whipping) cream
100 g (3½ oz) lightly salted butter
salt and pepper
Equipment:
potato masher

Peel the potatoes, cover in water and cook for 45 minutes. Drain*, then add the cream and cook for a further 10 minutes. Add the butter and mash using a potato masher. Season. Top with a sliver of butter when serving.

✳WITHOUT DRAINING?
The purple potato has very dense flesh. You can keep the cooking water to thin out the mash, if it is too thick.

20 feb

Ginger crème brûlée

Serves 6

PREPARATION TIME 10 MINUTES
COOKING TIME 1 HOUR 5 MINUTES
CHILLING TIME 1 HOUR

80 g (2¾ oz) fresh ginger
300 g (10½ oz/firmly packed 1⅓ cups) soft brown sugar
*   + extra for caramelising*
8 eggs, separated
1 litre (35 fl oz/4 cups) pouring
*   (whipping) cream*
Equipment:
kitchen blowtorch
6 ramekins

Preheat the oven to 120°C (235°F/Gas ½). Peel the ginger and dice it finely. Combine 150 g (5½ oz) of the sugar with 150 ml (5 fl oz) water in a saucepan and bring to the boil. Add the ginger and candy it* on a low simmer for 20 minutes. Drain the ginger (keep the syrup for other feasts). Whisk the egg yolks vigorously with the remaining sugar and the cream. (Use the whites for making meringues!) Divide the candied ginger between the six ramekins, cover with the crème brûlée mixture, cook in a bain-marie** for 45 minutes. Chill the crème brûlée for 1 hour. Sprinkle with the extra soft brown sugar before serving and caramelise it with the blowtorch.

✳CANDYING:
Cooking something in a syrup.

✳✳COOKING IN A BAIN-MARIE IN THE OVEN:
See the story of Marie Vachecrot (7th March, page 110).

21 feb

Slow-cooked pork belly

Serves 6

PREPARATION TIME 20 MINUTES
COOKING TIME 2 HOURS

1.5 kg (3 lb 5 oz) pork belly
1 bouquet garni
*1 onion studded with 4 cloves**
300 ml (10½ fl oz) veal stock
3 tablespoons tomato sauce (ketchup)
3 tablespoons soy sauce
2 tablespoons honey
4 garlic cloves, chopped
seasonal vegetables

Poach** the pork belly in a large volume of water with the bouquet garni and clove-studded onion. Cook uncovered on a very gentle simmer for 1–1½ hours — the belly needs to be tender. Take it out of the water. Preheat the oven to 160°C (315°F/Gas 2–3). Combine the veal stock with the tomato sauce, soy sauce, honey and garlic. Cut the belly into slices and lay in a dish, pour over the marinade, bake in the oven for 20 minutes, basting regularly. Reheat the seasonal vegetables*** in the cooking dish. *Cochonneries* (porkiness) for Valentine's week: it does you good!

✳WHY ARE THE CLOVES STUCK INTO THE ONION?
Cloves are hard and sticking them in the onion prevents them from disappearing into the dish and hiding in a mouthful to attack your palate.

✳✳POACH:
Cook in a liquid.

✳✳✳
VEGETABLES? *Serve with boiled potatoes and carrots.*

22 feb

Old-fashioned vegetable soup

Serves 6
PREPARATION TIME 20 MINUTES
COOKING TIME 45 MINUTES

4 carrots
4 potatoes
1 leek
1 celery stalk
¼ cabbage
1 swede (rutabaga)
1 parsnip
1 onion
100 g (3½ oz) butter
salt and pepper
200 ml (7 fl oz) pouring (whipping) cream
olive oil
snipped chives

✱WHY START THE COOKING COLD? Raising the cooking temperature of the vegetables bit by bit will only improve the blending of flavours.

Peel all of the vegetables, cut them into chunks. Put into a saucepan, cover with water, bring to the boil and cook over a gentle heat for 45 minutes*. Purée everything with the butter and season. Drizzle over the cream, some oil and scatter over the chives before serving.

23 feb

Individual raclettes

Serves 6
PREPARATION TIME 20 MINUTES
COOKING TIME 10 MINUTES

3 slices ham
3 slices prosciutto
3 potatoes, cooked
1 onion
6 slices speck
18 slices raclette cheese
paprika

✱BUILD THE MILLE-FEUILLES: Potato, speck, onion, raclette, ham, onion, raclette, prosciutto, onion, raclette and paprika, like a construction, you build up layers of ingredients.

Preheat the oven to 200°C (400°F/Gas 6). Cut the ham and prosciutto slices in half. Cut the potatoes and onion into rounds. On a sheet of baking paper, build raclette mille-feuilles*. Bake in the oven for about 10 minutes (the raclette should be soft). Serve immediately.

24 feb

Potato salad with Tomme cheese

Serves 6
PREPARATION TIME 30 MINUTES
COOKING TIME 20 MINUTES

600 g (1 lb 5 oz) waxy, yellow-fleshed potatoes
1 red onion
3 Diot* or pork sausages
50 g (1¾ oz/⅓ cup) pine nuts
150 g (5½ oz) Tomme de Savoie cheese
3 tablespoons canola oil
1 tablespoon sherry vinegar
1 tablespoon Viandox or veal jus
salt and pepper
1 bunch of flat-leaf (Italian) parsley, chopped

✱DIOT SAUSAGES: Fresh sausages containing root vegetables, turnips, beetroot and carrots.

✱✱COOKING ENGLISH-STYLE: Boil whole in water.

Peel the potatoes, cook them English-style** for 20 minutes, cut them into chunks. Thinly slice the onion. Slice the sausages into thin rounds, pan-fry them for 5 minutes, add the pine nuts, cook for a further 2–3 minutes. Use a vegetable peeler to create slivers of the Tomme de Savoie. Prepare the vinaigrette by combining the canola oil, sherry vinegar and Viandox. Combine all of the ingredients, season and sprinkle with parsley.

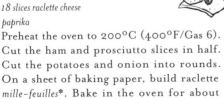

MARIE & LÉON

the half-day package

$\mathcal{I}$t's February, there's snow, the moon boots come out again: it's the week to go skiing. You're renting the studio from Saturday; like everybody else, you're planning to leave early to avoid the traffic (like everybody else).

You pack the car, a veritable jigsaw puzzle on a giant scale — you have to get a mountain of stuff into the tiny boot, a real brain-teaser that is best done alone, in order to avoid too scarring a confrontation. As Léon has known for some time, Marie likes not to forget anything. The car touches the ground, the boot is full, cooked roast pork, tinned food, a cassoulet in a two kilogram jar for Patrick, bars of chocolate and packets of chips (crisps) — it's important not to run short of anything in case they get trapped in ten centimetres of snow. Kevin's pillow is wedged between the snow boots and the sausages, the fondue pot finds a spot between Marie's legs and they're finally set for eight hours in the car: they've got 200 kilometres to go. A skiing trip has its rituals that must be observed: you don't get to go over 30 kilometres per hour on the journey between the house and the ski station (whose idea was it to leave so early!), there's melted cheese at every meal, some *vin de pays* to wash it down … *c'est la vraie vie.*

25 feb

Tartiflette

Serves 6

PREPARATION TIME 45 MINUTES
COOKING TIME 30 MINUTES

1.2 kg (2 lb 10 oz) potatoes
2 onions
200 g (7 oz) speck, cut into lardons
1 traditional farmhouse Reblochon cheese
150 g (5½ oz/⅔ cup) sour cream
salt and pepper
750 ml (26 fl oz/3 cups) Chignin–Bergeron
  or roussanne white wine

Preheat the oven to 180°C (350°F/Gas 4). Peel the potatoes, cut them into cubes and cook them in boiling water for about 10 minutes (they should stay firm). Slice the onions, brown them with the speck. Dice the Reblochon, combine with the sour cream and season. Put everything into a dish, cover with the wine, bake for about 15 minutes or until the top is golden and crusty.

26 feb Buckwheat pasta gratin

Serves 6

PREPARATION TIME 30 MINUTES

COOKING TIME 40 MINUTES

400 g (14 oz) small buckwheat pasta shapes

30 g (1 oz) butter

30 g (1 oz) plain (all-purpose) flour

500 ml (17 fl oz/2 cups) full-cream (whole) milk

1 dash ground nutmeg

pepper

150 g (5½ oz) Beaufort cheese

6 slices prosciutto

Equipment:

gratin dish

Preheat the oven to 160°C (315°F/Gas 2–3). Cook the pasta for about 20 minutes in a large volume of salted boiling water. Melt the butter in a saucepan, add the flour all at once*, add the milk, stir with a wooden spoon for 3 minutes, then add the nutmeg and season lightly (the prosciutto will add salt). Dice the Beaufort and slice the prosciutto. Mix the pasta with the béchamel sauce and the prosciutto, scatter over the cubes of Beaufort and bake for 20 minutes.

✳ WHY ALL AT ONCE? *It produces a good butter–flour mix to make the roux.*

27 feb Fondue

Serves 6

PREPARATION TIME 20 MINUTES

400 g (14 oz) Comté cheese

400 g (14 oz) Beaufort cheese

200 g (7 oz) Emmental cheese

1 garlic clove, halved

300 ml (10½ fl oz) Apremont or dry white wine

1 teaspoon nutmeg

1 teaspoon cornflour (cornstarch)

1 liqueur glass of kirsch

pepper

2 stale baguettes, cut into croûtons

Equipment:

fondue pot

✳ WHY RUB THE POT WITH THE GARLIC? *To scare off the vampires and give a good flavour.*

✳✳ WHAT'S THE CORNFLOUR FOR? *The cornflour will help the fondue to thicken. That way it will be easier to kidnap the melted cheese with the bread cubes.*

Cut all the cheeses into small cubes. Rub the fondue pot with the garlic clove*, add the white wine and nutmeg, then, bit by bit, the diced cheeses, stirring continuously. Blend the cornflour** with the kirsch, add this mixture to the fondue, stir. Once the mixture is smooth and creamy, season with pepper and use the bread croûtons for dipping.

28 feb Walnut tart

Serves 6

PREPARATION TIME 20 MINUTES

COOKING TIME 20 MINUTES

For the pastry:

150 g (5½ oz) butter

200 g (7 oz/1⅓ cups) plain (all-purpose) flour

100 g (3½ oz) sugar

100 g (3½ oz/1 cup) ground almonds

1 egg

For the filling:

150 g (5½ oz) sugar

50 g (1¾ oz) lightly salted butter

100 ml (3½ fl oz) pouring (whipping) cream

200 g (7 oz/2 cups) walnuts

Equipment:

rolling pin

For the pastry, preheat the oven to 180°C (350°F/Gas 4). Dice the butter and let it soften at room temperature. Combine the flour, sugar and ground almonds, add the butter, work the pastry together with the palm of your hand, add the egg and repeat the process. Wrap the pastry in plastic wrap, chill for 1 hour*. Roll the pastry into a thin circle on a piece of baking paper, bake for about 20 minutes — it should be a good golden brown.

To make the filling, put the sugar in a heavy-based saucepan with 1 tablespoon water, cook until the caramel is golden brown and translucent (the sugar will start off by crystallising, then little by little it will brown and finally become translucent). At that point, add the butter and cream, cook for a further 2 minutes so that the mixture becomes smooth, add the walnuts. Pour the mixture onto the tart base. Allow to cool, then serve.

✳ WHY CHILL THE PASTRY? *The chilled pastry will be easier to handle, since the butter will have become more solid.*

9.47

it doesn't happen every day

Recipe taken from Daniel Tardy's *The Short Guide to Living Well: From Cow Tripe to Cancoillotte, it's Good to Have Something in the Pot.*

As a homage to Polymnie Cancoyotte, the father of the famous comic book hero *le sapeur Camember,* who was born on 29th February, here is the very simple and delicious recipe for *fondue de Cancoillotte* (or Cancoyotte more appropriately).

Cancoillotte is a cheese from the Franche-Comté region, a rather smelly one, and with such a runny disposition that some wits like to say that they use it to put up the wallpaper in their house or to get friendly with themselves! It's sold in a pot, plain, with butter, flavoured with garlic or *vin jaune,* etc.

For two people who have forgotten Valentine's Day, on 28th February, when the clock (a *Comtoise* clock if possible) chimes the 12 strokes of midnight, light a large candle.

Put the cheese in an earthenware pot (or a fondue set) and heat it over the candle until morning. Purists will take turns to hold the pot with arms outstretched throughout the night, but if you have an appropriate stand, you can go to bed. Under normal circumstances, a rather extraordinary smell should wake you towards four in the morning! Don't open the windows! Hold fast! Remember that it's winter and that heating is very expensive! This is not the time to catch a sore throat! Get up, quickly boil four well-rounded potatoes with a real *saucisse de Morteau* (a smoked sausage, another typically Franc-Comtoise speciality). When the sausage is cooked, cut it in half and place the two halves, upright, on two warmed plates, between the two potatoes. Pour the hot cheese on top of the sausage, it should slowly trickle down until it gently (artistically even) covers the potatoes. Grate a little ginger. Savour with your partner, then go back to bed with joy in your hearts: it only happens every four years!

Note: This recipe is no doubt the source of the word *bissextile,* which very curiously is used to describe years that contain 29th February! Yes, this *bissextile* is a very bizarre word!

29 feb

Pork pot-au-feu
Serves 6

PREPARATION TIME 20 MINUTES
COOKING TIME 1 HOUR 30 MINUTES

6 Toulouse sausages
250 g (9 oz) smoked bacon
500 g (1 lb 2 oz) pork spare-ribs, brined*
500 g (1 lb 2 oz) pork neck or blade, brined*
1 bouquet garni
2 onions
6 parsnips
6 potatoes
3 tablespoons wholegrain mustard
1 bunch of flat-leaf (Italian) parsley, chopped

* BRINED: *Ask your butcher to do this for you but you'll need to order in advance.*

* * TO DEGREASE THE COOKING LIQUID: *You can skim it regularly during cooking to remove any impurities.*

Put the sausages, bacon, pork spare-ribs and neck in a large saucepan and cover with water. Add the bouquet garni and the onions and cook for 1 hour. Peel the parsnips and potatoes, add them whole to the pan (halve them if they're large), cook for a further 30 minutes. Remove the meat and vegetables to a dish. Reduce the cooking liquid**, add the mustard, then pour over the meats. Scatter over the parsley before serving.

MARIE & LÉON

darling lobster ...

In the beginning, Marie Vachecrot, a very ordinary cook married to Léon, a lover of fine food, spent her time in front of the family fish tank that was teeming with all kinds of fish, hypnotised by so much calm and serenity. Léon, who thought this attitude was a bit weird, decided to make his fish tank one of the more macho ones by adopting a good-natured lobster.

Léon's lobster, Omar, like the pope on his mule, proudly strutted about waving his claws in front of him, frightening Marie's rabble of fish as he went. Omar had got the upper hand, he led the peaceful life of the pasha, he had the benefit of Léon's very special attentions, he had respect. The spell was broken, Omar had eyes only for Léon, Léon had eyes only for Omar. This sentimental monopoly couldn't last, Marie saw red. A landing net, a chopping board and, like an executioner under the Pompidou regime, the blade slammed down between the eyes of Omar the lobster, who never saw anything coming. Omar thus found himself split between the vengeful smile of Marie and the sad but *gourmand* smile of Léon (even so, half each!). « *A cooked lobster is better than a dead lobster,*» cried Léon. Omar the lobster was thus sacrificed on the altar of pleasure, and in homage to our friend, millions of his kin have undergone the same treatment.

And that is how Marie, destined for the anonymity of her kitchen, became the Marie who went down in history.

They've gone completely mad! Next there'll be a 32nd August!

30 feb

Lobster with herb butter

Serves 6

PREPARATION TIME 20 MINUTES
COOKING TIME 10 MINUTES

1 executioner
3 good-looking lobsters, alive
olive oil
1 tablespoon pastis
1 French shallot (eschalot)
150 g (5½ oz) butter
50 g (1¾ oz) dry bread
½ bunch of tarragon, leaves picked
½ bunch of basil, leaves picked
salt and pepper

Preheat the oven to 180°C (350°F/Gas 4). Negotiate with the executioner to cut the live lobsters in half lengthways. Heat some olive oil in a frying pan, cook the lobsters, flesh side down, for 2 minutes, add the pastis, then place on a tray and bake in the oven for 5 minutes. Peel the shallot and process the shallot, butter, bread, tarragon and basil together, then season. Spread this butter generously on the lobster flesh, bake for a further 3 minutes. Enjoy immediately.

This month

March

01 — Albin
ONION AND CHIVE QUICHE

02 — Charles
GOAT'S CHEESE WITH SPECK

03 — Gwénolé
CABBAGE STUFFED WITH LAMB

08 — Onfroy
CUTTLEFISH SALAD WITH CORIANDER

09 — France
SPAGHETTI WITH GARLIC AND PROSCIUTTO

10 — Vivien
CALF'S LIVER WITH RASPBERRY VINEGAR

15 — Louise
TROUT WITH ALMONDS

16 — Bénédicte
CLASSIC CANNELLONI

17 — Patrick
BAKED ALASKA

22 — Léa
LAMB SHOULDER WITH GARLIC AND ROSEMARY

23 — Victorien
VEAL BLANQUETTE WITH VEGETABLES

24 — Berthe
PIKE QUENELLES

29 — Gladys
ROAST BEEF WITH ANCHOVIES

30 — Amédée
THIN CHOCOLATE TART

31 — Benjamin
CLASSIC ESCARGOT

04

Casimir

CLASSIC FRIED EGGS

05

Olive

ROAST MONKFISH

06

Colette

CRÈME CARAMEL

07

Félicité

HAZELNUT FONDANT CAKE

11

Rosine

MUSSELS WITH CHORIZO

12

Justine

LENTIL SALAD WITH SMOKED
DUCK BREAST

13

Rodrigue

ROAST CHICKEN
WITH GOAT'S CHEESE

14

Mathilde

RAZOR CLAMS
WITH TARRAGON

18

Cyrille

MONKFISH WITH
BEURRE BLANC

19

Joseph

CHOCOLATE MOUSSE

20

Printemps

VEGETARIAN TAGINE

21

Clémence

FLAGEOLET BEANS

25

Humbert

HARD-BOILED EGGS
WITH MAYONNAISE

26

Lara

ANDOUILLETTES
IN WINE

27

Albert

MINESTRONE

28

Gontran

CALF'S FEET SALAD

01 02 03 04

01 mar

Onion and chive quiche

Serves 6

PREPARATION TIME 20 MINUTES

COOKING TIME 20 MINUTES

5 onions
1 bunch of chives
3 eggs
400 ml (14 fl oz) full-cream (whole) milk
1 dash ground nutmeg
salt and pepper
1 sheet store-bought shortcrust pastry

✱WHY FILL THE SHELL HALFWAY? *Once the onions are arranged in the quiche they'll take up all the available space and so the level of the quiche mixture will rise.*

Preheat the oven to 160°C (315°F/Gas 2–3). Peel the onions, steam them for 10 minutes and cut them in half. Snip the chives. Beat the eggs until just combined, add the milk, nutmeg and chives, then season. Lay the sheet of pastry in a round tart tin, half-fill it with the egg mixture*, then arrange the onions evenly on top. Cook for 20 minutes.

02 mar

Goat's cheese with speck

Serves 6

PREPARATION TIME 10 MINUTES

COOKING TIME 10 MINUTES

12 slices speck
6 sprigs of thyme
6 rounds semi-firm goat's cheese
100 ml (3½ fl oz) olive oil

✱DRESSING THE NICE CRISP FRISÉE SALAD: *Make a mustard vinaigrette and add a teaspoon of Savora (honey mustard) sauce. Slice up a few onions if you're among friends, not recommended if you're a couple: you've already got the goat's cheese, so if you add onions on top of that …*

Preheat the oven to 160°C (315°F/Gas 2–3). Lay out the slices of speck two by two in the shape of crosses. Place a sprig of thyme in the middle of the cross, top with a round of goat's cheese. Fold over the cross and drizzle with olive oil. Line a baking tray with baking paper and bake for about 10 minutes. Serve as a starter with a crisp salad of frisée lettuce*.

03 mar

Cabbage stuffed with lamb

Serves 6

PREPARATION TIME 30 MINUTES

COOKING TIME 20 MINUTES

100 g (3½ oz) baguette
2 French shallots (eschalots)
6 garlic cloves
100 ml (3½ fl oz) olive oil + plus extra for drizzling
50 g (1¾ oz/⅓ cup) pine nuts
600 g (1 lb 5 oz) leftover cooked lamb
4 eggs
200 ml (7 fl oz) pouring (whipping) cream
salt and pepper
1 green cabbage
Equipment:
six 5 cm (2 inch) round cooking rings

✱LINING: *Lining a mould means to cover it with another ingredient or substance. You can line a mould with plastic wrap, butter, flour or even cabbage leaves. Watch out for wrinkles, they can be fatal when it comes to unmoulding. What's more, it looks sloppy!*

Dry the baguette in the oven for 15 minutes at 140°C (275°F/Gas 1). Chop the shallots and garlic. Crumble the baguette, sauté in the olive oil with the shallots and garlic until everything has browned. Add the pine nuts and allow them to brown. Increase the oven temperature to 180°C (350°F/Gas 4). Mince the lamb in a mincer or food processor, add the eggs, cream and the bread mixture. Season. Separate the cabbage leaves, remove the central rib. Bring some water to the boil with a little salt, blanch the cabbage leaves for 3 minutes, refresh them immediately. Drain the cabbage. Line a baking tray with baking paper. Line* each cooking ring with one or two cabbage leaves, then fill with the lamb mixture. Turn the cabbage leaves over to seal. Drizzle with extra olive oil and cook for 20 minutes. Can be eaten hot or cold.

04 mar

Classic fried eggs

Serves 6

PREPARATION TIME 5 MINUTES
COOKING TIME 3 MINUTES

12 free-range eggs
20 g (¾ oz) butter
sunflower oil
salt and pepper
wine vinegar
snipped chives

✳ WHY NOT BREAK THE EGGS DIRECTLY INTO THE FRYING PAN? *One is never safe from a rotten egg and you only realise it's rotten once you've broken it: if it is cracked directly into the frying pan, you have to throw out all of the eggs. For lovely shiny fried eggs, break them into ramekins, and put aside the ones with broken yolks for another use.*

Break the eggs into a bowl, two at a time*. Melt the butter with a little oil in a non-stick frying pan, let it get very hot. Pour in all of the eggs then cook for 2–3 minutes, season, add a dash of vinegar.

A good dipping soldier makes a good egg: brioche soldier with Saint-Morêt cheese and honey; white bread soldier with butter, wholegrain mustard and boiled ham; grissini soldier wrapped in smoked salmon; baguette soldier toasted and rubbed with tomato and garlic; *pain d'épice* (see page 512) soldier with Roquefort cheese; country-style bread soldier with tapenade, anchovies … and more!

05 mar

Roast monkfish

Serves 6

PREPARATION TIME 20 MINUTES
COOKING TIME 15 MINUTES

1 monkfish or other firm-fleshed white fish
2 garlic cloves
8 French shallots (eschalots)
100 g (3½ oz) sun-dried salty black olives
4 tinned anchovies in oil
10 slices speck
100 g (3½ oz) fresh spinach leaves
4 tablespoons olive oil

✳ PEEL THE SKIN FROM THE MONKFISH: *Slide a knife over the fillets and pull back the skin. I could already see you with a vegetable peeler in one hand and the fish in the other, looking desperately for a tip!*

✳ TAKE OUT THE FILLETS: *It's not about showing them a good time, but working along the central backbone with a sharp knife.*

Preheat the oven to 180°C (350°F/Gas 4). Peel the skin from the monkfish*, take out the fillets**. Peel the garlic and shallots; slice the shallots. Pit the olives and process with the anchovies and garlic. Lay out the speck slices so they overlap (the speck 'carpet' should match the length of a monkfish fillet), cover with spinach leaves. Lay one of the monkfish fillets over the spinach, spread it with the olive mixture, lay another fillet on top in the reverse direction (head-to-toe), roll it all up in the speck and tie up with kitchen string. Sauté the shallots in olive oil, place the fish parcel in the pan to brown on all sides. Place in a gratin dish and bake in the oven for 10 minutes.

06 mar

Crème caramel

Serves 6

PREPARATION TIME 20 MINUTES
COOKING TIME 45 MINUTES
CHILLING TIME 1 HOUR

400 g (14 oz) sugar
8 eggs
1 litre (35 fl oz/4 cups) full-cream (whole) milk
1 vanilla bean, seeds scraped
Equipment:
6 small ramekins

✳ DARK CARAMEL: *The caramel takes on different colours depending on how long it cooks. When the mixture starts to caramelise, let it cook for a further 2–3 minutes so that it takes on a slightly deeper colour.*

✳✳ THE SOLID STAGE: *The sugar will form a solid white mass.*

✳✳✳ WHY? *When you whisk the eggs with the sugar, the mixture will become pale and take on a creamy texture, a sign that the sugar is well incorporated into the egg yolk.*

Preheat the oven to 150°C (300°F/Gas 2). Combine 200 g (7 oz) of the sugar with 100 ml (3½ fl oz) water, cook in a heavy-based saucepan until you get a dark caramel* (the sugar will go through a wet stage, then a solid stage**, then it will start to caramelise). Pour the caramel into the base of each ramekin. Whisk the eggs with the remaining sugar until the mixure becomes pale and frothy***, add the milk into which you have scraped the vanilla seeds. Pour the custard mixture over the caramel in each ramekin, cook in a bain-marie in the oven for 45 minutes. Allow to cool, separate the custard from the sides using a knife, then unmould to serve.

MARIE & LÉON

cold shower and bain-marie

In the beginning, Marie Vachecrot, a very ordinary cook married to Léon, a lover of fine food, spent her time between her bathroom and her library, neglecting the kitchen to the great despair of her husband. One day, Marie decided, in order to satisfy Léon's ever more *gourmand* desires, to mix together some eggs, sugar and milk. She poured her mixture into some small ramekins that she had arranged on a tray filled with water (force of habit). She put this apparatus into the oven and returned to her favourite occupation, a nice soak in the *bain* (bath). Léon was surprised by the sweet aroma that filled the house when he arrived home. He rushed into the kitchen, teeth sharpened like bayonets and salivating like the Nile in flood at the sight of the gently burbling *petits pots de crème* (little custard pots). After 30 minutes of this, Léon was at the end of his tether and in a mad rage yelled: « *I'm hungry, get out of the bain, Marie.* »

And that is how Marie, destined for the anonymity of her kitchen, became the Marie who went down in history.

✳ZESTING:
Remove about 1 mm of skin from the citrus fruit. The zest shouldn't contain any white pith, just the rind of the fruit.

✳✳BAIN-MARIE:
A form of cooking that consists of placing a container of ingredients in a larger one filled with boiling water.

07 mar

Hazelnut fondant cake
Serves 6
PREPARATION TIME 10 MINUTES
COOKING TIME 10 MINUTES

200 g (7 oz) milk chocolate
100 g (3½ oz) butter
4 eggs
100 g (3½ oz) sugar
50 g (1¾ oz) cornflour (cornstarch)
100 g (3½ oz/¾ cup) hazelnuts
zest* of 1 orange
Equipment:
20 x 15 cm (8 x 6 inch) fondant mould

Preheat the oven to 160°C (315°F/Gas 2–3). Melt the chocolate and butter in a double-boiler or bain-marie**. Whisk the eggs with the sugar until the mixture is pale and frothy, then add the cornflour. Add the chocolate mixture and remaining ingredients. Pour into a buttered and floured mould, cook for about 10 minutes. Allow to cool before serving (the texture of the soft centre will depend on cooking time).

08 mar

Cuttlefish salad with coriander

Serves 6

PREPARATION TIME 20 MINUTES
COOKING TIME 5 MINUTES
RESTING TIME 1 HOUR

juice of 2 lemons
2 tablespoons fish sauce
3 tablespoons sunflower oil
1 tablespoon rice vinegar
2 tablespoons sugar
600 g (1 lb 5 oz) cuttlefish hoods*
6 bulb spring onions (scallions)
½ bunch of coriander (cilantro)

Combine the lemon juice, fish sauce, 2 tablespoons of the sunflower oil, the rice vinegar and sugar. Cut the cuttlefish hoods into equal-sized triangles, slash them** in a criss-cross pattern using a knife. Slice the spring onions, combine them with the vinaigrette. Heat the remaining sunflower oil in a frying pan, sear the cuttlefish for 2 minutes on each side (they should stay translucent inside), add them to the sauce with the spring onions. Chill for 1 hour before serving. Pick the leaves from the coriander finely chop and sprinkle over the cuttlefish.

✻WHERE CAN I GET CUTTLEFISH HOODS? *You can try a bakery or a dry-cleaner's, but the fishmonger remains the most likely place.*

✻✻WHY SLASH THE CUTTLEFISH? *Cuttlefish can quickly become rubbery, slashing will tenderise the flesh.*

09 mar

before

✻SEGMENTS: *Peel the lemon down to the flesh, making sure to remove all the pith. Slide a very sharp knife between the lemon segments so that you can take out just the flesh, remove the pips.*

Spaghetti with garlic and prosciutto

Serves 6

PREPARATION TIME 15 MINUTES
COOKING TIME 10 MINUTES

400 g (14 oz) spaghetti
3 tablespoons olive oil
3 slices prosciutto
6 garlic cloves
1 lemon
50 g (1¾ oz) caperberries
salt and pepper

Cook the spaghetti in boiling salted water with 1 tablespoon of the olive oil for 7 minutes. Refresh immediately. Cut the prosciutto into thin strips. Roughly chop the garlic. Peel the lemon and take out the segments*. Sauté the garlic in the remaining olive oil with the strips of prosciutto, add the spaghetti, lemon and capers, season.

after

10 mar

Calf's liver with raspberry vinegar

Serves 6

PREPARATION TIME 15 MINUTES
COOKING TIME 15 MINUTES

6 potatoes
80 g (2¾ oz) butter
100 ml (3½ fl oz) olive oil
1 slice stale white bread
1 bunch of flat-leaf (Italian) parsley
2 tablespoons raspberry vinegar
2 French shallots (eschalots)
6 thick pieces of calf's liver
salt and pepper

Peel the potatoes, cut them into thin slices. Sauté these in a frying pan with 50 g (1¾ oz) of the butter and 2 tablespoons of the oil for about 10 minutes, turning them over regularly. Process the bread with the parsley, remaining olive oil and raspberry vinegar. Finely chop the shallots, sauté them gently with the remaining butter, add the pieces of calf's liver, cook them for 2 minutes on each side (depending on how you like them cooked), season, remove the liver from the pan, deglaze* with the parsley oil. Serve the potatoes with a piece of liver on top. Make a *cordon*** of parsley oil.

✻DEGLAZE: *To pour a liquid into a pan or tray in order to pick up the bits stuck to the bottom.*

✻✻MAKE A CORDON: *Surround a meal with oil.*

11 mar

Mussels with chorizo

Serves 6

PREPARATION TIME 10 MINUTES
COOKING TIME 15 MINUTES

4 garlic cloves
4 French shallots (eschalots)
150 g (5½ oz) spicy chorizo
3 kg (6 lb 12 oz) mussels
2 tablespoons olive oil
200 ml (7 fl oz) white wine
50 g (1¾ oz) butter
1 bunch of coriander (cilantro)

Peel the garlic and shallots, slice them finely. Cut the chorizo into slices, then into 5 mm (¼ inch) thin strips. Clean the mussels*. Sweat** the shallots for about 3 minutes in the olive oil, then add the garlic, chorizo, wine and butter, simmer for 5 minutes. Add the mussels, cover and stir regularly for 5 minutes. Pick the coriander leaves and chop. Add just before serving. There's no need to season because the mussels are salty and the chorizo is spicy.

✳ CLEAN THE MUSSELS: *Ask the fishmonger to do this, or scrape them with a knife.*

✳✳ SWEAT: *Cook the shallots without colouring them.*

12 mar

Lentil salad with smoked duck breast

Serves 6

PREPARATION TIME 15 MINUTES
COOKING TIME 20 MINUTES

200 g (7 oz/1 cup) puy
    or tiny blue-green lentils
4 potatoes
1 bouquet garni*
1 French shallot (eschalot)
1 teaspoon mustard
1 tablespoon cider vinegar
80 ml (2½ fl oz/⅓ cup) walnut oil
100 g (3½ oz) air-dried duck breast
100 g (3½ oz) sun-dried tomatoes
1 bunch of flat-leaf (Italian) parsley
salt and pepper

string

✳ HOME-MADE BOUQUET GARNI: *Tie the green part of a leek, a bay leaf, a parsley stem and a fresh sprig of thyme together with kitchen string.*

✳✳ WHY COOK THE LENTILS AND POTATOES TOGETHER? *Lentils and potatoes have the same cooking time.*

Place the lentils and the peeled potatoes** with the bouquet garni in a saucepan of cold water, cook for 20 minutes, drain and slice the potatoes. Peel and slice the shallot. Combine the mustard with the vinegar and walnut oil, add the shallot. Finely slice the duck breast and sun-dried tomatoes, pick the parsley leaves and chop, mix all the ingredients together, then season. Serve warm or cold.

13 mar

Roast chicken with goat's cheese

Serves 6

PREPARATION TIME 15 MINUTES
COOKING TIME 1 HOUR

1 free-range chicken
6 Dutch carrots
6 French shallots (eschalots)
6 garlic cloves
100 ml (3½ fl oz) olive oil
1 tablespoon dried rosemary
1 fresh Sainte-Maure goat's cheese
salt and pepper

Preheat the oven to 160°C (315°F/Gas 2–3). Cut the chicken into eight portions (thighs, drumsticks, breasts and wings). Peel the carrots. Place the chicken in a roasting tin with the whole carrots, shallots and garlic cloves in their skins, drizzle with olive oil, sprinkle with the rosemary. Bake for 45 minutes, basting* the chicken regularly with its juices. Crumble the cheese over the chicken and bake for a further 15 minutes. Season and serve from the roasting tin.

✳ WHY DOES THE CHICKEN NEED TO BE BASTED? *So it doesn't dry out.*

14 mar

Razor clams with tarragon

Serves 6
PREPARATION TIME 2 HOURS
COOKING TIME 5 MINUTES

30 razor clams*
100 ml (3½ fl oz) wine vinegar
1 French shallot (eschalot)
1 bunch of tarragon, leaves picked
80 g (2¾ oz) butter
1 tablespoon pastis
salt and pepper

✳ RAZOR CLAM
SEASON? *They
are available all
year round.*

✳✳ WHY PURGE
THE RAZOR CLAMS?
*Like ostriches, razor
clams hide themselves
in the sand. Soak in
vinegar water to get
rid of their « holiday
souvenirs ».*

Two hours before serving, purge** the razor clams — to do this put the wine vinegar in a bowl with 500 ml (17 fl oz/2 cups) water and rinse well. Peel and slice the shallot, then process with the tarragon, butter and pastis. Gently sauté in a frying pan — as soon as the mixture starts to brown, add the drained clams, cook for 5 minutes, turning delicately. Season and serve immediately.

15 mar

Trout with almonds

Serves 6
PREPARATION TIME 10 MINUTES
COOKING TIME 10 MINUTES

1 good fisherman
6 good wild brown trout
50 g (1¾ oz/⅓ cup) plain (all-purpose) flour
6 French shallots (eschalots)
100 g (3½ oz) butter
100 g (3½ oz/1 cup) flaked almonds
salt and pepper
juice of 1 lemon

✳ HOW DO YOU
PREPARE THE FISH?
*Cut open the trout's
belly, cut the base of
the gills with scissors,
remove the guts of
the fish.*

Find a good fisherman (or a good fishmonger!) so he can catch you six beautiful wild brown trout. Clean the trout, discard the gills*, dust with flour. Peel the shallots, slice them roughly. Melt the butter in a frying pan and, once it is foamy, add the trout, shallots and almonds. Cook for 5 minutes on each side. Baste the trout regularly with the almond butter. Season. Pour the lemon juice into the pan to deglaze before serving.

16 mar

Classic cannelloni

Serves 6
PREPARATION TIME 30 MINUTES
COOKING TIME 30 MINUTES

6 garlic cloves
olive oil
1 bunch of flat-leaf (Italian) parsley, leaves picked
2 lemongrass stems
4 slices bread
200 ml (7 fl oz) pouring (whipping) cream
*800 g (1 lb 12 oz) leftover cooked meat,
    such as beef, lamb, pork or chicken*
1 teaspoon quatre-épices (four-spice mix)
salt and pepper
18 store-bought dried cannelloni tubes
400 g (14 oz) tinned tomatoes
2 tablespoons tomato paste (concentrated purée)
100 g (3½ oz) Comté cheese
Equipment:
piping (icing) bag

✳ FILLING THE
CANNELLONI: *Take
a cannelloni tube
in one hand, use
your thumb to
close off one end,
otherwise it'll be a
real shambles. Fill
the cannelloni tube
from the other end
using a piping bag.
In effect, once your
thumb is blocking off
the bottom end, a
real problem emerges
if you try to fill the
tube from that end,
you see?*

Preheat the oven to 160°C (315°F/Gas 2–3). Peel the garlic, chop it and lightly brown it in olive oil. Finely chop the parsley and lemongrass. Dip both sides of each bread slice briefly in the cream. Process the meat with the bread and cream, add the chopped garlic, parsley, lemongrass, *quatre-épices* and season. Put this mixture in a piping bag, fill* each cannelloni tube. Place in a gratin dish. Roughly process the tomatoes, then add the tomato paste and pour this mixture over the cannelloni. Dot with small pieces of cheese and bake in the oven for 30 minutes.

MARIE & LÉON

I don't understand

In the beginning, Marie Vachecrot, a very ordinary cook, married to Léon, a lover of fine food, spent her time on the ski slopes and in the *après-ski* bars, neglecting the kitchen to the great despair of her husband. One evening, filled with remorse at so much culinary negligence, Marie, who had taken care of all the red wine on the slopes (and not all the red slopes), finally decided to grant her husband his pleasure. « *Sponge fingers, jam, egg white, vanilla ice cream, that'll do the job nicely,* » thought Marie, between two grogs. « *There's my man home now. B'jour chéri, want some dessert? Made it myself, I'm just warming m'self with a drop of the good stuff, it is so cold around here.* » One false step, a fall caught just in time, some kirsch that goes up in flames, and an omelette that catches alight.

And that is how Marie, destined for the anonymity of her kitchen, became the Marie who went down in history.

17 mar

✱ Why light the warm kirsch in its saucepan and not afterwards? *Poured over the baked Alaska, the kirsch cools too quickly and won't flambé: jeers and mocking laughter shall fall down upon you like hail in March. Flambé before so you can be sure to flambé after!*

Baked Alaska
Serves 6
PREPARATION TIME 20 MINUTES
FREEZING TIME 30 MINUTES

200 g (7 oz) caster (superfine) sugar
200 ml (7 fl oz) kirsch
10 savoiardi (lady fingers) biscuits
350 g (12 oz) redcurrant jam
6 egg whites
1 litre (35 fl oz/4 cups) bourbon vanilla ice cream

Make a syrup with 100 g (3½ oz) of the sugar, 200 ml (7 fl oz) water and 100 ml (3½ fl oz) of the kirsch. Dip the biscuits into this syrup while it's still hot, arrange them on a plate that has the same dimensions as the tub of vanilla ice cream. Cover the biscuits with half of the redcurrant jam. Whip the egg whites to very stiff peaks, add the remaining sugar, continue to whip. Fill a piping (icing) bag with the whipped egg whites. Remove the ice cream from its tub, place it on the biscuits, cover the ice cream with the remaining redcurrant jam and cover with the whipped egg whites. Place in the freezer for 30 minutes. Heat the remaining kirsch and set it alight✱. While it's still alight, pour it over the baked Alaska.

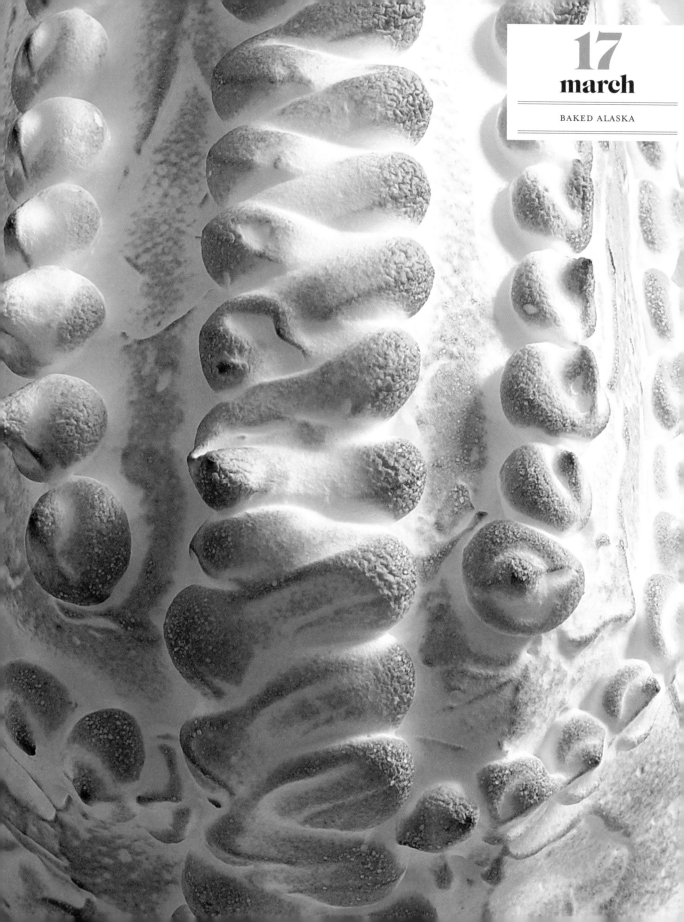

18
march

MONKFISH WITH
BEURRE BLANC

18 mar

Monkfish with beurre blanc

Serves 6
PREPARATION TIME 20 MINUTES
COOKING TIME 20 MINUTES

1.2 kg (2 lb 10 oz) whole monkfish or other
*   firm-fleshed white fish*
200 g (7 oz/1⅓ cups) podded fresh peas
200 g (7 oz) green beans
200 g (7 oz) snow peas (mangetout)
200 g (7 oz) fresh broad (fava) beans
2 French shallots (eschalots)
200 ml (7 fl oz) white wine
150 g (5½ oz) butter
olive oil
salt and pepper

*COOKING
TIMES FOR THE
VEGETABLES:
Peas 5 minutes,
beans 15 minutes,
snow peas
10 minutes, broad
beans 30 seconds.

**REFRESH:
Plunge into iced
water, immediately.

***CUT
THE BUTTER INTO
CUBES? *It will be*
easier to whisk in.

****BEURRE
BLANC: *Built on a*
reduction of white
wine and shallots.

Remove the skin from the monkfish, take out the fillets and cut each into six chunks. Cook the vegetables separately in boiling salted water until *al dente**. Refresh** immediately. Finely slice the shallots. Put the white wine on to boil, add the shallots and reduce until almost dry. Cut the butter into cubes***, whisk into the wine reduction over gentle heat (this will ensure the beurre blanc**** has a creamy texture). Reheat the vegetables and pan-fry the monkfish in olive oil until just cooked through, season and coat generously with the beurre blanc.

19 mar

Chocolate mousse

Serves 6
PREPARATION TIME 20 MINUTES
CHILLING TIME 2 HOURS

300 g (10½ oz) dark chocolate
200 ml (7 fl oz) pouring (whipping) cream
20 g (¾ oz) butter
5 eggs, separated
100 g (3½ oz) caster (superfine) sugar (optional)
*   + 1 tablespoon, extra*

*STABILISE
THE EGG WHITES:
Whip the egg whites
vigorously with
1 tablespoon caster
sugar and they'll
hold better.

**WHY A
SPATULA? *A rubber*
spatula lets you
delicately pick up the
egg whites without
breaking them so they
won't collapse.

Melt the chocolate in a double-boiler with the cream and butter (the water in the bottom pan should be barely simmering). Mix to obtain a smooth texture. Whisk the egg yolks with 100 g (3½ oz) of the sugar, if desired. Whip the egg whites to stiff peaks; stabilise them* with the extra tablespoon of caster sugar. When the chocolate has cooled to room temperature, add the yolks, then delicately fold in the egg whites using a rubber spatula**. Fill six small ramekins and chill for 2 hours before serving.

20 mar

Vegetarian tagine

Serves 6
PREPARATION TIME 20 MINUTES
COOKING TIME 20 MINUTES

3 Dutch carrots
1 bunch of radishes
1 bunch of baby turnips
3 onions
3 garlic cloves
1 lemon
olive oil
1 teaspoon ground coriander
1 teaspoon ground cumin
200 ml (7 fl oz) vegetable stock
100 g (3½ oz) green beans
100 g (3½ oz) snow peas (mangetout)
100 g (3½ oz) podded fresh peas
½ savoy cabbage
salt and pepper
Equipment:
tagine dish*

*THE ADVANTAGE
OF A TAGINE DISH:
It allows all the
different ingredients
to be gently cooked
or steamed so that
their flavours are
concentrated.

**MOISTEN:
Naughty!

Trim 1 cm (½ inch) from the tops of the carrots, radishes and turnips; peel them. Cut the carrots and turnips into halves or quarters lengthways (depending on size). Peel and slice the onions and garlic, cut the lemon into six, keeping the peel on. Sauté the onions and garlic in a little olive oil with the coriander and cumin, then add all of the vegetables and the lemon. Moisten** with the stock. Cover the tagine dish, cook over a gentle heat for about 20 minutes, season before serving.

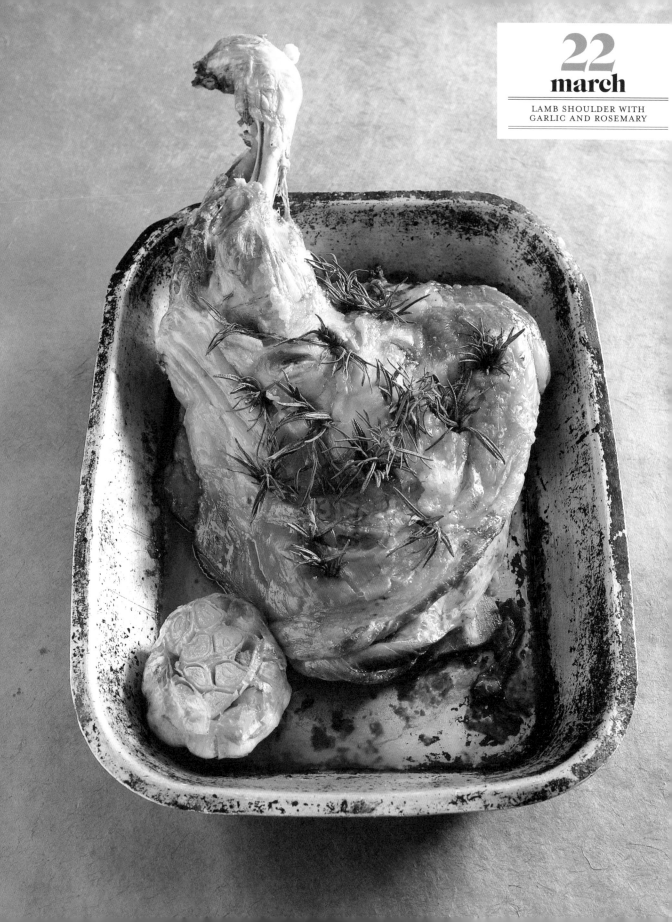

21 mar

Flageolet beans

Serves 6

PREPARATION TIME 10 MINUTES
SOAKING TIME 12 HOURS
COOKING TIME 1 HOUR

500 g (1 lb 2 oz) flageolet (green shell) beans
2 onions
1 piece old prosciutto
50 g (1¾ oz) butter
3 garlic cloves
1 bouquet garni
3 tablespoons sour cream
salt and pepper

✻SOAK THE
FLAGEOLET BEANS:
Like all dried beans,
flageolet beans
should be soaked in
about three times
their volume of water
so they can rehydrate
and become more
tender with cooking.

The day before, soak the flageolet beans in water*. Peel the onions and finely chop them. Cut the prosciutto into thin ſtrips. In a large saucepan, gently sauté the onions in the butter, add the garlic cloves whole, the flageolet beans and the bouquet garni. Add enough water to reach 2 cm (¾ inch) above the beans. Cook over gentle heat for 1 hour — the beans should ſtill be firm. Add the sour cream and season before serving.

22 mar

Lamb shoulder with garlic and rosemary

Serves 6

PREPARATION TIME 20 MINUTES
MARINATING TIME 1 NIGHT
COOKING TIME 1 HOUR

2 garlic bulbs
5 ſprigs of rosemary
2 lamb shoulders, bone in
  (it's meatball time if there is any left over)
olive oil
fleur de sel and pepper

✻STUD WITH
GARLIC: *Make*
small incisions in
the shoulders with a
knife, insert a half
clove into each hole.

✻✻WHY
PREPARE IT THE
DAY BEFORE? *To*
allow the flavours
of the garlic and
rosemary to infuse
the lamb.

The night before, peel one of the bulbs of garlic, cut each clove in half lengthways, cut the rosemary into 5 cm (2 inch) ſticks. Stud* the lamb shoulders all over with the garlic and rosemary. Drizzle with olive oil, season with *fleur de sel* and coarsely ground pepper, cover with plastic wrap and leave in the refrigerator overnight**. Preheat the oven to 200°C (400°F/Gas 6). Cut the other head of garlic horizontally, arrange it around the shoulders and bake in the oven for 1 hour for rare lamb. Baſte the shoulders regularly with their juices during cooking.

23 mar

Veal blanquette with vegetables

Serves 6

PREPARATION TIME 20 MINUTES
COOKING TIME 1 HOUR 30 MINUTES

1.2 kg (2 lb 10 oz) veal, cut into 5 cm (2 inch) cubes
50 g (1¾ oz) butter
1 tablespoon plain (all-purpose) flour
250 ml (9 fl oz/1 cup) white wine
1 litre (35 fl oz/4 cups) vegetable stock
1 onion studded with 4 cloves
1 bouquet garni
6 Dutch carrots
100 g (3½ oz) green beans
100 g (3½ oz) snow peas (mangetout)
100 g (3½ oz) podded fresh peas
3 savoy cabbage leaves, chopped
2 tablespoons crème fraîche
1 egg yolk
juice of 1 lemon
salt and pepper

✻AL DENTE:
Still a little criſp.

✻✻WHY SERVE
IMMEDIATELY?
It is important the
blanquette doesn't
boil after the crème
fraîche is added or
the egg will curdle.

In a very large flameproof casserole dish, sauté the veal in the butter, add the flour and allow to brown. Deglaze with the wine and ſtock. Add the onion and bouquet garni, cook at a bare simmer for 90 minutes, uncovered, keeping an eye on the liquid level (the pieces of meat should always be covered). Peel the carrots, keep the tops. Cook the vegetables separately in boiling salted water until *al dente*. Refresh immediately. Combine the crème fraîche with the egg yolk and lemon juice. Reheat the vegetables with the meat, turn off the heat, reſt for 5 minutes. Add the crème fraîche mixture. Season and serve immediately**.

MARIE & LÉON

the qu'nelle ...

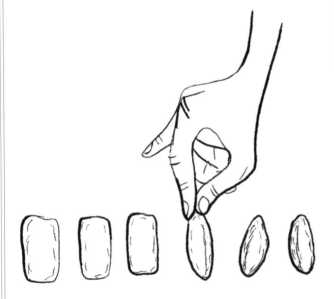

𝒯he pike quenelle is a typical Lyonnaise recipe, particularly enjoyed by Marie and Léon Vachecrot.

Quenelles are a serious business, there's no room for mistakes. The quenelle is the soul of the *canut* silk workers, the living memory of all those Lyonnaise *mères* (mothers). Those women who laboured in cramped kitchens to satisfy hordes of hungry *les gones* (local folk) have gone down in history thanks to the *qu'nelle*. So mind that you reflect on this with each mouthful, pay homage with each forkful, and support the OL (*Olympique Lyon*, Lyon's soccer team).

24 mar

✱WHY POUND IT?
The suet needs to be mashed to give it a smooth texture.

✱✱SHAPE:
Cocoon-shaped or bouchon (cork-shaped) are fine ... bouchons are very Lyonnaise.

✱✱✱ WHY CHILL? *The fat hardens and the quenelles are then easier to handle and stand up better during cooking.*

Pike quenelles
Serves 6
PREPARATION TIME 20 MINUTES
COOKING TIME 20 MINUTES
RESTING TIME 1 NIGHT

350 g (12 oz) pike or other firm-fleshed white fish
150 g (5½ oz) suet (calf kidney fat) or butter
4 eggs, separated
180 g (6¼ oz) plain (all-purpose) flour
300 ml (10½ fl oz) full-cream (whole) milk
1 dash ground nutmeg
salt and pepper
Equipment:
mortar and pestle

Remove any skin and bones from the pike flesh. Pound* the flesh together with the suet (for the purists) or the butter (for the tourists) to make a smooth paste. Combine the egg yolks with the flour, milk and nutmeg, then cook in a saucepan over gentle heat for about 10 minutes; allow to cool. Whip the egg whites to stiff peaks. Combine the fish with the egg yolk mixture, add the egg whites and season. Shape** the quenelles according to your fancy, then chill in the refrigerator overnight***. Poach the quenelles for 5–8 minutes in simmering water, then drain. Serve the quenelles with a lobster bisque and tomato sauce of your own making ...

25 mar

Hard-boiled eggs with mayonnaise

Serves 6

PREPARATION TIME 20 MINUTES
COOKING TIME 10 MINUTES

12 eggs
For the mayonnaise:
1 egg
1 tablespoon mustard
1 tablespoon wine vinegar
300 ml (10½ fl oz) sunflower oil
salt and pepper

Cook the eggs by carefully immersing them in boiling water, cook at a gentle simmer for 10 minutes, refresh in iced water. Remove the shells. To make the mayonnaise, put the egg, mustard and vinegar in a bowl, add the oil, season and process in a food processor or use a stick blender to combine.
To vary the classic mayonnaise add:

+ *juice and zest of 1 lime*
+ *1 tablespoon crème fraîche, 1 teaspoon curry powder, a touch of saffron*
+ *1 bunch of chives, 1 lemongrass stem, chopped*
+ *1 teaspoon pastis, 1 bunch of tarragon*
+ *1 tablespoon tomato sauce (ketchup), 1 tablespoon Cognac*

26 mar

Andouillettes in wine

Serves 6

PREPARATION TIME 10 MINUTES
COOKING TIME 20 MINUTES

6 AAAAA (Association Amicale des Amateurs d'Andouillettes Authentiques*) andouillettes
120 g (4¼ oz/½ cup) wholegrain mustard
1 tablespoon soft brown sugar
250 ml (9 fl oz/1 cup) white wine
6 French shallots (eschalots)
1 bay leaf
1 sprig of thyme

❋ AAAAA: *A real association called the Friendly Association of Authentic Andouillette Lovers.*

❋❋ WHITE WINE CARAMEL: *Once you have obtained a caramel, you add 1 glass of white wine to stop the caramel cooking any further.*

Preheat the oven to 160°C (315°F/Gas 2–3). Spread the andouillettes with mustard. Lay them in a gratin dish. Make a caramel* with the brown sugar, deglaze with the wine. Peel the shallots, cut them in half, arrange them in the dish with the bay leaf and thyme. Pour over the white wine caramel and bake in the oven for 20 minutes.

27 mar

Minestrone

Serves 6

PREPARATION TIME 10 MINUTES
COOKING TIME 20 MINUTES

For the pesto:
1 bunch of basil
1 tablespoon pine nuts
1 garlic clove
50 g (1¾ oz/½ cup) grated parmesan cheese
2 tablespoons olive oil
salt and pepper
For the soup:
200 g (7 oz) green beans
200 g (7 oz/1⅓ cups) podded fresh peas
100 g (3½ oz) snow peas (mangetout)
1 bunch of radishes, keep the tops for prettiness
2 onions
1 tablespoon olive oil
1 litre (35 fl oz/4 cups) vegetable stock
100 g (3½ oz) spaghetti

Make the pesto by processing the basil, pine nuts, garlic, parmesan and olive oil. Season. To make the soup, cook the vegetables separately in a saucepan of boiling salted water until *al dente*. Refresh immediately*. Peel and slice the onions, sauté gently in the oil, then add the stock. Break the spaghetti into 2 cm (¾ inch) lengths and cook in the vegetable stock. Allow to cool, add the vegetables, season. Serve cold or hot, with the pesto.

❋ WHY REFRESH THE VEGETABLES? *So they stay crisp and retain their colour.*

28 mar

Calf's feet salad

Serves 6

PREPARATION TIME 30 MINUTES
COOKING TIME 4 HOURS

2 brown onions
1 white onion
4 blanched calf's feet*
1 bouquet garni
3 celery stalks, halved
1 bunch of radishes
6 chives
50 g (1¾ oz) cornichons
1 tablespoon Dijon mustard
1 tablespoon wine vinegar
125 ml (4 fl oz/½ cup) olive oil
salt and pepper

Peel all of the onions and slice the white onion. Put the calves' feet in a large volume of water with the whole onions, the bouquet garni and celery and cook for 4 hours. Remove the meat from the feet while still warm and cut into cubes. Cut the radishes into thin slices. Snip the chives and chop the cornichons. Combine the mustard with the vinegar and gradually add the oil. Combine the calves' feet with all of the ingredients and dress with the mustard vinaigrette. Season.

✳AND HOW DO YOU PREPARE CALF'S FEET? *Calves' feet are generally sold blanched and cut in two. The cooking time is rather long, but the result is worth the effort.*

29 mar

Roast beef with anchovies

Serves 6

PREPARATION TIME 15 MINUTES
COOKING TIME 20 MINUTES

1 kg (2 lb 4 oz) mushrooms
6 French shallots (eschalots)
50 g (1¾ oz) butter
sunflower oil
1.2 kg (2 lb 10 oz) roasting beef, tied with kitchen string
12 tinned anchovies in oil, drained

Preheat the oven to 180°C (350°F/Gas 4). Clean the mushrooms* and trim the stems. Peel and slice the shallots. Melt the butter with a little oil directly in a roasting tin. Add the shallots, mushroom and beef and turn to brown the beef on all sides. Transfer to the oven and cook for about 15 minutes for rare. Add the anchovies. Before serving, let the beef rest for a good 5 minutes**.

✳HOW TO CLEAN MUSHROOMS? *Rub with a damp cloth.*

✳✳WHY REST THE ROAST BEEF? *To relax the flesh, it will then be more tender and tasty.*

30 mar

Thin chocolate tart

Serves 6

PREPARATION TIME 20 MINUTES
CHILLING TIME 1 HOUR
COOKING TIME 10 MINUTES

For the pastry:
200 g (7 oz/1⅓ cups) plain (all-purpose) flour
100 g (3½ oz) caster (superfine) sugar
50 g (1¾ oz/½ cup) ground almonds
1 pinch salt
120 g (4¼ oz) butter, cubed and softened
1 egg yolk
For the chocolate topping:
1 orange
50 g (1¾ oz) butter
150 ml (5 fl oz) pouring (whipping) cream
140 g (5 oz) dark chocolate

Preheat the oven to 180°C (350°F/Gas 4). Sift* the flour with the sugar, ground almonds and salt. Add the cubes of butter in stages. Add the egg yolk, work the pastry using your palm to give it a crumbly texture. Shape it into a ball, cover with plastic wrap, chill for 1 hour**. Roll the pastry out on a sheet of baking paper to make a very thin circle 2 mm (1/16 inch) thick all over. Cook for about 10 minutes — the pastry should be a nice golden brown.

For the chocolate topping, zest and juice the orange, add to the butter, cream and chocolate, melt all of these together and coat the tart. Leave at room temperature for 30 minutes before serving.

✳SIFT: *Put the flour, sugar and ground almonds through a sieve, so that each grain is separate, this avoids lumps forming.*

✳✳WHY CHILL THE PASTRY FOR AN HOUR? *The butter will harden and the pastry will be easier to roll.*

MARIE & LÉON

the hunting of the snail

*I*t's chaos this rainy morning as boxes within the Vachecrot household are turned upside-down in search of rubber boots — waxed ones, preferably yellow — and a wicker basket. Léon is going snail-hunting, and the snail is a sly one, mind.

No mercy shall be shown to the beast: garden snail, Roman snail or giant African snail, it shall be genocide.

Helix pomatia just has to behave itself and the garlic and parsley aren't far away. *« After all, you can't get too bothered over a creature that's autosexual! »*, says Léon, gearing up for the fight. Léon is wound up like a clock, the rain has stirred the male warrior within, the testosterone is flowing, the beard is three days' old, his hands tremble. First, a dose of white wine, as if granting a last request (in case he doesn't come back from the journey), and a hip flask in the pocket, to use as disinfectant in case of injury. *« Pear eau-de-vie is very healing, if I happen to hurt myself! »*

All systems are on red alert — the signal is given and he's off. Léon springs forward, head first, gathering speed with a determined step, white froth at the corners of his mouth. The step was slippery, Léon over-hasty, takes a hard fall, the flask is broken and Léon returns home. It is a victory for the gastropod (we did warn that the snail is a sly one)!

31 mar

✱Shells and snails, where can I get them? At the shops! You can clean the snail shells after using them, turn them over regularly so that they dry properly and start all over again. Make sure you have some cardamom on hand so you can speak without killing vampires!

Classic escargot

Serves 6

PREPARATION TIME 1 HOUR
COOKING TIME 10 MINUTES

3 garlic cloves
1 French shallot (eschalot)
1 bunch of flat-leaf (Italian) parsley, leaves picked
250 g (9 oz) butter, softened
salt and pepper
72 good tinned snails (or in a jar), unflavoured
72 empty snail shells

Preheat the oven to 160°C (315°F/Gas 2–3). Peel the garlic and shallot, mince them finely. Finely chop the parsley. Combine the butter, garlic, shallot and parsley; season generously. Put a snail in each shell*, cover with garlic butter. Arrange the snails on a piece of foil, crumpled to keep them in place. Bake in the oven for 5–10 minutes — the butter should start to become foamy. Eat very hot.

This month

April

the greengrocer
FRISÉE LETTUCE
TOMATOES
EGGPLANTS (AUBERGINES)
FENNEL
CELERY
POTATOES
SNOW PEAS (MANGETOUT)
GREEN BEANS
BULB SPRING ONIONS
(SCALLIONS)
PEAS
GREEN AND WHITE ASPARAGUS
BROAD (FAVA) BEANS
CARROTS
BABY SPINACH LEAVES
RADISHES
RASPBERRIES
STRAWBERRIES

the fishmonger
SALMON
SMOKED HADDOCK
RED MULLET
MUSSELS
PRAWNS (SHRIMP)
PIKE

the butcher-deli
LAMB LEG
LAMB SHOULDER
FREE-RANGE CHICKEN
VEAL RUMP
VEAL SWEETBREADS
RACK OF VEAL
PROSCIUTTO
SPECK

the cheese-seller
GOAT'S CHEESE

the grocer
POLENTA
ARBORIO RICE
CONFIT GIZZARDS

---

01 Hugues
KINOU TERRINE WITH AGRETTES

02 Alexandrine
ONION TART

03 Richard
LITTLE CUSTARD POTS

08 Julie
FRISÉE LETTUCE WITH CONFIT GIZZARDS

09 Gautier
ASPARAGUS AND PEA RISOTTO

10 Fulbert
VEAL TARTARE WITH ORANGE SALAD

15 Paterne
PIKE TERRINE

16 Benoît
ROAST CHICKEN WITH HERBS

17 Anicet
CRÈME BRÛLÉE WITH BERRI

22 Alexandre
BAKED RACK OF VEAL

23 Georges
SPICY BROAD BEAN PURÉE

24 Fidèle
STRAWBERRY GÂTEAU

29 Catherine
STRAWBERRY VACHERIN

30 Robert
PRAWN AND LEMONGRASS SOUP

01

04
Isidore

LEMON CHICKEN TAGINE

05
Irène

CURED SALMON

06
Célestin

CRUDITÉ OF BROAD BEANS

07
Jean-Baptiste

LAMB SHOULDER WITH HERBS

11
Stanislas

7-HOUR LEG OF LAMB

12
Jules

FRENCH-STYLE PEAS

13
Ida

SALAD OF BABY SPINACH
AND SMOKED HADDOCK

14
Maxime

RED MULLET
WITH ROASTED ONIONS

18
Parfait

CREAM OF ASPARAGUS SOUP

19
Emma

OMELETTE WITH FRESH HERBS

20
Odette

ESCALOPES OF VEAL
SWEETBREADS

21
Anselme

MUSSELS IN SAUCE POULETTE

25
Marc

SAUTÉ OF GREEN ASPARAGUS

26
Alda

POLENTA WITH
BROWN BUTTER

27
Zita

TOMATO AND
GOAT'S CHEESE QUICHE

28
Valérie

GRILLED ASPARAGUS
WITH SPECK

02 03 04 05

MARIE & LÉON

kinou, kinou, kinou ...

The *terrine de kinou* is part of the culinary tradition of the isles of Fémalamangé.

It was in the course of an expedition in his boat that the great explorer Léon Vachecrot lost his heart to this delicacy. The *kinou*, a wild and very ugly animal (some say mythical because it's hard to find!), proliferates in the *agrettes* (the monk's beard shrubs that surround the Fémalamangé islands). It is hunted a bit like the *dahu* (goaty kind of creature) of the Savoie: you call it with the cry of « kinou, kinou, kinou », it pokes its head out of the *agrettes*, and then kapow! a good whack on the head, a sort of Tyson-style hook to the temple and it's a guaranteed K.O. One *kinou* for six is perfect. And if you're talking *kinou*, you're talking *agrettes*, it's a bit like Dolce & Gabbana or Laurel and Hardy, you can't imagine one without the other. You don't catch an *agrette*, you pull the plant up (it's best to keep the children well away during this manœuvre, the *agrette* doesn't like it and lets out a cry, a sort of *ouillouillouille*, which may shock sensitive ears).

A well-judged combination of the two, a few basic ingredients, *Merguez* sausage, Saint-Nectaire cheese and a banana. And that is how the *terrine de kinou*, lost in the obscurity of *la gastronomie Fémalamangée* became the *terrine de kinou* that went down in history.

✳ Blutter:
Violently thump the agrette until it says 'stop'.

✳✳
Troupille:
Said when one no longer knows what to say, if indeed one ever knew before.

01 april

Kinou terrine with agrettes

Serves 6

PREPARATION TIME 20 MINUTES
COOKING TIME (IT DEPENDS ON THE KINOU)

1.2 kg (2 lb 10 oz) kinou
6 agrettes, nice and firm (the soft ones are too soft)
12 litres (420 fl oz) pouring (whipping) cream
1 banana
1 farmhouse Saint-Nectaire cheese
3 Merguez sausages
salt and pepper

The day before, put the *kinou* on to soak in the 12 lítres of cream (the *kinou* is best eaten with plenty of fat). *Blutter** the *agrettes*, *troupille*** them the old-fashioned way, set aside. Once the *kinou* has absorbed the cream, ít's ready. Process the *troupilled agrettes* with the banana and the Saint-Nectaire, season. Make a hole in the *kinou*, gently insert the agrette stuffing, shape in a terrine dish, push down well, ít should go in. Decorate with fresh Merguez, cover. Cook on a high heat until the *kinou* explodes. Eat very hot.

02 april

Onion tart

Serves 6

PREPARATION TIME 20 MINUTES
COOKING TIME 20 MINUTES

250 g (9 oz) block store-bought butter puff pastry
2 tablespoons herbes de Provence (Provençal herb mix)
6 large onions
2 tablespoons olive oil
1 tablespoon honey
50 g (1¾ oz/⅓ cup) pine nuts
salt
Equipment:
six 10 cm (4 inch) round cooking rings

Preheat the oven to 180°C (350°F/Gas 4). Roll out the butter pastry over the herbs*. Cut out individual circles to fit the cooking rings, prick them with a fork**. Peel and slice the onions, then sauté them in the olive oil until they caramelise. Next, add the honey and pine nuts, let them brown. Bake the bases for 10 minutes. Remove from the oven, top with the onion mixture and bake for a further 5–10 minutes until crisp. Season.

✳WHY IN THAT ORDER RATHER THAN SCATTERING THE HERBS OVER THE PASTRY? *This way the herbes de Provence will get into the pastry and really give it flavour.*

✳✳WHY PRICK THE PASTRY? *So it doesn't puff up too much.*

03 april

Little custard pots

Serves 6

PREPARATION TIME 15 MINUTES
COOKING TIME 45 MINUTES

1 litre (35 fl oz/4 cups) full-cream (whole) milk
7 eggs
180 g (6¼ oz) sugar
Equipment:
six 250 ml (9 fl oz/1 cup) ramekins

Preheat the oven to 120°C (235°F/Gas ½).

Chocolate: Melt 200 g (7 oz) dark chocolate (70% cocoa) in the milk, add 1 teaspoon ground cinnamon. Whisk the eggs with the sugar, add the chocolate mixture. Pour into the pots, cook in a bain-marie for 45 minutes.

Coffee: Combine 80 ml (2½ fl oz/⅓ cup) strong espresso coffee with the milk and add 100 ml (3½ fl oz) amber rum*. Whisk the eggs with the sugar, add the coffee mixture. Pour into the pots, cook in a bain-marie for 45 minutes.

Vanilla: Bring the milk to the boil with 1 split vanilla bean, add 1 teaspoon ground cardamom. Whisk the eggs with the sugar, add the vanilla mixture. Pour into the pots, cook in a bain-marie for 45 minutes.

✳WHAT'S AMBER RUM? *Amber rum is a rum that's aged in a wooden barrel, which gives it a unique colour.*

04 april

Lemon chicken tagine

Serves 6

PREPARATION TIME 15 MINUTES
COOKING TIME 50 MINUTES

800 g (1 lb 12 oz) chicken breast fillets
3 tomatoes
1 eggplant (aubergine)
1 fennel bulb
4 French shallots (eschalots)
4 garlic cloves
2 lemons
olive oil
1 teaspoon ground ginger
1 teaspoon ground coriander
1 teaspoon cinnamon
1 tablespoon sugar
250 ml (9 fl oz/1 cup) chicken stock
salt and pepper
Equipment:
*tagine dish**

✳CAN YOU PUT A TAGINE DISH ON ANY TYPE OF HEAT? *Normally yes, but it's good to check first. Some ceramics can't handle too intense a heat.*

Cut the chicken into pieces. Cut the tomatoes and eggplant into cubes, slice the fennel. Peel and roughly slice the shallots and garlic. Cut the lemons into eight segments and remove the pips. In a tagine dish, sauté the chicken in some oil with the spices, sugar, garlic and shallots until it caramelises. Next, add all of the vegetables and stock. Season, cover, and cook over low heat for 45 minutes. Serve immediately.

05 april

Cured salmon

Serves 6

PREPARATION TIME 10 MINUTES
RESTING TIME 48 HOURS

800 g (1 lb 12 oz) salmon (the thick end of the fillet)
1 tablespoon coarse salt
1 teaspoon coarsely ground black pepper
1 tablespoon sugar
1 bunch of dill, leaves picked and chopped
1 lime
50 g (1¾ oz) sour cream
1 tablespoon olive oil
salt and pepper
100 g (3½ oz) podded fresh peas
1 bulb spring onion (scallion), thinly sliced

Lay the salmon in a dish, cover with the coarse salt, pepper, sugar and chopped dill. Chill for 48 hours to purge* the moisture. Wipe the salmon dry with paper towels, remove the skin and cut into 5 cm (2 inch) pieces. Zest and juice the lime, combine the juice with the sour cream, add the olive oil and season. Serve two slices of salmon per person, spread one slice with the sour cream mixture and top with the raw fresh peas, spring onion and lime zest.

✲WHY DOES THE SALMON NEED TO BE PURGED? *Its water content will be reduced and its flavours concentrated.*

06 april

Crudité of broad beans

Serves 6

PREPARATION TIME 30 MINUTES
COOKING TIME 15 SECONDS

1 kg (2 lb 4 oz) fresh broad (fava) beans
100 g (3½ oz) lightly salted butter
toasted bread

Pod the broad beans, plunge them into boiling salted water* for 15 seconds. Refresh immediately. Carefully remove the skins from the broad beans — it's important to have people around you as it's a long process, very long … Enjoy the broad beans on toasted bread with a little butter, a twist of the pepper mill and a drop of an aniseed beverage … Feels like summer's coming!

✲WHY DIP THE BEANS? *To make them easier to peel.*

07 april

Lamb shoulder with herbs

Serves 6

PREPARATION TIME 20 MINUTES
COOKING TIME 50 MINUTES

1 French shallot (eschalot)
1 garlic clove
50 g (1¾ oz) lightly salted butter
3 sprigs of thyme, leaves picked
6 sprigs of rosemary
2 boneless lamb shoulders
1 garlic bulb
olive oil

Preheat the oven to 180°C (350°F/Gas 4). Peel the shallot and the garlic. Process the butter with the shallot, garlic and thyme leaves. Cut the rosemary into 3 cm (1¼ inch) lengths. Spread the herb butter all over the shoulders and scatter with the rosemary. Tie each shoulder with kitchen string. Cut the garlic bulb in half and arrange it around the lamb, then drizzle olive oil over the whole thing. Bake in the oven for 40–50 minutes.

08 april

Frisée lettuce with confit gizzards

Serves 6

PREPARATION TIME 15 MINUTES
COOKING TIME 5 MINUTES

200 g (7 oz) gizzards preserved in duck fat
  or chicken livers, trimmed
3 French shallots (eschalots)
50 g (1¾ oz/⅓ cup) almonds, halved
3 tablespoons raspberry vinegar
10 radishes
1 tablespoon wholegrain mustard
2 tablespoons walnut oil
2 tablespoons sunflower oil
1 frisée lettuce

Finely slice the gizzards and shallots. Sauté together in some duck fat*, add the almonds, then deglaze with 2 tablespoons of the raspberry vinegar. Cut the radishes into thin sticks. Combine the mustard and oils with the remaining vinegar and dress the lettuce with this vinaigrette. Pour the gizzards and hot cooking juices over the salad, then scatter over the radish.

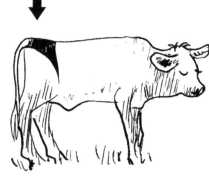

beak — pancreas — œsophagus — cloaca — crop — kidneys — stomach — intestines — *gizzard* — liver

*WHERE TO
GET IT? *Use the
fat the gizzards are
preserved in, about
1 tablespoon.*

09 april

Asparagus and pea risotto

Serves 6

PREPARATION TIME 10 MINUTES
COOKING TIME 25 MINUTES

6 green asparagus spears
3 French shallots (eschalots)
3 tablespoons olive oil
350 g (12 oz/1⅔ cups) arborio rice
700 ml (24 fl oz) vegetable stock
150 g (5½ oz/1 cup) podded fresh peas
50 g (1¾ oz/½ cup) grated parmesan cheese
salt and pepper

Trim the ends off the asparagus spears, cut into thin slices. Peel and slice the shallots, sauté them in a saucepan in some olive oil, then add the rice and allow the rice to become pearly*. Moisten with some of the vegetable stock and cook for 15 minutes over gentle heat, regularly stirring and adding stock as it is absorbed. Add the asparagus and peas, cook for a further 5 minutes. Add the parmesan, cook for a further 2 minutes, then season.

*PEARLY RICE:
*Sauté the rice in
the oil so it becomes
translucent.*

10 april

Veal tartare with orange salad

Serves 6

PREPARATION TIME 30 MINUTES

3 oranges
3 bulb spring onions (scallions)
50 g (1¾ oz) cornichons
1 tablespoon Dijon mustard
1 tablespoon tomato sauce (ketchup)
1 teaspoon Cognac
3 tablespoons olive oil
900 g (2 lb) fresh veal, such as quasi de veau*
50 g (1¾ oz) large salted capers, rinsed and drained
10 chives, snipped
salt and pepper

*QUASI DE VEAU?
WHAT'S THAT?
*This is a cut of veal
located on the rump;
the equivalent
of rump steak
in beef terms.*

Zest 1 orange, remove the peel and pith of the others and take out the segments. Thinly slice the spring onions, mix with the orange segments. Slice the cornichons. Combine the mustard with the tomato sauce, Cognac, olive oil and orange zest. Cut the veal into small cubes, combine with the sauce, cornichons, capers and chives. Season. Serve chilled, with the orange salad.

MARIE & LÉON

Easter lamb and beef

In the beginning, Marie Vachecrot, a very ordinary cook married to Léon, a lover of fine food, was secretly jealous of her neighbours on the same floor, Pascal and Ginette Leglu.

The story goes back to April 2002 when, having been invited to dinner along with the Mizous (some other neighbours), Marie found herself at the table with the rest of the party, an entirely pleasant group, all in throes of rapture over the leg of lamb served by Pascal. It was, in effect, very well made lamb, « *But to make a song and dance about it, well, no need to get carried away ...* » she thought. The story could have ended there, but as soon as the next year came round, at around the same time, her favourite butcher put up a large sign in the window display: « *agneau Pascal de qualité* » (quality Pascal (Easter) lamb).

It was as if the whole village was conspiring against her: wherever there was meat sold in a store, you'd read « *Pascal lamb* » here, « *Pascal lamb* » there. « *Pascal lamb* », nyah nyah nyah, what was it about Pascal's lamb that was causing all this hoopla? The same refrain returned each year like a boomerang in the face. Marie couldn't stand it anymore, she had to find a way to deal with so much culinary aggression. She pushed her rage down deep inside (easy!), a genuine jealousy of this Pascal who was subject to such great gastronomic acclaim.

April 2008: another invitation to dine at the Leglus. Trembling, her hands clammy, Marie was dreading more provocation from Pascal and his lamb, but in fact, a rare *rosbif*, simple and tasty, was served to the delighted taste buds of the day's gathering. Marie could not help but feel an *ouf* of relief ... The Pascal lamb issue having quieted down, she left her neighbours' apartment and went home peacefully with Léon on her arm. Pascal's lamb a distant memory, Marie scanned the window of her favourite butcher shop and there, arrghhh, writ large in the window display, « *agneau Pascal et boeuf Pascal de qualité* ». It was too much! She too wanted her 15 minutes of fame, she too wanted her name writ large on a sign at the butcher shop, she too wanted to leave the anonymity of her kitchen to go down in history ... Maybe one day she'll understand!

11 april

7-hour leg of lamb

Serves 6

PREPARATION TIME 15 MINUTES
COOKING TIME 7 HOURS

1.2 kg (2 lb 10 oz) lamb leg, bone in
olive oil
6 garlic cloves
6 French shallots (eschalots)
1 sprig of rosemary
1 tablespoon herbes de Provence *(Provençal herb mix)*
500 ml (17 fl oz/2 cups) white wine
salt and pepper

Preheat the oven to 100°C (200°F/Gas ½). Place the lamb leg in a heavy flameproof casserole dish. Place over high heat and colour on both sides. Peel the garlic and shallots, add to the lamb dish with the rosemary, *herbes de Provence* and white wine. Season. Cover, cook in the oven for 7 hours*. Baste from time to time with the juices, adding a little water, if necessary. The lamb should be very tender.

✱ ARE YOU SURE IT WON'T BURN? *If you check it regularly, it won't burn.*

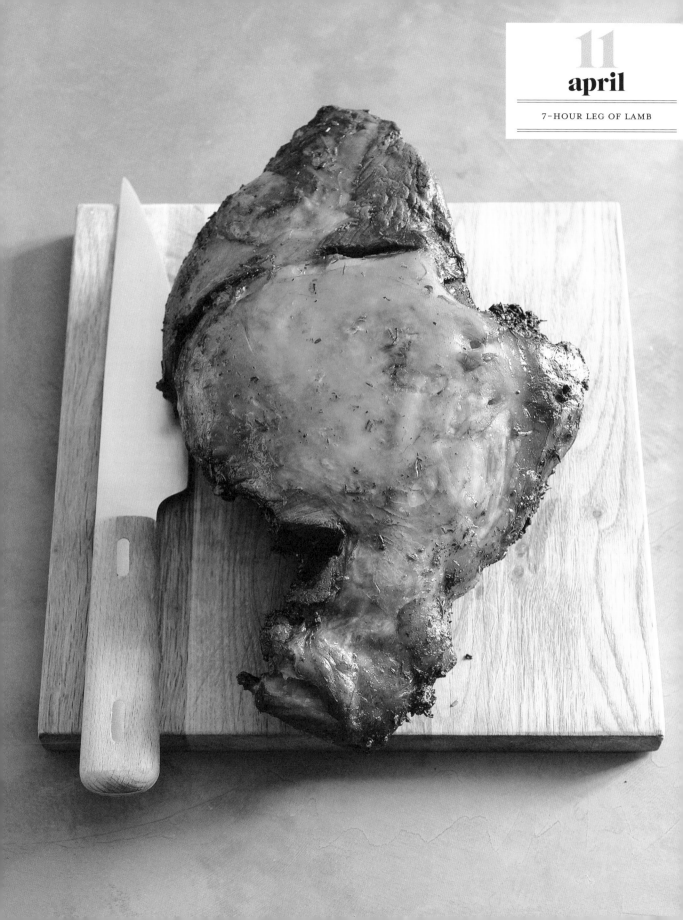

12
april

FRENCH-STYLE PEAS

12 april

French-style peas

Serves 6

PREPARATION TIME 30 MINUTES
COOKING TIME 10 MINUTES

3 onions
3 slices prosciutto
3 lettuce leaves
50 g (1¾ oz) butter
600 g (1 lb 5 oz) podded fresh peas
1 teaspoon sugar
200 ml (7 fl oz) vegetable stock
salt and pepper

✱WHAT'S THE
LETTUCE FOR?
*Nothing, it's just a
conversation-starter!
(and it also
adds flavour).*

Peel and slice the onions. Slice the prosciutto
and the lettuce*. Sauté the onions in the butter
with the prosciutto, add the peas, lettuce and
sugar, moisten with the vegetable stock. Cook
for about 10 minutes, then season.

13 april

Salad of baby spinach and smoked haddock

Serves 6

PREPARATION TIME 15 MINUTES
MARINATING TIME 1 HOUR

300 g (10½ oz) smoked haddock or trout*
2 French shallots (eschalots)
1 tablespoon rice vinegar
125 ml (4 fl oz/½ cup) olive oil
juice of 2 lemons
1 teaspoon ground ginger
1 tablespoon sugar
500 g (1 lb 2 oz) baby spinach leaves
6 chives, snipped

✱WHAT EXACTLY
IS SMOKED
HADDOCK?
*Smoked haddock is
haddock, smoked!*

Finely slice the smoked haddock*, lay it out
on a plate. Peel and slice the shallots into
thin rings. Combine the vinegar, oil, lemon
juice, ginger, sugar and shallots and pour this
marinade over the haddock. Chill for 1 hour.
Place the baby spinach leaves and haddock
slices in serving dishes, dress with the marinade
and scatter over the chives.

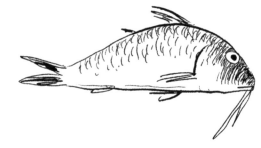

14 april

Red mullet with roasted onions

Serves 6

PREPARATION TIME 15 MINUTES
COOKING TIME 15 MINUTES

6 brown onions
50 g (1¾ oz) lightly salted butter, cubed
1 bunch of thyme
6 whole red mullets (rouget barbet)
olive oil
10 bay leaves
fleur de sel

✱WHY CLEAN
THEM? *I don't like
eating fish guts,
but purists don't
clean mullet.*

Light the barbecue coals. Cut a cross in the
top of the onions to open them up, insert a
piece of butter and a sprig of thyme. Wrap the
onions in foil, put them in the embers for
15 minutes. Clean the fish*, oil them, place
them on the barbecue grill for 3 minutes each
side, throw the bay leaves under the fish. Serve
with *fleur de sel* and olive oil.

15 april

Pike terrine

Serves 6

PREPARATION TIME 45 MINUTES
COOKING TIME 1 HOUR

½ savoy cabbage
1 good-sized whole pike or firm-fleshed white fish
50 g (1¾ oz) fresh ginger
2 French shallots (eschalots)
1 bunch of chives
5 eggs
200 ml (7 fl oz) pouring (whipping) cream
2 tablespoons pastis
150 g (5½ oz) small prawns (shrimp), peeled and deveined
1 lime

Preheat the oven to 160°C (315°F/Gas 2–3). Separate the cabbage leaves, blanch them in boiling salted water for 5 minutes. Refresh immediately. Prepare the pike*. Peel and chop the ginger, shallots and chives. Process the pike with the eggs, cream and pastis. Combine with the prawns, ginger, shallots and chives, add the zest and juice of the lime. Season. Line a terrine dish with cabbage leaves, fill with the pike mixture. Cook in a bain-marie for 1 hour.

✱How do I prepare the pike? *Fillet the pike, remove the skin, take out the bones using a pair of tweezers.*

16 april

Roast chicken with herbs

Serves 6

PREPARATION TIME 20 MINUTES
COOKING TIME 1 HOUR

6 garlic cloves
6 French shallots (eschalots)
1 large chicken (or 2 small ones)
100 ml (3½ fl oz) olive oil
fleur de sel and pepper
1 bunch of basil
1 bunch of thyme
4 sprigs of rosemary
4 celery stalks, including the leaves
250 ml (9 fl oz/1 cup) white wine

Preheat the oven to 200°C (400°F/Gas 6). Peel the garlic and shallots. Cut the chicken in half. Lay it in a gratin dish, skin side up, brush with olive oil and sprinkle with some salt. Bake for 30 minutes. Take the chicken out of the oven. Reduce the oven temperature to 140°C (275°F/Gas 1). Add all of the herbs to the chicken dish with the celery, shallots, garlic and wine. Cover with a sheet of foil* and bake for a further 30 minutes. Serve the chicken coated with the herb jus.

✱What's the foil for? *The foil will prevent the herbs from drying out.*

17 april

Crème brûlée with berries

Serves 6

PREPARATION TIME 10 MINUTES
COOKING TIME 45 MINUTES

8 egg yolks
150 g (5½ oz) caster (superfine) sugar
1 litre (35 fl oz/4 cups) pouring (whipping) cream
100 g (3½ oz/¾ cup) raspberries
100 g (3½ oz/⅔ cup) strawberries
80 g (2¾ oz/firmly packed ⅓ cup) soft brown sugar
Equipment:
6 small ramekins
kitchen blowtorch (optional)

Preheat the oven to 120°C (235°F/Gas ½). Combine the egg yolks with the caster sugar, then add the cream. Divide this custard between the ramekins. Scatter over the berries, cook in a bain-marie in the oven for 45 minutes (the custard should be firm). Allow to cool*. Sprinkle over the brown sugar, scorch with a blowtorch to caramelise, or pass it under a hot grill (broiler). Serve immediately.

✱Why let it cool before adding the brown sugar? *You want the crème brûlée to have a crunchy toffee on top. If the custard is hot, the caramel won't harden, it will be soft, and Amélie Poulain will be very sad.*

18 april

Cream of asparagus soup

Serves 6

PREPARATION TIME 15 MINUTES
COOKING TIME 35 MINUTES

2 bunches of green asparagus
2 onions
3 large potatoes, peeled
80 g (2¾ oz) lightly salted butter
300 ml (10½ fl oz) pouring (whipping) cream
salt and pepper
1 bulb spring onion (scallion)
olive oil
balsamic vinegar
Equipment:
chinois (fine cone-shaped strainer)

Trim the ends off the aparagus spears. Set aside six aparagus tips (cut 5 cm/2 inches from the top), cook the rest in boiling salted water for 10 minutes. Refresh immediately. Slice the onions. Cut the potatoes into cubes. Cook them with the onions for 15 minutes in boiling water. Add the asparagus, cook for a further 5 minutes. Drain the water until it's the same level as the vegetables, purée them and put through a *chinois**. Add the butter and cream, cook for a further 5 minutes, season. Slice the reserved asparagus tips and the spring onion, dress with olive oil. Serve in a bowl garnished with the asparagus salad. Drizzle with a little balsamic vinegar.

*WHY STRAIN AS WELL AS PURÉE? *Asparagus contains fibres that may not have puréed, the* chinois *will help get rid of them.*

19 april

Omelette with fresh herbs

Serves 6

PREPARATION TIME 5 MINUTES
COOKING TIME 5 MINUTES

12 free-range eggs
150 ml (5 fl oz) pouring (whipping) cream
salt and pepper
½ bunch of basil
½ bunch of tarragon
½ bunch of chives, snipped
4 bulb spring onions (scallions)
50 g (1¾ oz) butter
1 tablespoon sunflower oil

Beat the eggs with the cream, then season. Strip the leaves from the herbs, keeping them whole. Slice the spring onions, add them to the omelette with the herbs. Melt the butter with the oil in a frying pan, pour in the omelette, stir the middle with a fork* and cook to the consistency you like.

*WHY STIR WITH THE FORK? *It will help the omelette cook evenly.*

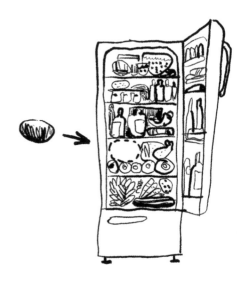

20 april

Escalopes of veal sweetbreads

Serves 6

PREPARATION TIME 2 HOURS
COOKING TIME 20 MINUTES

800 g (1 lb 12 oz) veal sweetbreads
100 ml (3½ fl oz) wine vinegar
500 ml (17 fl oz/2 cups) full-cream (whole) milk
1 carrot
150 g (5½ oz/1 cup) podded fresh peas
200 g (7 oz) green beans
150 g (5½ oz) snow peas (mangetout)
salt and pepper
1 French shallot (eschalot), sliced
80 g (2¾ oz) lightly salted butter
200 ml (7 fl oz) veal stock

Plunge the sweetbreads into a saucepan of cold water with the wine vinegar, bring to the boil, then rinse immediately. Place the sweetbreads into a clean saucepan with the milk and add just enough water to cover. Simmer for 20 minutes*. Rinse the sweetbreads, remove their membrane, roll them up into a large sausage shape in plastic wrap and refrigerate for 90 minutes**. Peel the carrot and finely dice. Cook the green vegetables separately in boiling salted water: keep them *al dente*. Cut slices of sweetbread, season them. Sweat the shallot in the butter in a non-stick frying pan, add the sweetbreads, brown, then add all of the vegetables and deglaze with the veal stock.

*WHAT ARE THE VINEGAR BATH AND MILK BATH FOR? *The vinegar will purge the sweetbreads; poaching in milk will give them creaminess.*

**WHY PUT IT IN THE REFRIGERATOR? *To give it a more compact shape.*

MARIE & LÉON

hen, chicken, little chicken ...

*I*n the beginning, Marie Vachecrot, a very ordinary cook married to Léon, a lover of fine food, despaired of being able to do justice to the sophisticated palate of her dear husband.

No matter how much she tried every day to wield her spoon with the greatest determination, cooking remained, in spite of everything, a dark black hole. Léon, a patient man, but no more than that, would lose no time seizing the pots and pans to turn the dining nightmare into an impromptu feast. A well-made hen, a few mature vegetables (one generally goes hand-in-hand with the other!), some stock, and Henry IV can rest easy. The *poule au pot* is ready, the meal can be served. Marie, a little annoyed at her husband's culinary dexterity, couldn't stop herself from adding some cream to the cooking liquid, a case of making her mark on the dish ... The well-built hen was transformed into a high-class bird and Léon, moved by so much pleasure, was heard to say, his hand resting on one of Marie's more generous curves: « *Our* sauce poulette — *it's good!* »

And that is how Marie, destined for the anonymity of her kitchen, became the Marie who went down in history.

21 april

Mussels in sauce poulette*

Serves 6
PREPARATION TIME 10 MINUTES
COOKING TIME 10 MINUTES

4 garlic cloves
4 French shallots (eschalots)
3 kg (6 lb 12 oz) mussels
1 bunch of flat-leaf (Italian) parsley
50 g (1¾ oz) butter
250 ml (9 fl oz/1 cup) white wine
500 ml (17 fl oz/2 cups) pouring (whipping) cream
1 teaspoon cornflour (cornstarch)

❋WHY IS IT CALLED A SAUCE POULETTE? *Originally, sauce poulette was made from the cooking broth of a poule au pot. This stock was used as the basis of a creamy béchamel sauce.*

Peel and chop the garlic and shallots. Clean the mussels. Chop the parsley. In a large saucepan, sauté the garlic and shallots in the butter. Add the white wine and let it reduce. Add the mussels and the cream, cook for 5 minutes, stirring well. Blend the cornflour in a little water, add to the pan and cook for a further 5 minutes. Scatter with the chopped parsley to serve.

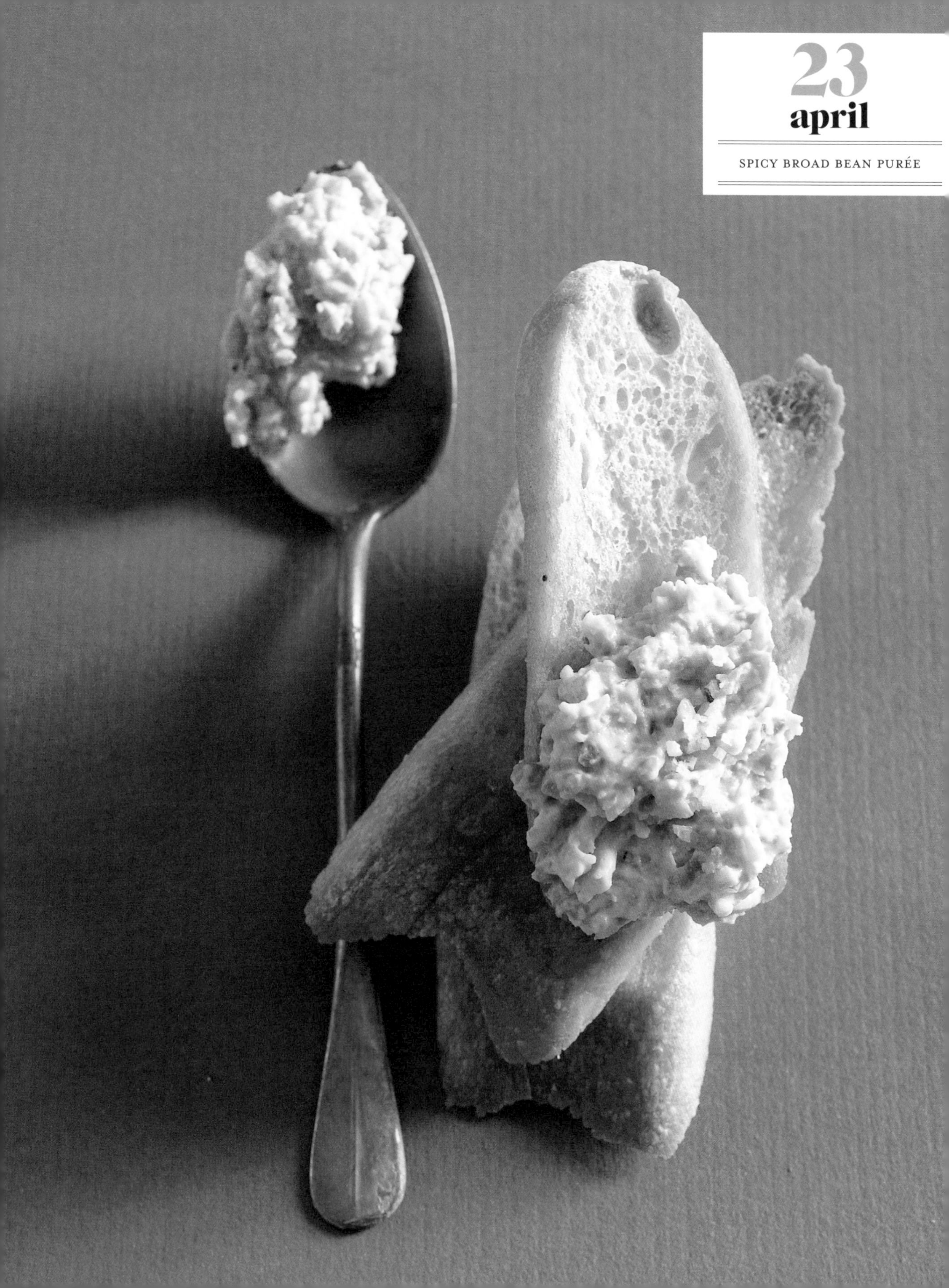

23
april

SPICY BROAD BEAN PURÉE

22 april

Baked rack of veal

Serves 6

PREPARATION TIME 10 MINUTES
COOKING TIME 45 MINUTES

1 rack of veal with 4 cutlets
100 g (3½ oz) butter
1 teaspoon whole mixed peppercorns, crushed
6 garlic cloves
6 French shallots (eschalots)
1 bunch of sage
250 ml (9 fl oz/1 cup) white wine
salt

Preheat the oven to 200°C (400°F/Gas 6). In a flameproof casserole dish, sauté the veal on all sides in 50 g (1¾ oz) of the butter. Add the crushed peppercorns and cook in the oven for 30 minutes. Take the rack out of the oven. Reduce the oven temperature to 140°C (275°F/Gas 1). Add the garlic, shallots, sage and wine to the dish. Bake for 15 minutes, then turn off the oven and leave for a further 15 minutes*. Take the rack out of the oven and set it on a board. Heat the casserole dish with the remaining butter and 125 ml (4 fl oz/½ cup) water, scraping up all the bits on the bottom. Serve the rack in slices with the cooking juices drizzled over the top.

*WHY NOT SERVE IMMEDIATELY? So the meat in the rack can relax.

23 april

Spicy broad bean purée

Serves 6

PREPARATION TIME 45 MINUTES
COOKING TIME 1 MINUTE

1 kg (2 lb 4 oz) broad (fava) beans
150 ml (5 fl oz) olive oil
a few drops of Tabasco sauce
1 French shallot (eschalot), chopped
6 chives, snipped
fleur de sel
slices of toasted baguette

Pod the broad beans, plunge them into boiling salted water for 1 minute. Refresh immediately*. Carefully remove the skins from the beans. Crush the beans with the olive oil, Tabasco sauce, shallot and chives. Season. Spread on toasted baguette, to serve.

*WHY REFRESH? To set the green colour of the broad beans.

24 april

Strawberry gâteau

Serves 6

PREPARATION TIME 30 MINUTES
COOKING TIME 20 MINUTES
CHILLING TIME 6 HOURS

For the base:
220 g (7¾ oz/1¾ cups) icing (confectioners') sugar
125 g (4½ oz/1¼ cups) ground almonds
4 egg whites
50 g (1¾ oz) caster (superfine) sugar
For the filling:
3 gelatine leaves
200 g (7 oz) crème pâtissière (see page 200, 07 May)
200 ml (7 fl oz) pouring (whipping) cream
1 tablespoon vanilla sugar
500 g (1 lb 2 oz/3⅓ cups) strawberries
300 g (10½ oz) marzipan
Equipment:
1 round springform cake tin

Preheat the oven to 160°C (315°F/Gas 2–3). To make the base, combine the icing sugar with the ground almonds, sift*. Beat the egg whites with the caster sugar to very stiff peaks. Delicately fold the whites into the almond mixture — it should be shiny. On a sheet of baking paper, inside the cake tin, make a circle of *macaron***, let it form a crust***. Cook for 10 minutes. Let it cool, unmould and place the *macaron* circle on a serving plate.

To make the filling, soften the gelatine in water. Gently heat the crème pâtissière, incorporate the gelatine. Allow to cool. Whip the cream and vanilla sugar into a chantilly, fold it delicately into the crème pâtissière. Hull the strawberries, halve them lengthways. Place the ring back over the *macaron* circle, line the side with the cut strawberries. Combine the remaining strawberries with the crème pâtissière, fill the ring with this mixture. Chill for 2 hours. Roll out the marzipan, cut out a circle the same size as the gâteau, lay it on top. Give it a blast from a kitchen blowtorch to brown the marzipan.

*SIFT? Pass through a sieve to separate each grain of the ground almonds and icing sugar, thus eliminating lumps!

**HOW DO I MAKE THE CIRCLE? Using a piping (icing) bag.

***LET IT FORM A CRUST? 30 minutes exposed to the air.

25 april

Sauté of green asparagus

Serves 6

PREPARATION TIME 20 MINUTES
COOKING TIME 10 MINUTES

2 bunches of green asparagus
3 French shallots (eschalots)
3 tablespoons olive oil
*3 sprigs of lemon thyme***
salt and pepper

Peel the end of the asparagus spears using a vegetable peeler, cut them in half. Peel and slice the shallots. In a non-stick frying pan, sauté the shallots in the olive oil, add the asparagus and the lemon thyme. Let it brown for around 10 minutes: the asparagus should stay al dente. Season.

✳LEMON THYME?
It's readily available and it grows everywhere, in the garden or on a balcony.

26 april

Polenta with brown butter

Serves 6

PREPARATION TIME 20 MINUTES
COOKING TIME 30 MINUTES

3 garlic cloves
6 French shallots (eschalots)
1 litre (35 fl oz/4 cups) full-cream (whole) milk
80 g (2¾ oz/⅔ cup) sultanas (golden raisins)
200 g (7 oz/1⅓ cups) polenta
salt and pepper
100 g (3½ oz) butter

Peel and chop the garlic and shallots. Add both to the milk with the sultanas. Bring to the boil, allow to simmer for 5 minutes. Add the polenta in a steady stream (the cooking time will depend on the type of polenta*) and cook until the milk is absorbed. Season. Cook the butter for 5 minutes over high heat until it is a nut-brown colour. Scrape up any particles stuck to the bottom of the pan. Sauce the polenta with a tablespoon of brown butter.

✳WHY'S THAT?
Polenta can be fine or coarse in texture.

27 april

Tomato and goat's cheese quiche*

Serves 6

PREPARATION TIME 20 MINUTES
COOKING TIME 30 MINUTES

For the pastry:
200 g (7 oz/1⅓ cups) plain (all-purpose) flour
50 g (1¾ oz/½ cup) ground almonds
120 g (4¼ oz) butter
1 teaspoon ground cumin
1 egg
1 pinch salt
For the filling:
200 g (7 oz) cherry tomatoes
1 Valençay-style
* or soft goat's cheese, cubed*
3 eggs
300 ml (10½ fl oz) pouring (whipping) cream
6 chives, snipped
salt and pepper

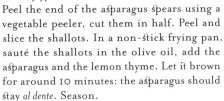

✳HOW CAN I RUIN THIS RECIPE?
To ruin this quiche, replace the flour with lard, the tomatoes with pigs' ears — substitute your own leftovers in other words!

Preheat the oven to 180°C (350°F/Gas 4). To make the pastry, combine the flour, ground almonds, butter, cumin and salt, then add the egg. Roll out the pastry and use it to line a baking paper-lined pie dish.
For the filling, scatter in the cherry tomatoes and goat's cheese. Combine the eggs with the cream and chives, season, then pour into the pastry case. Bake for 30 minutes.

28 april

Grilled asparagus with speck

Serves 6

PREPARATION TIME 20 MINUTES
COOKING TIME 10 MINUTES

18 white asparagus spears
18 slices speck
18 salt-packed anchovies
1 bunch of flat-leaf (Italian) parsley, leaves picked
olive oil

Preheat the oven to 180°C (350°F/Gas 4). Trim 1 cm (½ inch) from the end of the asparagus spears and peel. Cook the asparagus in boiling salted water for 5 minutes. Drain, then cut each spear in half. Wrap each spear half in a half-slice of speck. Arrange in a gratin dish. Scatter the anchovies on top and bake for 5 minutes. Chop the parsley, scatter over the asparagus and drizzle over some olive oil.

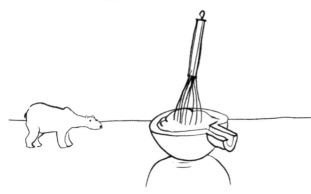

29 april

Strawberry vacherin

Serves 6

PREPARATION TIME 20 MINUTES

1 kg (2 lb 4 oz) strawberries
juice of 1 lemon
300 ml (10½ fl oz) pouring (whipping) cream
1 tablespoon vanilla sugar, or to taste
3 large store-bought meringues

✳TIP FOR WHIPPING CREAM: *Have the bowl and cream well chilled.*

✳✳WHY? *Otherwise the coulis will bleed into the cream and it won't be very chic.*

Hull the strawberries, slice them in half. Purée 300 g (10½ oz/2 cups) of the strawberries with the lemon juice to make a coulis. Whip the cream into a chantilly with the vanilla sugar*. Crush the meringues. Build the vacherin layer by layer in a glass: strawberries, coulis, meringue, chantilly. Repeat. Serve immediately**.

30 april

Prawn and lemongrass soup

Serves 6

PREPARATION TIME 10 MINUTES
COOKING TIME 45 MINUTES

18 large prawns (shrimp)
2 tablespoons olive oil
3 garlic cloves, peeled
1 bouquet garni
1 bunch of coriander (cilantro)
3 celery stalks
3 lemongrass stems, white part only
2 onions
200 g (7 oz/1⅓ cups) podded fresh peas
2 tablespoons soy sauce

✳WHY SMASH THE GARLIC CLOVES? *Smashing up the garlic cloves will allow for a good spread of flavours, the pieces will be different sizes, creating an element of surprise.*

Peel and devein the prawns, reserve the heads. Sauté the heads in the olive oil with the garlic cloves smashed using a rolling pin, add 1 litre (35 fl oz/4 cups) water, the bouquet garni and coriander. Simmer for 30 minutes. Strain the broth through a *chinois* (fine cone-shaped strainer). Slice the celery, lemongrass and onions and add them to the broth. Cook for a further 10 minutes, then add the prawns and peas and cook for a further 5 minutes. Stir in the soy sauce before serving.

May

the greengrocer

RED AND GREEN CAPSICUMS
(PEPPERS)

PURPLE ARTICHOKES

TOMATOES

BULB SPRING ONIONS
(SCALLIONS)

PEAS, BROAD (FAVA) BEANS
AND SNOW PEAS (MANGETOUT)

BABY TURNIPS

GREEN ASPARAGUS

BABY SPINACH AND
ROCKET (ARUGULA) LEAVES

FENNEL

CUCUMBERS

RASPBERRIES

STRAWBERRIES

ROCKMELON

RHUBARB

the fishmonger

MUSSELS

PRAWNS (SHRIMP) AND SCAMPI

SQUID AND SMALL CUTTLEFISH

CLAMS AND RAZOR CLAMS

WHITING

POLLOCK (LIEU JAUNE)

JOHN DORY

SALMON

the butcher-deli

RIB STEAK

RACK AND SADDLE OF LAMB

RABBIT

VEAL BREAST

DUCK BREAST

ROASTING VEAL

SPICY CHORIZO

the cheese-seller

PECORINO

PARMESAN

MASCARPONE

SAINT-MARCELLIN

the grocer

CAMARGUE BLACK RICE

HARICOT BEANS

01
Florine

PAELLA

02
Zoé

PIZZA TIME

03
Jacques

MELON AND CUCUMBER
GAZPACHO

08
Désiré

SLOW-COOKED BREAST
OF VEAL

09
Pacôme

ASPARAGUS AND BULB SPRING
ONION SALAD

10
Solange

CHILLI CUTTLEFISH

15
Denise

MACAROONS WITH BERRIES

16
Honoré

ARTICHOKE AND PECORINO
SALAD

17
Pascal

RACK OF LAMB WITH PESTO
AND TURNIPS

22
Émilie

MOTHER-IN-LAW ROAST VEAL

23
Didier

GRATIN DAUPHINOIS

24
Donatien

BERRY FRUIT SALAD

29
Ursule

ARTICHOKES BARIGOULE

30
Ferdinand

BLACK RICE PAELLA

31
Pétronille

RIB STEAK

04
Odilon

RABBIT TERRINE

05
Sylvain

SALMON TARTARE

06
Prudence

RHUBARB TART

07
Gisèle

STRAWBERRY TARTS

11
Estelle

SCAMPI TERRINE

12
Achille

VEAL CARPACCIO WITH
CAPERBERRIES

13
Rolande

POLLOCK WITH BABY SPINACH

14
Matthias

CHOUX SHOWER

18
Éric

MELON AND PROSCIUTTO
CARPACCIO

19
Yves

BLACK FOREST CAKE

20
Bernardin

CUCUMBER, MINT AND
FENNEL SALAD

21
Constantin

CHILLI DUCK KEBABS

25
Sophie

BACON AND COMTÉ KEBABS

26
Bérenger

JOHN DORY IN A SALT CRUST

27
Augustin

RICE SALAD FOR A BIG TABLE

28
Germain

SADDLE OF LAMB WITH
HARICOT BEANS

01 02 03 04

MARIE & LÉON

manifesto for paella

1st May and all's well — we've got the day off. It's Labour Day and we'll celebrate without it. A *premier Mai* that falls on a Wednesday and it's an all-week weekend.

Planning to lie-in, the shutter blinds are lowered, the alarm clock's on snooze, Marie and Léon Vachecrot are at the top of their game.

At 11.30 am, our young lovers stretch themselves out like two napping sea cows. Lunch is planned for 12.30 pm, time's getting on. On 1st May, you don't work, you ask people over.

The day's gathering looks to be sunny, a one-course meal to match the day (we don't want to overdo it, union conditions you know ... *siouplais!*). The rosé has been chilling since the night before — they've got their priorities in order at the Vachecrot household; the ice-cubes are made — they're organised in the Vachecrot household. Friends are on their way over — they know how to entertain in the Vachecrot household.

On 1st May you demonstrate ... your good humour and *savoir-vivre*, « *You'll have an anis won't you Georges?* » On 1st May you take a stand ... « *Personally I always put the ice in the carafe rather than in the glass.* » On 1st May we're all together, united in front of the paella. Thank you, 1st May!

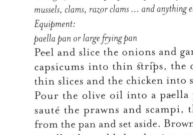

01 may

Paella
Serves 6
PREPARATION TIME 20 MINUTES
COOKING TIME 45 MINUTES

3 onions
1 garlic bulb
2 red capsicums (peppers)
150 g (5½ oz) spicy chorizo
1 free-range chicken
150 ml (5 fl oz) olive oil
6 large prawns (shrimp)
6 large scampi
300 g (10½ oz) squid tubes, cleaned
300 g (10½ oz/1⅓ cups) short-grain rice
500 ml (17 fl oz/2 cups) white wine
1 teaspoon saffron threads
salt
200 g (7 oz/1⅓ cups) podded fresh (or frozen) peas
mussels, clams, razor clams ... and anything else you like!
Equipment:
paella pan or large frying pan

Peel and slice the onions and garlic. Cut the capsicums into thin strips, the chorizo into thin slices and the chicken into small pieces. Pour the olive oil into a paella pan, briefly sauté the prawns and scampi, then remove from the pan and set aside. Brown the chicken on all sides, add the chorizo, squid, onion, garlic and capsicum. Add the rice, sauté until pearly*, moisten with the white wine, add the saffron, cook over a low heat, regularly moistening with water. When the rice is almost cooked (about 20 minutes), season generously and add the peas. Five minutes before the end of cooking, arrange the prawns and scampi, as well as any mussels or clams ... pushing them into the rice (where they'll finish cooking). Serve when the rice just starts to catch on the base of the pan.

❋ PEARLY RICE? *When you sauté the rice in the olive oil, it will become translucent.*

May without a long weekend ... never!'

02 may

Pizza time

Serves 6

PREPARATION TIME 10 MINUTES
RESTING TIME 2 HOURS
COOKING TIME 15 MINUTES

2 teaspoons dried yeast
500 g (1 lb 2 oz/3⅓ cups) plain (all-purpose) flour
1 teaspoon salt
3 tablespoons olive oil
1 teaspoon sugar
tomato passata (puréed tomatoes)
Gruyère cheese

✳ WHY LUKEWARM WATER? *It allows the yeast to grow.*

✳✳ WHY COVER THE DOUGH WITH A CLOTH AND LET IT REST? *The damp cloth will prevent the dough from forming a crust while the resting time will allow the dough to rise.*

Combine the yeast with 250 ml (9 fl oz/1 cup) lukewarm water* and set aside for 5 minutes for the yeast to develop. Mix the yeast, flour, salt, olive oil and sugar together to make a very smooth dough. Cut the dough into six portions, cover with a damp cloth and set aside at room temperature for 2 hours** before rolling. Preheat the oven to 230°C (450°F/Gas 8). Pizza is the veritable basis of the gourmet imagination: prepare a multitude of ingredients to put in the middle of the table. Start with tomato passata and finish with cheese — the rest is up to you …

03 may

Melon and cucumber gazpacho

Serves 6

PREPARATION TIME 15 MINUTES

2 cucumbers
1 rockmelon (cantaloupe), Cavaillon if in season
1 bulb spring onion (scallion)
10 mint leaves
100 ml (3½ fl oz) sherry vinegar
150 ml (5 fl oz) olive oil
salt
Tabasco sauce
2 sprigs of dill, plus extra to garnish
juice of 1 lemon

✳ WHY PEEL ONLY ONE CUCUMBER? *The skin is left on the other one to add a bit of crunch and colour.*

Peel one of the cucumbers*, as well as the melon, then cut into small pieces. Purée the cucumbers with the spring onion and mint, then add the vinegar and olive oil. Season with salt and Tabasco sauce. Purée the melon with 2 sprigs of dill and the lemon juice, and season. Put a layer of the cucumber gazpacho in the bottom of a glass, top with a layer of the melon gazpacho, add a few leaves of dill. Serve iced.

04 may

Rabbit terrine

Serves 6

PREPARATION TIME 1 HOUR
COOKING TIME 3 HOURS
CHILLING TIME 24 HOURS

3 onions
2 carrots
3 garlic cloves
50 g (1¾ oz) fresh ginger
1 rabbit with giblets
1 blanched calves' foot
1 sprig of thyme
1 sprig of rosemary
250 ml (9 fl oz/1 cup) white Port
½ bunch of tarragon
1 French shallot (eschalot)
salt and pepper
Equipment:
terrine mould

Peel and slice the onions and carrots. Peel and chop the garlic and ginger. Cut the rabbit into pieces. Place the rabbit pieces, calves' foot, onion, carrot, thyme, rosemary, garlic and ginger in a large saucepan, pour in the Port and enough water to cover. Bring to the boil, then reduce the heat and cook for 3 hours over low heat. Pick off the leaves from the tarragon, slice the French shallot. Once the rabbit has cooled to lukewarm, carefully separate the flesh from the bones (watch out for the small bones). Recover the herbs and onion, combine them with the rabbit meat, tarragon and shallot, then season well and set aside. Reduce the cooking liquid with the calves' foot and strain. Fill a terrine with the rabbit mixture and cover with the reduced cooking liquid. Make holes in the terrine using a fork*. Cover and chill for 24 hours before serving.

✳ WHY MAKE HOLES IN THE TERRINE? *Pricking the terrine with a fork will allow the liquid to get right into the terrine.*

05 may

Salmon tartare

Serves 6

PREPARATION TIME 15 MINUTES

3 sprigs of coriander (cilantro)
2 bulb spring onions (scallions)
½ red capsicum (pepper)
1 celery stalk
6 chives
8 basil leaves
juice of ½ lime
100 ml (3½ fl oz) olive oil
salt and pepper
800 g (1 lb 12 oz) fresh salmon fillet

Pick the leaves from the coriander. Finely slice the spring onions, capsicum and celery. Snip the chives into long pieces. Purée the basil with the lime juice and olive oil, then season. Chop the salmon into 1 cm (½ inch) dice, then combine with the celery, capsicum, spring onion, chives and coriander. Just before serving, dress with the lime and basil vinaigrette*.

✳ WHY DRESS ONLY AT THE LAST MINUTE? *The salmon is better raw and the lime will tend to cook it, so that's why you dress it at the last minute.*

06 may

Rhubarb tart

Serves 6

PREPARATION TIME 20 MINUTES
COOKING TIME 25 MINUTES

For the pastry:
250 g (9 oz/1⅔ cups) plain (all-purpose) flour
100 g (3½ oz) sugar
125 g (4½ oz) butter, softened
3 tablespoons pouring (whipping) cream
2 tablespoons raspberry coulis
2 tablespoons bilberry or blueberry coulis
For the rhubarb filling:
100 g (3½ oz) sugar
1 kg (2 lb 4 oz) rhubarb
100 g (3½ oz) butter, melted
100 g (3½ oz/1 cup) ground hazelnuts
1 egg

Preheat the oven to 180°C (350°F/Gas 4). Make a syrup for the filling by combining the sugar with 200 ml (7 fl oz) water. Peel the rhubarb*, cut it into 10 cm (4 inch) lengths, cook in the syrup over gentle heat for 5 minutes. Combine the butter, ground hazelnuts and egg. To make the pastry, combine the flour, sugar and butter. Bring the pastry dough together with the cream (it should be smooth). Roll out the pastry and lay it in a tin, fill with rhubarb and top with the hazelnut mixture. Bake for about 20 minutes. Drizzle over the coulis to serve.

✳ WHY PEEL THE RHUBARB AND HOW? *Rhubarb skin is stringy so it should be peeled off with a knife. Make an incision into the skin, pull away and discard the fibres.*

07 may

Strawberry tarts

Serves 6

PREPARATION TIME 20 MINUTES
CHILLING TIME 1 HOUR
COOKING TIME 20 MINUTES

For the pastry:
180 g (6¼ oz/1¼ cups) plain (all-purpose) flour
80 g (2¾ oz/⅓ cup) sugar
30 g (1 oz/¼ cup) ground almonds
120 g (4¼ oz) lightly salted butter, diced and softened
1 egg
For the crème pâtissière:
2 egg yolks
80 g (2¾ oz/⅓ cup) sugar
1 tablespoon plain (all-purpose) flour
1 tablespoon cornflour (cornstarch)
250 ml (9 fl oz/1 cup) full-cream (whole) milk
For the strawberries:
800 g (1 lb 12 oz) strawberries, hulled
icing (confectioners') sugar

Preheat the oven to 180°C (350°F/Gas 4). For the pastry, combine the flour, sugar and ground almonds. Incorporate the butter, using the palm of your hand to work the pastry, then add the egg. Wrap the pastry in plastic wrap and chill for 1 hour. Roll out the cold pastry on a sheet of baking paper to 5 mm (¼ inch) thick all over. Cut out circles, bake for about 15 minutes, or until the pastry is golden*. For the crème pâtissière, whisk the egg yolks with the sugar until pale and frothy, then add the flour and cornflour. Boil the milk**, pour it over the egg mixture and combine well. Cook for 8 minutes over gentle heat, stirring constantly. Allow to cool.
To serve, place 1 tablespoon of the crème patissière on each pastry round, arrange the strawberries on top and dust with icing sugar.

✳ TIP FOR BLIND BAKING THE PASTRY: *To prevent them puffing up, place the tart bases inside cake rings on a sheet of baking paper, cover with dried fruit and nuts and make sure the pastry is quite cold when it goes into the oven.*

✳✳ WHY DOES THE MILK NEED TO BOIL? *Boiling milk will help to incorporate the yolks well.*

08 may

Slow-cooked breast of veal

Serves 6

PREPARATION TIME 20 MINUTES
COOKING TIME 5 HOURS

3 French shallots (eschalots)
1 garlic clove
50 g (1¾ oz/½ cup) grated parmesan cheese
100 ml (3½ fl oz) olive oil
50 g (1¾ oz/⅓ cup) pine nuts
1 bunch of basil
1.2 kg boneless veal breast
1 tablespoon herbes de Provence (Provençal herb mix)
salt and pepper

Preheat the oven to 100°C (200°F/Gas ½). Peel and finely chop the shallots and garlic. Process the parmesan with the olive oil, pine nuts, garlic and basil. Lay the veal breast on the bench (flesh side up), spread the breast with the basil mixture, scatter with shallots and the *herbes de Provence*, season generously. Roll the breast up firmly and tie with kitchen string. Cook in the oven for 5 hours* — you should be able to pierce the veal easily with the point of a knife when done.

✽ COOKING AT A LOW TEMPERATURE: *The temperature needs to stay constant and not go over 100°C (200°F/ Gas ½). Baste the meat regularly with its juices.*

09 may

Asparagus and bulb spring onion salad

Serves 6

PREPARATION TIME 15 MINUTES

2 bunches of green asparagus
3 tomatoes
3 bulb spring onions (scallions)
80 ml (2½ fl oz/⅓ cup) olive oil
juice of 1 lemon
1 tablespoon cider vinegar
1 handful of rocket (arugula) leaves
1 bunch of dill, leaves picked
salt and pepper

Trim the ends of the asparagus and cut the spears into 5 cm (2 inch) lengths. Make a cross-shaped incision in the base of the tomatoes*, blanch them for 15 seconds in boiling water and peel. Seed the tomatoes and cut the flesh into 1 cm (½ inch) cubes. Slice the spring onions. Combine the oil with the lemon juice and cider vinegar. Combine all the vegetables and leaves, dress with the vinaigrette, then season.

✽ WHY CUT A CROSS IN THE TOMATOES BEFORE BLANCHING THEM? *It makes it easy to peel off the skin!*

10 may

Chilli cuttlefish

Serves 6

PREPARATION TIME 30 MINUTES
COOKING TIME 5 MINUTES

1 kg (2 lb 4 oz) small cuttlefish
100 g (3½ oz/⅔ cup) plain (all-purpose) flour
1 tablespoon piment d'Espelette (Basque chilli por or mild chilli powder
50 g (1¾ oz) butter
2 tablespoons sunflower oil

✽ PREPARE THE CUTTLEFISH: *It takes time to prepare cuttlefish. Separate the head from the body, remove the beak, reserve the tentacles, clean the cuttlefish bodies, taking care to pull out the cartilaginous bone and rinse well.*

Prepare the cuttlefish*. Rinse and pat dry paper towels. Combine the flour with *piment d'Espelette* and dust the cuttlefish. the butter and oil in a frying pan over heat, brown the cuttlefish for 5 minu it's better to cook them in several batches to overcrowd the pan.

11 may

Scampi terrine

Serves 6

PREPARATION TIME 30 MINUTES
COOKING TIME 1 HOUR

12 fresh scampi
1 lime
1 orange
100 g (3½ oz/⅔ cup) podded fresh peas
100 g (3½ oz) podded broad (fava) beans
800 g (1 lb 12 oz) whiting fillets
4 eggs
200 ml (7 fl oz) pouring (whipping) cream
3 French shallots (eschalots), sliced
salt and pepper
a few cabbage leaves, blanched

✱WHY DO PEAS NEED TO BE BLANCHED AS WELL AS COOKED IN THE BAIN-MARIE? *To set the chlorophyll in the vegetables.*

✱✱WHY DO THE BROAD BEANS NEED TO BE PEELED? *The skin isn't edible: it's tough and bitter.*

Preheat the oven to 160°C (315°F/Gas 2–3). Remove the scampi from the shells. Zest the citrus, remove the skin and pith and cut into segments. Blanch* the peas and broad beans for 30 seconds in boiling salted water, peel the broad beans**. Process the whiting with the eggs, cream, shallots, citrus zest and segments, peas and broad beans, season. Line a terrine tin with the cabbage, half-fill with the whiting mixture, arrange the scampi in a pyramid in the middle of the terrine, cover with the remaining whiting mixture. Seal with the cabbage, cook in a bain-marie for 1 hour.

12 may

Veal carpaccio with caperberries

Serves 6

PREPARATION TIME 20 MINUTES
COOKING TIME 5 MINUTES

600 g (1 lb 5 oz) roasting veal
50 g (1¾ oz) butter
2 lemons
100 ml (3½ fl oz) olive oil
1 tablespoon Port
10 caperberries
*6 chive flowers**
2 sprigs of lemon thyme, leaves picked
fleur de sel and pepper

✱WHERE DO YOU FIND THE CHIVE FLOWERS? *In the garden!*

✱✱WHY PUT THE ROAST IN THE FREEZER? *It makes it easier to carve.*

In a frying pan, brown the veal roast in the butter on all sides without cooking it. Put it in the freezer for 30 minutes**. Remove the skin and pith of the lemons and cut out the skinless segments. Combine the olive oil with the Port. Cut the caperberries into rounds. Slice the veal thinly, arrange the slices on individual plates, dress with the Port mixture, scatter with the lemon thyme, chive flowers, lemon segments, caperberries and season.

13 may

Pollock with baby spinach

Serves 6

PREPARATION TIME 15 MINUTES
COOKING TIME 15 MINUTES

2 garlic cloves
3 carrots
6 bulb spring onions (scallions)
2 tablespoons plain (all-purpose) flour
6 thick fillets of pollock (lieu jaune)
or firm-fleshed white fish, skin on
1–2 tablespoons olive oil
600 g (1 lb 5 oz) baby spinach leaves
125 ml (4 fl oz/½ cup) white wine
60 g (2¼ oz) butter
salt and pepper

✱TIP FOR KEEPING WARM: *Keep them in front of an open oven, covered with foil.*

Peel and chop the garlic. Peel and cut the carrots into thin sticks. Chop the spring onions. Flour the pollock fillets, cook them for about 10 minutes in olive oil in a non-stick frying pan. Keep them warm*. In the same pan, sauté the garlic, carrots and bulb spring onions, add the baby spinach leaves and the white wine. Reduce for 2–3 minutes, then add the butter and season.

MARIE & LÉON

great is the mystery of faith

Today is a big day for Kevin, it's his first communion. Léon and Marie have invited the whole family, it's a big sit-down meal, with name and menu printed alongside each person's serviette. The table has sprouted on top of two trestles, the white sheets are doing duty as a tablecloth, the wedding silver's been brought out, the *Moustiers* dinner service dusted off, there are Champagne flutes, wine glasses, water glasses, it's classy! Freshly cut flowers from the garden are placed in the middle of the table, a floral arrangement is improvised with roses and greenery — super-classy! It's a high-wire act.

The whole family has answered the call. Cousin Georges has left his offices, Marinette and Fernand have come 200 kilometres, Uncle Jacques arrived the day before. Everything's a-bubbling, in the kitchen as in the glasses. A good sparkling found at the last wine fair, 12 bottles for the price of six. By way of *apéritif*, there are sausages in flaky pastry, anchovies in flaky pastry, cheese in flaky pastry, it's a symphony of nibbles — hot, lukewarm or cold, the choice is vast. Uncle Jacques has opened up his box of jokes, « *That's blondes for you …* » Marinette can't get over seeing the little one so big, « *When I think that just yesterday I was carrying him in my arms.* » Fernand has discreetly turned on the TV to sneak a look at the Monaco Grand Prix, « *He's really good that Hamilton, I can see him winning this year.* » Georges, account manager with a major (yellow!) bank, doesn't understand why the small shareholders are nervous about the current crisis, « *You should buy Eurotunnel, it's a blue-chip investment, 15% guaranteed per annum.* » It's a circus this Sunday lunch, coming from all sides. Kevin concentrates on his new video game, which has come straight from Paris, thank you, cousin Georges. Marie and Léon concentrate on the *pièce montée*: three failed caramels, bandages on every finger, a blistered lip (ah, the bad reflex of putting your finger in your mouth when it's covered with caramel), but never mind, there'll be *choux* whether as a *pièce montée* or a *pièce démontée*.

14 may

Choux shower

Serves 6

PREPARATION TIME 15 MINUTES
COOKING TIME 30 MINUTES

For the choux pastry:
65 g (2¼ oz) butter
125 g (4½ oz) plain (all-purpose) flour
4 eggs
1 egg yolk, lightly beaten

Preheat the oven to 160°C (315°F/Gas 2–3). Bring 250 ml (9 fl oz/1 cup) water to the boil with the butter, add the flour all at once and mix together with a spatula. Cook over low heat until the mixture comes away from the sides. Remove from the heat and add the eggs one by one. Form small choux with 2 teaspoons and arrange on a baking tray lined with baking paper (they'll expand by a third), brush them with the last egg yolk. Bake for 30 minutes (without opening the oven*). Then leave them for 10 minutes more with the oven half-open.

For chantilly choux puffs: Whip 500 ml (17 fl oz/2 cups) pouring (whipping) cream with 150 g (5½ oz/⅔ cup) caster (superfine) sugar, then fill the choux puffs using a piping (icing) bag.

For choux to make a *pièce montée* (like a *croquembouche*): Fill with crème pâtissière (see page 200) using a piping (icing) bag. Then dip them into a caramel**. Be careful: it burns!

✳ WHY NOT OPEN THE OVEN DURING COOKING TIME? *To avoid ending up with a thin pancake.*

✳✳ A TIP FOR COATING THE CHOUX: *The ideal to avoid burning yourself is to impale the choux on a toothpick and dip them in the caramel one by one like that.*

> **'The artichoke is the striptease of the vegetable world, after the outer layers are removed, you reach the heart in the hope it's not too hairy.'**

15 may
Macaroons with berries
Serves 6

PREPARATION TIME 20 MINUTES
COOKING TIME 10 MINUTES

220 g (7¾ oz/1¾ cups) icing (confectioners') sugar
125 g (4½ oz/1¼ cups) ground almonds
4 egg whites
50 g (1¾ oz/¼ cup) caster (superfine) sugar
200 g (7 oz) crème pâtissière (see page 200)
berry sorbet
200 g (7 oz/1⅔ cups) raspberries
200 g (7 oz/1⅓ cups) strawberries, hulled and sliced
3 tablespoons raspberry coulis
3 tablespoons bilberry or blueberry coulis

Preheat the oven to 160°C (315°F/Gas 2–3). Combine the icing sugar and the ground almonds and pass through a sieve*. Beat the egg whites with the caster sugar to very stiff peaks. Delicately fold the sugar-almond mix into the egg whites: the mixture should be shiny. Make six macaroons on a baking tray lined with baking paper, leave for 30 minutes to form a crust. Cook for 10 minutes. Allow to cool. Make a circle of crème pâtissière** on a plate, place a scoop of berry sorbet on top, then some berries, top with a macaroon and some coulis.

✱ WHY SIEVE?
To avoid lumps and make it easier to fold the almond mixture into the egg whites.

✱✱ HOW DO I MAKE THE CIRCLE?
With patience or a piping (icing) bag.

16 may
Artichoke and pecorino salad
Serves 6

PREPARATION TIME 30 MINUTES
COOKING TIME 10 MINUTES

18 purple artichokes
juice of 1 lemon
olive oil
120 g (4¼ oz) pecorino cheese
1 handful of rocket (arugula) leaves
3 bulb spring onions (scallions)
fleur de sel

Peel the stem of the artichokes. Cut off the top of the artichoke heads. Remove the larger leaves so that you keep only the lighter leaves and the hearts. Cut them in two, remove the choke, keep them in water with some lemon juice added*. Cook the artichoke in olive oil for 5–7 minutes: they should stay *al dente*. Make shavings of pecorino, combine them with the rocket and the sliced spring onion, add the artichoke, drizzle with some olive oil then season with *fleur de sel*.

✱ WHY KEEP THEM IN WATER WITH LEMON JUICE?
Artichokes oxidise very quickly, so the lemon will slow down this oxidisation.

17 may
Rack of lamb with pesto and turnips
Serves 6

PREPARATION TIME 20 MINUTES
COOKING TIME 20 MINUTES

3 bunches of baby turnips
50 g (1¾ oz) butter
1 tablespoon sugar
2 lamb racks containing 8 cutlets each
olive oil
1 handful of rocket (arugula) leaves
1 bunch of basil
80 g (2¾ oz) parmesan cheese
juice of 1 lemon
2 garlic cloves
salt and pepper

Preheat oven to 180°C (350°F/Gas 4). Trim the turnip tops to 1 cm (½ inch)* and peel the turnips. Place in a saucepan with the tops upward, cover with water, add the butter and sugar and cover with a sheet of baking paper**. Cook over low heat until the water has completely evaporated, then glaze***. Drizzle the lamb with olive oil and cook them in the oven for about 15 minutes. Purée the rocket with the basil, parmesan, lemon juice and garlic, then season. Take the racks out of the oven and rest for 5 minutes. Cut into cutlets, drizzle over the pesto and serve with the glazed turnips.

✱ WHY KEEP THE TOPS? *For aesthetic reasons — it's pretty, no?*

✱✱ WHY COOK THE TURNIPS COVERED WITH BAKING PAPER WHEN YOU WANT TO EVAPORATE THE LIQUID? *It allows the turnips to cook evenly.*

✱✱✱ GLAZE THE TURNIPS: *Roll them in the cooking juices, that way they'll become nice and shiny.*

18 may

Melon and prosciutto carpaccio

Serves 6

PREPARATION TIME 15 MINUTES

2 rockmelons (cantaloupes), Cavaillons *if in season*
3 slices prosciutto
1 teaspoon honey
2 tablespoons walnut oil
1 bunch of chives, snipped
2 sprigs of oregano, leaves picked
fleur de sel

Cut the melons in half, remove the seeds. Cut them into thin slices, remove the skin. Cut the prosciutto into a chiffonade*. Combine the honey and walnut oil. Arrange the melon in a rosetta pattern, brush with the honey and walnut oil, arrange the slivers of prosciutto, pieces of chive and oregano leaves on top, season with *fleur de sel*.

A PROSCIUTTO CHIFFONADE? Slice the prosciutto into thin strips.

19 may

Black Forest cake

Serves 6

PREPARATION TIME 30 MINUTES
COOKING TIME 20 MINUTES

350 g (12 oz) good-quality dark chocolate
100 g (3½ oz) butter
6 eggs, separated
250 g (9 oz) sugar
2 tablespoons cornflour (cornstarch)
100 ml (3½ fl oz) kirsch
400 ml (14 fl oz) pouring (whipping) cream
2 tablespoons vanilla sugar
200 g (7 oz) amarena cherries*
   or bottled morello cherries, drained

Preheat the oven to 180°C (350°F/Gas 4). Melt 250 g (9 oz) chocolate in a double-boiler with the butter. Shave the remaining chocolate and set aside. Whisk the egg yolks with 150 g (5½ oz) sugar until pale and frothy, add the cornflour, then the melted chocolate mixture. Whip the egg whites to soft peaks, fold into the chocolate mixture. Pour into a buttered and floured round cake tin and bake for 20 minutes. Unmould the cake, cut it into three horizontal layers. Make a syrup with the remaining sugar, kirsch and 100 ml (3½ fl oz) water. Soak each layer in the syrup. Whip the cream into a firm chantilly with the vanilla sugar. Arrange the cherries on two of the layers, cover with some chantilly and assemble the cake. Cover with the remaining chantilly and scatter with the chocolate shavings.

AMARENA CHERRIES: These are cherries that have been preserved in syrup.

20 may

Cucumber, mint and fennel salad

Serves 6

PREPARATION TIME 20 MINUTES

2 cucumbers
coarse salt
2 fennel bulbs
juice of 2 lemons
3 bulb spring onions (scallions), sliced
1 bunch of coriander (cilantro)
100 ml (3½ fl oz) olive oil

Peel the cucumbers, cut them in half lengthways, remove the core of seeds. Slice them finely and place them in a colander with a little coarse salt so they degorge*. Cut the fennel in half, slice as finely as possible. Combine the fennel with the lemon juice, add the spring onion, coriander, cucumber and olive oil**.

WHY DEGORGE THE CUCUMBER? The cucumber should be degorged for about 1 hour to draw out its juices and make it more digestible. If you don't ... burp ... degorge the cu ... burp, pardon ... cumber you run the risk of ... being reminded ... burp ... the whole day.

WHEN IS IT SEASONED? You should taste the salad before seasoning it, because the degorged cucumbers are already salted.

MARIE & LÉON

Jacquy's team

*H*ow to find and choose a good *magret de canard* (duck breast)? The best are obviously enjoyed in the Landes region. (Just as for that matter the best nougats are found in Montélimar, the best sardines in Marseille, the best camemberts in Normandie, the best *bêtise* candies in Cambrai, the best *rosette* sausages in Lyon ...)

But in the Landes area there's Jacquy, and Jacquy, believe me, is precious, so he's called direct on 06 64 18 ... « *Ah! These tunnels, they cut you off every time!* » He's told what time they're arriving and everything is ready. The barbecue has reddened the vine shoots (us too), the *magrets* are impatient (us too), Marie and Léon Vachecrot got the day wrong (stay calm), but there are friends aplenty: Bernard, world champion in bottle-opening and serving from the trough; Pompon, whiskovore *emeritus*, world champion in spoonerisms and very fond of his region. Nowhere else does the pear *eau-de-vie* have a taste of terrine, and their wives, smiling in the face of all the bawdiness, applaud their nonsense ... *Magrets* are truly good.

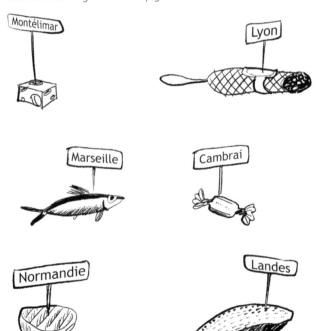

Montélimar — Lyon — Marseille — Cambrai — Normandie — Landes

21 may

Chilli duck kebabs
Serves 6

PREPARATION TIME 15 MINUTES
COOKING TIME 10 MINUTES

3 duck breast fillets, skin off
1 red capsicum (pepper)
1 green capsicum (pepper)
6 bulb spring onions (scallions)
2 garlic cloves
2 tablespoons soy sauce
1 tablespoon olive oil
1 pinch piment d'Espelette (Basque chilli powder)
   or mild chilli powder

Preheat the oven to 200°C (400°F/Gas 6) or barbecue to hot. Cut the duck breasts in half lengthways, then cut each half into six pieces. Cut the capsicums into 2 cm (¾ inch) squares. Halve the spring onions. Finely chop the garlic, combine with the soy sauce and olive oil. Thread the ingredients onto the skewers, brush with the soy sauce mixture, dust with chilli powder. Cook on the barbecue or in the oven for a few minutes to sear the duck breasts — they should stay red in the middle.

23 may

Gratin dauphinois

Serves 6

PREPARATION TIME 15 MINUTES
COOKING TIME 45 MINUTES

1 kg (2 lb 4 oz) potatoes, peeled
600 ml (21 fl oz) pouring (whipping) cream
salt and pepper
1 dash nutmeg

Preheat the oven to 180°C (350°F/Gas 4).

Classic: Thinly slice the potatoes, arrange them in a gratin dish, combine the cream with the salt, pepper and a good dash of nutmeg, pour this mixture over the potatoes, bake in the oven for 45 minutes.

Beaufort: Cut 200 g (7 oz) Beaufort cheese into thin slivers, finely slice 6 garlic cloves. Arrange the potatoes, the cheese and garlic in layers in a gratin dish. Season the cream and pour it over the lot, bake in the oven for 45 minutes.

Bacon and onion: Slice 4 large onions, sauté them in a little oil with 150 g (5½ oz) speck. Arrange the potatoes, onions and speck in layers in a gratin dish. Season the cream and pour it over the lot, bake in the oven for 45 minutes.

22 may

Mother-in-law roast veal

Serves 6

PREPARATION TIME 20 MINUTES
COOKING TIME 55 MINUTES

1.2 kg (2 lb 10 oz) roasting veal, tied with kitchen string
3 tablespoons olive oil
250 ml (9 fl oz/1 cup) white wine
1 sprig of rosemary
2 French shallots (eschalots)
6 garlic cloves
60 g (2¼ oz) butter
800 g (1 lb 12 oz) oyster mushrooms*, cleaned**
salt and pepper

*Mushrooms in May? *Yes, they're available all year round. Oyster mushrooms are a cultivated mushroom.*

**Cleaning the mushrooms: *Rinse the mushrooms briefly in water and blot them dry with a clean cloth.*

In a flameproof casserole dish, brown the veal roast on all sides in the olive oil. Add the white wine, rosemary and shallots, whole, and cover. Cook over low heat for 45 minutes. Remove the roast from the casserole dish, keep warm. Peel and slice the garlic, sauté it in the casserole dish in the butter, add the mushrooms, cook over high heat for 5 minutes, season. Serve the roast on a dish surrounded by the mushrooms.

24 may

Berry fruit salad

Serves 6

PREPARATION TIME 15 MINUTES

300 g (10½ oz/2 cups) strawberries
150 ml (5 fl oz) pouring (whipping) cream
100 g (3½ oz) vanilla sugar
2 tablespoons Amaretto liqueur
150 g (5½ oz/⅔ cup) mascarpone cheese
300 g (10½ oz/2⅓ cups) raspberries

*No berries to hand? *You can replace the berries of the season with any other seasonal fruit.*

Hull the strawberries*. Whip the cream to a stiff chantilly with the vanilla sugar. Fold the Amaretto into the mascarpone, then the chantilly. Place a few of the berries into some glasses, then some mascarpone cream, then repeat.

may

BACON AND COMTÉ KEBABS

25 may

Bacon and Comté kebabs

Serves 6

PREPARATION TIME 15 MINUTES
COOKING TIME 10 MINUTES

600 g (1 lb 5 oz) Comté cheese
12 slices speck
1 teaspoon honey
2 tablespoons soy sauce
1 tablespoon Viandox or veal jus
coarsely ground black pepper

Cut the Comté into 1 cm (½ inch) wide sticks. Place them on skewers, lengthways. Wrap a slice of speck around each kebab. Combine the honey, soy sauce and Viandox, brush each kebab with this mixture. Scatter with the coarsely ground black pepper. Place the kebabs on a hot barbecue, cook them on each side until the cheese starts to melt.

26 may

John dory in a salt crust

Serves 6

PREPARATION TIME 20 MINUTES
COOKING TIME 15 MINUTES

2 large whole John dory, cleaned
3 sprigs of dill
1 tablespoon fennel seeds
1 bunch of basil
1 bunch of chervil
2 tablespoons olive oil
500 g (1 lb 2 oz) coarse salt
500 g (1 lb 2 oz/3⅓ cups) plain (all-purpose) flour

Preheat the oven to 180°C (350°F/Gas 4). Clean the John dory, place the dill and fennel seeds inside the cavity. Finely chop the herbs. Oil the John dory and roll in the chopped herbs. Combine the coarse salt and flour, then add just enough water to make a malleable dough. Roll out half the salt dough, lay the John dory on top and cover with another piece of dough, shaping the dough around the fish. Bake in the oven for 15 minutes. Cut the salt crust* at the table using a bread knife.

✱CUT THE SALT CRUST: *Don't panic, the mixture of flour and coarse salt lets you cut it cleanly without spraying crystals everywhere.*

27 may

Rice salad for a big table

Serves 6

PREPARATION TIME 20 MINUTES
COOKING TIME 20 MINUTES

300 g (10½ oz/1⅓ cups) rice
100 g (3½ oz/⅔ cup) podded fresh peas
100 g (3½ oz) snow peas (mangetout)
100 g (3½ oz) green beans
3 tomatoes
1 French shallot (eschalot)
50 g (1¾ oz) bottarga (cured fish roe)
1 egg
1 tablespoon Dijon mustard
zest and juice of 1 lemon
100 ml (3½ fl oz) olive oil
200 ml (7 fl oz) sunflower oil
salt and pepper

Cook the rice in a large saucepan of boiling water for the time indicated on the packet. Rinse it immediately. Cook the peas, snow peas and beans in boiling salted water for 7–8 minutes: they should stay *al dente*. Cut the tomatoes into cubes, slice the shallot and the bottarga into shavings. Place the egg in a straight-sided bowl with the mustard, lemon zest and juice. Add the oils, then process with a stick blender to make a mayonnaise*. Season. Mix everything together and serve chilled.

✱FOR EASY MAYONNAISE: *A whole egg is used instead of just the yolk, so the mayo comes together more easily.*

'The purple artichoke is like a fast woman, undressed at the outset.'

28 may

Saddle of lamb with haricot beans

Serves 6

SOAKING TIME 1 NIGHT
PREPARATION TIME 20 MINUTES
COOKING TIME 2 HOURS

250 g (9 oz/1¼ cups) dried white haricot beans
1 boneless fine saddle of lamb
3 French shallots (eschalots)
1 bunch of flat-leaf (Italian) parsley, leaves picked
1 garlic bulb + 2 garlic cloves, extra
1 sprig of rosemary
2 onions
1 bouquet garni
1 tomato, chopped
salt and pepper

The day before, soak the beans in cold water. Preheat the oven to 200°C (400°F/Gas 6). Lay out the lamb saddle, cut in half down the middle (along the fillets). Peel the shallots, chop them with the parsley. Spread the lamb with this mixture and season. Roll up each half-saddle tightly and tie with kitchen string. Halve the garlic bulb horizontally. Cook the lamb for about 15 minutes with the garlic and rosemary. Drain the beans, then cook in boiling water with the onions, extra garlic, bouquet garni and tomato for about 2 hours. Drain the beans, reheat in the cooking dish with the lamb, then season.

29 may

Artichokes barigoule

Serves 6

PREPARATION TIME 30 MINUTES
COOKING TIME 10 MINUTES

18 purple artichokes
2 tablespoons lemon juice
2 tablespoons olive oil
4 garlic cloves, sliced
3 French shallots (eschalots), sliced
2 sprigs of thyme
fleur de sel

❋ WHY REMOVE THE LARGE LEAVES? *The lighter leaves and the hearts are the most tender parts, so it's a matter of keeping the best!*

Peel the stem of the artichokes. Cut off the top of the artichoke heads. Remove the large leaves*, keep the lighter leaves and hearts. Cut them in half, discard the choke and keep them in water with the lemon juice. Cook the artichokes in the olive oil for 5–7 minutes with the garlic, shallots and thyme — they should stay al dente. Season with *fleur de sel*.

30 may

Black rice paella

Serves 6

PREPARATION TIME 15 MINUTES
COOKING TIME 45 MINUTES

6 onions
10 garlic cloves
2 tablespoons olive oil
800 g (1 lb 12 oz) squid tubes, cleaned and chopped
350 g (12 oz) black Camargue* or short-grain rice
250 ml (9 fl oz/1 cup) white wine
salt and pepper

❋ WHAT'S SPECIAL ABOUT BLACK RICE? *It's a firmer variety of Camargue rice that suits paella well.*

Peel and slice the onions and garlic, sauté them in olive oil in a paella pan with the squid, add the black rice*. Sauté for 5 minutes, moisten with the white wine, then add about 1 litre (35 fl oz/4 cups) water, season. Cook over low heat for 45 minutes — the rice should be very soft and the liquid completely evaporated.

MARIE & LÉON

barbecue: a story about men

Today is barbecue day: « *Barbecuing is men's business so you have a day off, Marie. I, Léon, shall take care of everything.* »

The sun is shining and as 10 o'clock chimes, Léon hurries to set up the barbecue and coals. As for Marie, she's busy in the kitchen cleaning the grill, put away any old how, namely dirty, after her man's last *merguez* party with his *boules*-playing mates.

10:10 am: the grill is clean, a quick dash in the car to the butcher to buy the rib steaks for lunch, Léon forgot.

10:45 am: back home, Marie washes the vegetables, prepares the meat and the utensils essential for lunch to go smoothly.

11:30 am: Marie sets the table, opens the rosé, brings out the aniseed *apéritifs*. « *Don't forget the ice, Marie.* »

11:55 am: Marie puts the vegetables on to cook, takes the meat out to her husband. Léon puts the steaks on the barbecue and pours a round of drinks.

12:30 pm: Marie checks that her vegetables are ready, calls out to Léon: « *The steaks are burning!* » Léon brings the overcooked meat to the table, pours drinks.

12:40 pm: Marie carves and serves the meat, brings out the vegetables, serves them, quickly eats and goes back into the kitchen to prepare the dessert. Léon pours drinks.

1:30 pm: Marie clears the table and puts it away, makes the coffee. Léon pours drinks.

2:30 pm: Marie does the dishes and sweeps the floor, Léon leaves the barbecue outside, « *It's still hot, a person could burn themselves,* » goes to have a nap, « *I'm exhausted darling, happy then you didn't have to cook?* » Faced with Marie's affronted look, Léon concludes that his wife is never happy.

31 may

Rib steak

Serves 6

PREPARATION TIME 20 MINUTES
COOKING TIME YOUR CALL

Light the barbecue coals. Choose a rib roast weighing 1.5 kg (3 lb 5 oz), well aged*, marbled to perfection, from a noble breed (a good rib roast is worth two average ones, so go for quality, and next time we'll make sardines!). When the embers are nice and red, sear the rib steak for 3 minutes on each side to seal**, finish the cooking at your leisure***. Serve with your choice of condiments from the list below.

* AGED AND MARBLED? *Aged beef is beef wise enough to take its time before being put on sale, the flesh has relaxed, the meat has become more tender, me too for that matter. Marbled meat is meat that shows a good balance of lean and fat.*

** WHY SEAL? *To trap the juices.*

*** HOW DO YOU CHECK FOR DONE-NESS BY TOUCH? *The firmer the meat is to the touch, the more cooked it is.*

Tarragon butter: Combine 100 g (3½ oz) lightly salted butter with 1 finely chopped French shallot (eschalot) and 1 bunch chopped tarragon.

Béarnaise: Reduce 100 ml (3½ fl oz) wine vinegar with 1 bunch of chopped tarragon. Remove from the heat and add 2 egg yolks. Whisk until it becomes pale and frothy over gentle heat (the yolks mustn't coagulate). Gradually add 200 g (7 oz) melted butter, whisking constantly, season and serve immediately.

Saint-Marcellin cheese: Melt 2 mature Saint-Marcellin cheeses in 200 ml (7 fl oz) pouring (whipping) cream. Reduce until you have a smooth, creamy sauce.

Onions: Sauté 4 sliced onions in olive oil, add 1 tablespoon soft brown sugar, moisten with 250 ml (9 fl oz/1 cup) red wine, add 1 teaspoon of tomato paste (concentrated purée) and let it reduce.

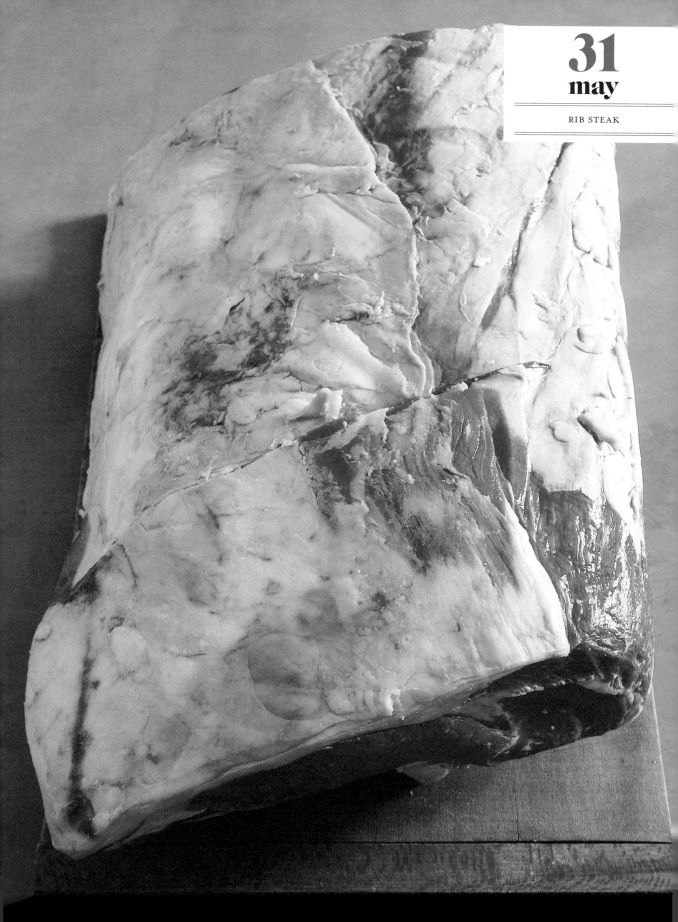

June

the greengrocer

ZUCCHINI (COURGETTES)

RED, GREEN AND YELLOW
CAPSICUMS (PEPPERS)

BULB SPRING ONIONS
(SCALLIONS)

TOMATOES

CUCUMBERS

EGGPLANTS (AUBERGINES)

BROAD (FAVA) BEANS

SNOW PEAS (MANGETOUT)

PEAS

GREEN BEANS

GREEN ASPARAGUS

ROCKET (ARUGULA) LEAVES

MUNG BEAN SHOOTS

ALFALFA SPROUTS

HERBS AND SPICES

CHERRIES

RHUBARB

STRAWBERRIES

RASPBERRIES

BILBERRIES OR BLUEBERRIES

the fishmonger

MACKEREL AND SARDINES

SMOKED SALMON

TUNA

ANCHOVY FILLETS

SMALL SQUID
AND CUTTLEFISH

RASCASSE (SCORPION FISH)

the butcher-deli

BEEF STEAK

VEAL ESCALOPE

CHICKEN

RABBIT

DUCK

MINCED BEEF

BACON LARDONS

PORK NECK

PORK SPARE-RIBS

LAMB LEG

the grocer

ARBORIO RICE

SEMOLINA

01 Justin	02 Blandine	03 Kevin
ZUCCHINI SALAD	MARINATED CAPSICUMS	SPAGHETTI BOLOGNESE
08 Médard	09 Diane	10 Landry
VEGETABLE TERRINE	PENNE AND SMOKED SALMON SALAD	FIRST TABOULEH
15 Augustin	16 François	17 Hervé
CHERRIES IN RED WINE	RABBIT IN MUSTARD SAUCE	PISSALADIÈRE
22 Alban	23 Audrey	24 Jean-Baptiste
RHUBARB AND BERRY COMPOTE	SUMMERTIME SPRING ROLLS	CLASSIC GAZPACHO
29 Pierre	30 Martial	01
STIR-FRIED CUTTLEFISH WITH GARLIC	CORIANDER MEATBALLS	

04
Clotilde
COCONUT CHICKEN KEBABS

05
Igor
MACKEREL À LA GRENOBLOISE

06
Norbert
EGGPLANT FRITTERS

07
Gilbert
CHERRY CLAFOUTIS

11
Barnabé
MARINATED SARDINES

12
Guy
SESAME TUNA CARPACCIO

13
Antoine
GRILLED VEGETABLES

14
Élisée
CHICKEN IN GARLIC CRUST

18
Léonce
DUCK TERRINE

19
Jude
CLASSIC LASAGNE

20
Silvère
SARDINES GRILLED
WITH ROSEMARY

21
Été
TUNA WITH SAUCE VIERGE

25
Prosper
SWEET AND SOUR
PORK SPARE-RIBS

26
Anthelme
PANNA COTTA

27
Fernand
SQUID RISOTTO

28
Irénée
RASCASSE WITH LEMON

01 june

Zucchini salad

Serves 6

PREPARATION TIME 20 MINUTES

6 small firm zucchini (courgettes)
1 bunch of peppermint
3 bulb spring onions (scallions)
100 ml (3½ fl oz) olive oil
1 lemon
salt and pepper

✳TECHNIQUE FOR CUTTING INTO SPAGHETTI: *Cut the zucchini into long thin slices, then cut the slices into strips.*

Cut the zucchini into spaghetti, keeping the skin on*. Pick off the peppermint leaves. Slice the green part of the spring onion, finely slice the white part. Combine the peppermint and vegetables, add the olive oil and lemon juice, then season.

02 june

Marinated capsicums

Serves 6

PREPARATION TIME 45 MINUTES
COOKING TIME 10 MINUTES
CHILLING TIME 24 HOURS

12 garlic cloves
200 ml (7 fl oz) full-cream (whole) milk
3 red capsicums (peppers)
3 green capsicums (peppers)
3 yellow capsicums (peppers)
fleur de sel
1 teaspoon peppercorns
3 bulb spring onions (scallions)
3 bay leaves
3 sprigs of rosemary
300 ml (10½ fl oz) olive oil

✳WHY COOK THE GARLIC IN THE MILK? *It softens the taste and gives it a creamy quality.*

✳✳WHY PUT THE CAPSICUMS IN A PLASTIC BAG? *The moisture produced by being enclosed in the bag will help the skin come away from the flesh easily.*

Preheat the oven to 200°C (400°F/Gas 6). Peel the garlic, cook it in the milk* over low heat for 10 minutes, rinse and slice. Bake all of the capsicums whole in the oven for 10 minutes, or until they brown, then enclose them in a plastic bag** for 10 minutes. Remove the skin and seeds from the capsicums and tear the flesh. Quarter the spring onions. Place layers of capsicum and garlic in a sterilised jar, seasoning with pepper and *fleur de sel* and adding the spring onion. Repeat to fill two more jars. Add a bay leaf and a sprig of rosemary, cover with olive oil. Chill for 24 hours before eating. Capsicums will keep for up to 1 week in the refrigerator.

03 june

Spaghetti bolognese

Serves 6

PREPARATION TIME 20 MINUTES
COOKING TIME 20 MINUTES

4 x 185 g (6½ oz) beef steaks or escalopes of veal or chicken
6 tomatoes
4 onions
olive oil
1 tablespoon tomato paste (concentrated purée)
2 tablespoons tomato sauce (ketchup)
1 bunch of basil, leaves picked
500 g (1 lb 2 oz) spaghetti
salt and pepper

Cut the steaks* into thin strips, then small cubes. Dice the tomatoes. Peel and slice the onions. Sauté the meat in olive oil with the onions, let them brown, then add the tomatoes, the tomato paste and tomato sauce, cook for 10 minutes. Roughly slice the basil. Cook the spaghetti in boiling water with some olive oil added, according to the instructions on the packet, then refresh immediately. Reheat the spaghetti in olive oil, season, pour over the bolognese sauce and scatter with strips of basil.

✳WHY NOT BEEF MINCE? *I prefer to have some good meat to chew on rather than minced meat!*

'A rainy June makes the grapevine smile, but not too much in case it lasts!'

04 june — Coconut chicken kebabs

Serves 6

PREPARATION TIME 20 MINUTES
MARINATING TIME 2 HOURS
COOKING TIME 10 MINUTES

6 chicken breast fillets
200 ml (7 fl oz) coconut milk
1 bunch of coriander (cilantro), leaves picked
2 tablespoons honey
salt and pepper

Cut the chicken breast into strips and thread them onto kebab skewers. Purée the coconut milk with the coriander and honey, season. Cover the kebabs with this mixture and refrigerate for 2 hours. Cook on a hot barbecue for 1 minute on each side, then dip into the marinade again and repeat*.

ONE MORE FOR THE ROAD...

✳WHY COOK THE KEBABS TWICE? *So the chicken can soak up plenty of the marinade.*

05 june — Mackerel à la Grenobloise*

Serves 6

PREPARATION TIME 20 MINUTES
COOKING TIME 15 MINUTES

6 fine and reputable whole mackerel!
4 French shallots (eschalots)
100 g (3½ oz) soft white sandwich bread
150 ml (5 fl oz) pouring (whipping) cream
1 bunch of flat-leaf (Italian) parsley
salt and pepper
olive oil
2 lemons
80 g (2¾ oz) butter
6 slices of stale baguette, cubed
50 g (1¾ oz) caperberries

✳WHY GRENOBLOISE? *Since the mackerel is in the habit of hurtling down the snowy slopes of Grenoble at full speed in a fuchsia pink ensemble during the winter months, it has earned the nickname mackerel à la Grenobloise.*

Preheat the oven to 180°C (350°F/Gas 4). Clean the mackerel, rinse and wipe dry. Peel and slice the shallots. Process the sandwich bread with the cream and parsley, add the shallots, then season. Stuff the mackerels with this mixture. Lay them in a dish, drizzle over some olive oil and bake for 10 minutes. Remove the skin and pith of the lemons, cut out the segments. Melt the butter until it is a nut brown, then brown the baguette cubes and add the lemon segments and the caperberries. Pour this mixture over the mackerels.

06 june — Eggplant fritters

Serves 6

PREPARATION TIME 20 MINUTES
COOKING TIME 20 MINUTES

3 firm eggplants (aubergines)
salt and pepper
6 tomatoes
6 garlic cloves
2 French shallots (eschalots)
50 g (1¾ oz) fresh ginger
100 ml (3½ fl oz) olive oil
3 eggs, separated
200 g (7 oz/1⅓ cups) plain (all-purpose) flour
200 ml (7 fl oz) full-cream (whole) milk
1 litre (35 fl oz/4 cups) vegetable oil

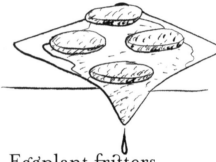

Cut the eggplants into 5 mm (¼ inch) thick slices, season. Cut a cross in the base of the tomatoes and plunge into boiling water for 30 seconds, then remove the skins and chop the flesh. Peel the garlic, shallots and ginger, chop them all together. Sauté in the olive oil, add the tomatoes, let them stew down for 20 minutes over low heat. Season, then purée. Whip the egg whites to stiff peaks. Combine the yolks with the flour, add the milk, then gently fold in the egg whites. Heat the vegetable oil to 160°C (315°F), dip the eggplant slices in the fritter batter, then brown in the oil for 2 minutes on each side*. Serve with the tomato coulis.

✳SO IT'S NOT TOO GREASY: *After deep-frying, placing the fritters on some paper towels will remove the excess oil.*

07 june

Cherry clafoutis

Serves 6

PREPARATION TIME 10 MINUTES
COOKING TIME 30 MINUTES

500 g (1 lb 2 oz) ripe cherries
240 g (8¾ oz) caster (superfine) sugar
60 g (2¼ oz) plain (all-purpose) flour
3 eggs
200 ml (7 fl oz) full-cream (whole) milk
100 ml (3½ fl oz) pouring (whipping) cream
20 g (¾ oz) butter
icing (confectioners') sugar

Preheat the oven to 180°C (350°F/Gas 4). Combine the cherries with 100 g (3½ oz) of the caster sugar. Combine the flour with the eggs, 120 g (4¼ oz) of the caster sugar, the milk and cream. Use the butter to grease a round tart tin and dust with the remaining caster sugar*. Add the cherries, then pour in the cream mixture and bake for 30 minutes. Dust with icing sugar once cooked.

✳ WHY COAT THE TIN WITH SUGAR? *It gives a caramel note to the clafoutis.*

08 june

Vegetable terrine

Serves 6

PREPARATION TIME 30 MINUTES
COOKING TIME 1 HOUR

2 carrots
1 red capsicum (pepper)
1 zucchini (courgette)
100 g (3½ oz) broad (fava) beans
50 g (1¾ oz) fresh ginger
2 French shallots (eschalots)
5 eggs
400 ml (14 fl oz) pouring (whipping) cream
1 dash ground nutmeg
salt and pepper

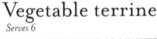

Preheat the oven to 160°C (315°F/Gas 2–3). Peel the carrots, cut them into thin sticks, cook them in boiling salted water for 5 minutes (they should stay firm). Cut the capsicum and the (unpeeled) zucchini into thin strips. Blanch the broad beans, peel them. Peel and finely chop the ginger and the shallots. Whisk the eggs and cream together, then add the nutmeg, ginger and shallots, season. Line a terrine dish with baking paper, fill with the vegetables without packing them down, cover with the egg mixture and cook in a bain-marie for 1 hour*.

✳ HOW IS THE TERRINE UNMOULDED? *Thanks to the baking paper, the terrine unmoulds very easily.*

09 june

Penne and smoked salmon salad

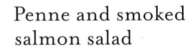

Serves 6

PREPARATION TIME 20 MINUTES
COOKING TIME 10 MINUTES

400 g (14 oz) penne rigate
1 red onion
1 lemon
1 teaspoon mustard
1 egg
100 ml (3½ fl oz) olive oil
150 ml (5 fl oz) sunflower oil
salt and pepper
150 g (5½ oz) smoked salmon
1 handful of rocket (arugula) leaves

✳ ANY INSTRUCTIONS FOR THE MAYO? *You get all the ingredients and blend or mix them together energetically!*

✳✳ WHY AT THE LAST MINUTE? *The salad leaves are added at the last minute so that they stay nice and crisp.*

Cook the penne according to the instructions on the packet: keep them *al dente* and allow to cool. Finely slice the onion. Zest and juice the lemon. Combine the mustard, egg, lemon juice and both oils, blend to make a stiff mayonnaise*, then season generously. Slice the salmon into thin strips, combine all of the ingredients and dress with the lemon mayonnaise. Scatter over the lemon zest. Serve chilled and add the rocket at the last minute**.

10
june

FIRST TABOULEH

'Stay healthy in June, wear a swimsuit in July.'

10 june — First tabouleh

Serves 6

PREPARATION TIME 45 MINUTES
CHILLING TIME 1 HOUR

1 cucumber

4 tomatoes

3 French shallots (eschalots)

10 mint leaves

300 g (10½ oz/2½ cups) medium-grain semolina

150 ml (5 fl oz) olive oil

juice of 1 orange

zest and juice of 2 lemons

1 bunch of flat-leaf (Italian) parsley

salt and pepper

✳WHY NOT LEAVE THE SEEDS? *The seeds are full of water and indigestible, so they're shown the door!*

✳✳THE SEMOLINA ISN'T COOKED FIRST? *The semolina is in fact cooked by the juices and olive oil.*

Cut the cucumber in half lengthways. Remove the core of seeds*, then peel one of the halves. Cut both cucumber halves into thin strips, then each strip into small cubes. Cut each tomato into six segments, remove the seeds and chop the flesh. Peel and finely slice the shallots and mint. Combine the semolina** with all of these ingredients, add the olive oil, the orange juice and the zest and juice of the lemons. Chill for 1 hour, stirring regularly. Pick off the parsley leaves and add before serving, then season.

11 june — Marinated sardines

Serves 6

PREPARATION TIME 45 MINUTES
MARINATING TIME 24 HOURS

18 very fresh sardines

zest and juice of 2 oranges

3 tablespoons soy sauce

2 tablespoons fish sauce

200 ml (7 fl oz) olive oil

6 bulb spring onions (scallions)

fleur de sel

coarsely ground black pepper

✳HOW DO YOU FILLET SARDINES YOURSELF? *Make an incision where the head meets the body, slide the knife along the backbone via the back, remove the first fillet, carefully remove the backbone and take out the second fillet.*

✳✳WHY RINSE THE SARDINES? *To firm the fragile flesh back up.*

Scale and fillet the sardines* and remove as many of the bones as possible. Rinse the fillets under iced water**, blot them dry with some paper towels. Combine the orange zest and juice with the soy sauce, fish sauce and olive oil. Finely slice the spring onions. Arrange the sardines in a dish, cover them with spring onion and pour over the marinade. Season with *fleur de sel* and coarsely ground black pepper. Chill for 24 hours before eating.

12 june — Sesame tuna carpaccio

Serves 6

PREPARATION TIME 15 MINUTES
COOKING TIME 10 MINUTES

2 tomatoes

100 g (3½ oz) snow peas (mangetout)

100 g (3½ oz) green beans

2 bulb spring onions (scallions)

10 tinned anchovies in oil

1 teaspoon Dijon mustard

1 tablespoon white wine

200 ml (7 fl oz) olive oil

400 g (14 oz) tuna loin*

50 g (1¾ oz/⅓ cup) sesame seeds

Cut a cross in the base of the tomatoes and plunge them into boiling water for 30 seconds, remove the skins and dice the flesh. Cook the snow peas and beans separately in boiling salted water for 7–10 minutes, refresh immediately. Slice the spring onions, cut the snow peas into triangular pieces and the beans into short lengths. Mix the vegetables together. Process the anchovies with the mustard, wine and 150 ml (5 fl oz) of the olive oil, season the vegetables with half of the vinaigrette. Roll the tuna in the sesame seeds, pan-fry it briefly, then slice very thinly. Serve with the vegetables and the rest of the anchovy vinaigrette.

✳WHAT IS TUNA LOIN? *It's simply a tuna fillet.*

'Grilled vegetables for a summer's day give a clear conscience for a nice rosé.'

13 june — Grilled vegetables

Serves 6
PREPARATION TIME 20 MINUTES
COOKING TIME 20 MINUTES

2 zucchini (courgettes)
1 eggplant (aubergine)
1 bunch of green asparagus
6 bulb spring onions (scallions)
3 young fennel bulbs
2 red capsicums (peppers)
1 bunch of basil
200 g (7 oz) cherry tomatoes
olive oil
balsamic vinegar
fleur de sel

* PAINT? *Coat the vegetables with olive oil using a brush.*

** WHY INDIVIDUALLY? *As the cooking times are a delicate matter, avoid filling the barbecue up with vegetables. Proceed in stages.*

Cut the zucchini and eggplant into rounds. Peel the asparagus spears, cut them in half lengthways. Halve the spring onions and fennel bulbs, cut the capsicums into strips. Pick off the basil leaves. Paint* all of the vegetables with the olive oil, grill them individually** on the barbecue. Serve with the basil leaves, a dash of olive oil and balsamic vinegar. Season with *fleur de sel*.

14 june — Chicken in garlic crust

Serves 6
PREPARATION TIME 30 MINUTES
COOKING TIME 1 HOUR

600 g (1 lb 5 oz/4 cups) plain (all-purpose) flour
600 g (1 lb 5 oz) coarse salt
200 ml (7 fl oz) white wine
1 free-range chicken
10 garlic cloves
1 bunch of basil
1 bunch of thyme

* HOW TO STUFF? *It's quite simply a matter of placing the ingredients mentioned inside the chicken.*

Preheat the oven to 180°C (350°F/Gas 4). Combine the flour and salt, bind with the white wine to make a pliable dough. Stuff* the chicken with half of the garlic cloves and the basil. Slice the remaining garlic. Roll out the dough, scatter with thyme sprigs and garlic. Place the chicken on the dough, breast side down, wrap it up, pressing around the joints. Bake in the oven for 1 hour. Break the crust in front of your guests … What a delicious aroma!

15 june — Cherries in red wine

Serves 6
PREPARATION TIME 10 MINUTES
COOKING TIME 30 MINUTES

1 kg (2 lb 4 oz) cherries
600 ml (21 fl oz) red wine
1 cinnamon stick
1 teaspoon ground ginger
1 teaspoon ground aniseed
80 g (2¾ oz/¼ cup) honey
300 ml (10½ fl oz) pouring (whipping) cream
80 g (2¾ oz/⅓ cup) caster (superfine) sugar
2 tablespoons kirsch
Equipment:
6 verrine glasses

* WHY TWO BATHS IN THE RED WINE? *The first stage is to cook the cherries and during the second stage, they'll marinate in the red wine reduction.*

Remove the cherry stems, place the cherries in a saucepan with the red wine, spices and honey, and bring to the boil. Simmer gently for 10 minutes, then take out the cherries. Reduce the red wine for about 20 minutes. Return the cherries to the red wine*, then chill. Whip the cream with the sugar until it has a smooth, rich texture, add the kirsch. Arrange the cherries in the glasses and add a spoonful of cream.

MARIE & LÉON

come, little rabbit ...

$\mathcal{K}$evin, 16, and his late rabbit.

I love my rabbit

To hold tenderly

My hand it gets lost in

His fluffy tummy

He's as soft as soft

He is tender to perfection

Run as he wants

I'll catch him again

He's warm, that's normal

It's what animals like, so

After he's skinned

Into the saucepan he'll go

Emotion tickles the nose

Like the mustard I smell

It's a feast for dinner

I love him just as well

16 june

＊A TIP FOR CUTTING UP THE RABBIT: *Remove the thighs and front legs before cutting the body into sections.*

＊＊WHAT'S THE EGG YOLK FOR? *It will bind the sauce.*

＊＊＊WHY MUSTN'T IT BOIL? *The egg coagulates and the sauce will curdle.*

Rabbit in mustard sauce
Serves 6
PREPARATION TIME 20 MINUTES
COOKING TIME 45 MINUTES

1 large rabbit
2 garlic cloves
3 French shallots (eschalots)
2 zucchini (courgettes)
3 tablespoons olive oil
1 tablespoon plain (all-purpose) flour
200 ml (7 fl oz) white Port
1 sprig of rosemary
400 ml (14 fl oz) pouring (whipping) cream
300 g (10½ oz/2 cups) podded fresh peas
1 tablespoon Dijon mustard
1 egg yolk
salt and pepper

Cut the rabbit into eight portions*. Peel and slice the garlic and the shallots. Cut the zucchini into sticks. Brown the pieces of rabbit in a flameproof casserole dish with the olive oil, garlic and shallots, then add the flour and cook for a further 5 minutes. Moisten with the Port, add the rosemary, cover and cook for 20 minutes. Next, add the cream, zucchini and peas, cook for a further 15 minutes. Take out the rabbit and vegetables. Off the heat, add the mustard, then the egg yolk** to the sauce, whisk well, season, pour the sauce back over the rabbit (careful! the sauce mustn't boil***) and serve.

17 june

Pissaladière

Serves 6

PREPARATION TIME 20 MINUTES

COOKING TIME 25 MINUTES

3 sprigs of rosemary

50 g (1¾ oz/½ cup) black olives, pitted

200 g (7 oz) block store-bought butter puff pastry

6 onions

olive oil

fleur de sel

50 g (1¾ oz) tinned anchovies in oil

50 g (1¾ oz/½ cup) sun-dried black olives

Preheat the oven to 180°C (350°F/Gas 4). Pick off the rosemary leaves, process them with the pitted black olives. Scatter this mixture over the pastry*. Roll the pastry into a rectangle. Peel and slice the onions, soften them in the olive oil for 5 minutes, season with *fleur de sel*. Cover the pastry with this mixture, arrange the anchovies in a criss-cross pattern, then the sun-dried olives. Bake in the oven for 20 minutes. Serve hot or cold.

✻ BEFORE
ROLLING IT?
The rosemary and black olives will be pushed into the pastry as it's rolled out.

18 june

Duck terrine

Serves 6

PREPARATION TIME 20 MINUTES

COOKING TIME 1 HOUR 30 MINUTES

CHILLING TIME 24 HOURS

4 French shallots (eschalots)

100 g (3½ oz) speck, chopped into lardons

100 g (3½ oz) air-dried duck breast

400 g (14 oz) duck meat

*200 g (7 oz) pork neck**

1 teaspoon juniper berries

1 teaspoon piment d'Espelette *(Basque chilli powder) or mild chilli powder*

1 bunch of basil, leaves picked and chopped

3 tablespoons Armagnac

150 ml (5 fl oz) good red wine

salt

2 bay leaves

1 sprig of rosemary

Preheat the oven to 160°C (315°F/Gas 2–3). Peel and slice the shallots. Sauté the speck with the shallots for 5 minutes. Cut the duck into thin strips. Put the duck and pork neck through a mincer, crush the juniper berries, combine all of the ingredients, except the bay leaves and rosemary, and season. Press the mixture into a terrine dish, place the bay leaves and rosemary on top, cook in a bain-marie (uncovered**) for 90 minutes. Chill for 24 hours before serving.

✻ IS PORK NECK
EASY TO FIND?
Yes, it's also called pork scotch filllet. You could also use some back fat, instead.

✻✻ COOKING
TIP: *I like it when the top of the terrine is browned, it gives it an extra texture.*

19 june

Classic lasagne

Serves 6

PREPARATION TIME 30 MINUTES

COOKING TIME 1 HOUR

3 garlic cloves

3 onions

6 tomatoes

80 ml (2½ fl oz/⅓ cup) olive oil

400 g (14 oz) beef, hand chopped for texture!

1 tablespoon herbes de Provence (Provençal herb mix)

1 tablespoon tomato paste (concentrated purée)

salt and pepper

50 g (1¾ oz) butter

50 g (1¾ oz) plain (all-purpose) flour

800 ml (28 fl oz) full-cream (whole) milk

1 bay leaf

2 sprigs of thyme

1 good dash ground nutmeg

300 g (10½ oz/2¼ cups) grated Gruyère cheese

200 g (7 oz) store-bought lasagne sheets

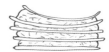
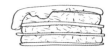

I don't have one!

Preheat the oven to 180°C (350°F/Gas 4). Peel and chop the garlic and onions. Dice the tomatoes. Sauté the garlic and onions in olive oil for 5 minutes, then add the beef and cook for 10 minutes. Add the tomatoes, *herbes de Provence* and tomato paste, cook over low heat for 15 minutes, then season. Melt the butter in a saucepan, add the flour, cook for 3 minutes, then add the milk, bay leaf and thyme and boil for 5 minutes, stirring. Add the nutmeg and season. In a gratin dish, make layers of béchamel sauce, meat, Gruyère and lasagne sheets. Continue the process, finishing with a layer of béchamel sauce*, then Gruyère. Bake for 30 minutes.

✻ WHY FINISH
WITH A LAYER
OF BÉCHAMEL?
If you finish with a layer of lasagne, it will dry out.

20 june

Sardines grilled with rosemary

Serves 6

PREPARATION TIME 20 MINUTES
COOKING TIME 20 MINUTES

36 sardines
36 sprigs of rosemary
olive oil
fleur de sel

Clean the sardines, rinse them well and blot dry using paper towels. Skewer* each sardine with a sprig of rosemary. Grill the sardines on a very hot barbecue. Drizzle the sardines with some olive oil, season with *fleur de sel*. Eat with your fingers, speak with the accent of the South and drink aniseed beverages.

✳ HOW SHOULD THE SARDINES BE SKEWERED? *Have the hardest part of the rosemary sprig exit through the mouth of the sardine, that way the rosemary needles stay in the stomach.*

21 june

Tuna with sauce vierge

PREPARATION TIME 30 MINUTES
COOKING TIME 15 MINUTES

2 tomatoes
2 bulb spring onions (scallions)
1 bunch of chives
1 lemongrass stem, white part only
1 carrot
1 teaspoon coriander seeds
olive oil
*6 thick tuna fillets**
fleur de sel
800 g (1 lb 12 oz) baby spinach leaves

Cut a cross in the base of the tomatoes and plunge into boiling water for 30 seconds, remove their skin and dice the flesh. Finely slice the spring onions, snip the chives and lemongrass. Peel the carrot, chop it into a fine dice. Crush the coriander seeds, combine with the preceding ingredients and cover with olive oil. Sear the tuna fillets in olive oil, keeping them very rare, season with *fleur de sel*, pour over the *sauce vierge*. Sauté the spinach in olive oil for 2 minutes, season. Serve immediately.

✳ WHICH TUNA TO CHOOSE? *If you can, choose yellowfin or albacore, varieties which are not as over-fished.*

22 june

Rhubarb and berry compote

Serves 6

PREPARATION TIME 20 MINUTES
COOKING TIME 10 MINUTES

600 g (1 lb 5 oz) rhubarb
120 g (4¼ oz/⅓ cup) maple syrup
200 g (7 oz/1⅓ cups) strawberries
200 g (7 oz/1½ cups) raspberries
juice of 1 lemon
2 tablespoons vanilla sugar

Peel the rhubarb*, cook in a saucepan with a small amount of water (just half-covered) and the maple syrup for about 10 minutes. Stir with a fork and chill. Purée the berries with the lemon juice and vanilla sugar. In serving glasses arrange a layer of rhubarb and a layer of berries.

✳ HOW DO YOU PEEL THE RHUBARB? *You gently pull away the fibres using a knife.*

MARIE & LÉON

44 years old, a spring roll

Marie Vachecrot is 44 years old and not a wrinkle to be seen. She is incredibly beautiful, our Marie, and Léon takes no small pride in this fact.

For her birthday, Léon wants to mark the occasion, he wants to offer her the unique and perfect present, one which will stay in her memory for years to come, one she'd be happy to see again every year. A diamond? « *No, way overrated.* » A watch? « *There are clocks everywhere at home.* » A lawnmower? « *Maybe, why not?* » A breadmaking machine? « *She's on a diet.* » A knot board? « *She gets sea-sick.* » ... An Asian cooking course, now there's an idea, there's a real gem, that's the one.

It's a date at the Imperial Chopstick restaurant for an Introduction to Spring Rolls. Marie nervously presents herself on the day at 12 noon, Avenue de Choisy in the XIIIth Arrondissement.

« *Bonjoure, a drink?* » Marie's in her element straight away (we'll come back to that another time), the ingredients are in front of her, her cup, in which a lychee floats, doesn't have time to lose its chill. Nothing like total immersion to soak up all this gastronomical culture. « *You take rice-paper wrapper ...* », the aromas change, she's in a Beijing market, there's movement around her. « *No problem to start again ...* », Marie loses herself in her emotions, she's on a journey. « *Très bien, très très bien, Marie, spring roll very good, très bon ...* » But what's happening? A flash, a discovery, an encounter. The local Asian supermarket survives Marie's assaults, the shopping jeep is overflowing, training at lunchtime and dinner-time at home, it's Imperial Chopsticks in the Vachecrot household. Thank you, Léon.

23 june

Summertime spring rolls

Serves 6

PREPARATION TIME 30 MINUTES

For the spring rolls:
1 cucumber
300 g (10½ oz) fresh salmon
soy sauce
6 rice-paper wrappers
200 g (7 oz) mung bean shoots
100 g (3½ oz/1⅔ cups) alfalfa sprouts
For the sauce:
2 garlic cloves, peeled
1 red bird's eye chilli
1 carrot
6 sprigs of coriander (cilantro)
3 tablespoons fish sauce
3 tablespoons soy sauce
3 tablespoons lemon juice
1 tablespoon sugar

✳ WHY A DAMP CLOTH? *So the rice-paper wrapper doesn't stick to the cloth.*

✳✳ HOW SHOULD THEY BE STORED? *To keep them to eat later, wrap them individually in plastic wrap.*

Have a damp cloth ready*. Peel the cucumber, cut into sticks after removing the core of seeds. Cut the salmon into thick strips, brush them with soy sauce. Dip the rice-paper wrapper into hot water, turning it carefully so that all the sheet is covered. Place it on the damp cloth, arrange the salmon, cucumber, bean shoots and alfalfa on the wrapper and roll it up, keeping it nice and tight**.

For the sauce: finely slice the garlic and chilli, finely shred the carrot, pick off the coriander leaves. Combine all the ingredients and serve with the spring rolls.

24 june

Classic gazpacho

Serves 6

PREPARATION TIME 30 MINUTES

6 tomatoes

2 cucumbers

1 bunch of basil

3 bulb spring onions (scallions)

20 g (¾ oz) fresh ginger

150 ml (5 fl oz) balsamic vinegar

150 ml (5 fl oz) olive oil

salt and pepper

Cut a cross in the base of the tomatoes and plunge into boiling water for 30 seconds, remove their skin and cut each into 6 segments, remove the seeds. Peel one of the cucumbers, cut them in quarters lengthways, remove the core of seeds. Finely dice half of the unpeeled cucumber. Pick off the basil leaves, chop 2 of the leaves to mix with the diced cucumber. Finely chop the spring onions and ginger. Purée the tomatoes and remaining cucumber, basil, vinegar and olive oil, season. Add the ginger and the spring onions*. Serve** garnished with the diced cucumber and basil and drizzled with olive oil.

*Purée again? *No.*

**How should it be served? *It's good well chilled, so it's easy to make ahead of time.*

25 june

Sweet and sour pork spare-ribs

Serves 6

PREPARATION TIME 20 MINUTES

COOKING TIME 1 HOUR 15 MINUTES

1.2 kg (2 lb 10 oz) pork spare-ribs

6 garlic cloves

2 French shallots (eschalots)

150 g (5½ oz) tomato sauce (ketchup)

3 tablespoons soy sauce

3 tablespoons rice vinegar

3 tablespoons olive oil

1 tablespoon tandoori spices

Preheat the oven to 160°C (315°F/Gas 2–3). Cook the pork spare-ribs for 45 minutes in a large saucepan of water, skimming* regularly. Rinse. Peel and finely chop the garlic and the shallots. Combine them with the tomato sauce, soy sauce, rice vinegar, olive oil and tandoori spices. Lay the ribs in a gratin dish, coat with the marinade. Bake for 30 minutes, basting the ribs with the sauce. Serve when the flesh comes away from the bones.

*And why do we need to skim? *To remove the coagulated blood, we're not vampires!*

26 june

Panna cotta

Serves 6

PREPARATION TIME 10 MINUTES

CHILLING TIME 2 HOURS

4 gelatine leaves

1 vanilla bean

800 ml (28 fl oz) pouring (whipping) cream

180 g (6¼ oz) sugar or 3 tablespoons honey

100 g (3½ oz) raspberries

100 g (3½ oz) bilberries or blueberries

100 g (3½ oz/⅔ cup) strawberries

juice of 1½ lemons

Equipment:

6 verrine glasses

Soak the gelatine leaves in cold water for 2 minutes to soften them. Split the vanilla bean in half, scrape the seeds into the cream. Bring the cream to the boil with the sugar, mix together well. Add the drained gelatine and whisk. Pour the cream into the glasses, then chill for 2 hours before serving. Purée the berries separately, add the juice of ½ lemon to each coulis. Pour some coulis over each panna cotta before serving*. You can flavour the panna cotta however you like (chocolate, green tea, alcohol, fruit compote ...). Get to work!

*Why just before serving? *If you pour over the coulis too far ahead of time, it could dry out and it won't look pretty.*

27
june

SQUID RISOTTO

27 june

Squid risotto

Serves 6

PREPARATION TIME 15 MINUTES
COOKING TIME 25 MINUTES

3 French shallots (eschalots)
3 green asparagus spears
1 red capsicum (pepper)
3 tablespoons olive oil
400 g (14 oz) small squid, prepared* and sliced
350 g (12 oz/1⅔ cups) arborio rice
200 ml (7 fl oz) white wine
500 ml (17 fl oz/2 cups) vegetable stock
50 g (1¾ oz/½ cup) grated parmesan cheese
salt and pepper

Peel and slice the shallots, cut the asparagus spears into rounds after trimming the ends, and dice the capsicum. Heat the olive oil in a wide saucepan and sauté the shallots, asparagus and capsicum. Add the squid and rice, allow the rice to become pearly. Moisten with the white wine and a little vegetable stock. Cook for 20 minutes over low heat, regularly moistening with the vegetable stock. Add the parmesan, cook for a further 2 minutes. Season.

*WHAT DOES READY-TO-COOK SQUID LOOK LIKE? *They're squid that have been cleaned.*

28 june

Rascasse with lemon

Serves 6

PREPARATION TIME 10 MINUTES
COOKING TIME 15 MINUTES

1 x 800 g (1 lb 12 oz) rascasse (scorpion fish)
*   or red snapper*
3 onions
4 lemons
salt and pepper
200 ml (7 fl oz) olive oil

Preheat the oven to 200°C (400°F/Gas 6). Scale, clean and rinse the *rascasse*. Peel and chop the onions. Cut the lemons into thin slices, cover the fish with the lemon slices and chopped onions, season and generously drizzle with olive oil. Bake for 15 minutes. Serve*.

*SUGGESTED ACCOMPANIMENT: *A sauté of vegetables with lemon.*

29 june

Stir-fried cuttlefish with garlic

Serves 6

PREPARATION TIME 20 MINUTES
COOKING TIME 10 MINUTES

600 g (1 lb 5 oz) cuttlefish hoods, cleaned
1 teaspoon curry powder
6 garlic cloves
1 bunch of coriander (cilantro)
vegetable oil
4 French shallots (eschalots), sliced
1 tablespoon pastis
1 tablespoon soy sauce
Equipment:
wok

*WHY DO WE NEED TO MAKE INCISIONS? *To tenderise the cuttlefish.*

**WHY QUICKLY? *Cooking the cuttlefish too slowly will tighten the flesh and it will be tougher.*

Finely slice the cuttlefish into rings. Make incisions* all along the external side of each cuttlefish slice and roll them in the curry powder. Peel and finely slice the garlic. Pick off the coriander leaves. Sauté the garlic and shallots in a wok: they should be golden. Add the cuttlefish, sear it quickly**, add the pastis and flambé the alcohol, then add the soy sauce and coriander.

MARIE & LÉON

*I*n the beginning, Marie Vachecrot, a very ordinary cook married to Léon, a fine food lover, was known for the mediocrity of her dinner parties to the great despair of her guests.

One day, Léon, determined to prove to his friends that Marie wasn't such a terrible *cordon bleu*, decided to take care of the shopping personally. He returned in raptures with a magnificent leg of milk-fed lamb. « *Produce of such quality can't be turned into a gastronomic nightmare!* » he thought. Marie disappeared into the kitchen with the precious treasure, put it straight in the oven without further ado and a few hours later, not knowing how it should be prepared, carved it up, minced it and mixed it with some herbs and spices to make some nice big meatballs. Léon, impatient to see his sweet and lovely leg of lamb on the table, poked his nose into the kitchen. And there ... balls! Marie had sacrificed the Sunday joint for an edible round of *pétanque*. This culinary blunder became a culinary wonder, all the most knowledgeable foodie circles swearing by them alone.

And that is how Marie, destined to the anonymity of her kitchen, became the Marie who went down in history.

30 june

✱ HOW DO YOU MAKE MEATBALLS? *Wash your hands twice rather than once, rub your dry hands with flour, take a tablespoon of mixture, roll it between the palms of your hands, repeat. Greet your guests with your unwashed hands (hilarious!), then wash them.*

Coriander meatballs

Serves 6

PREPARATION TIME 30 MINUTES
COOKING TIME 30 MINUTES

3 French shallots (eschalots)
1 bunch of coriander (cilantro)
500 g (1 lb 2 oz) leftover roast lamb leg
200 ml (7 fl oz) pouring (whipping) cream
100 g (3½ oz) soft white sandwich bread
1 tablespoon cumin
2 eggs
½ bunch of chives, snipped
salt and pepper
1 red capsicum (pepper)
1 green capsicum (pepper)
2 tomatoes
250 ml (9 fl oz/1 cup) white wine

Preheat the oven to 160°C (315°F/Gas 2–3). Peel and slice the shallots. Pick the coriander leaves. Process the leftover lamb with the cream, bread, coriander and cumin. Add the eggs, shallots and chives, then season. Make meatballs*, place them in a gratin dish. Dice the capsicums and tomatoes, place them around the meatballs, add the wine. Bake for 30 minutes.

July

01 Thierry
DUCK WITH HONEY

02 Eugénie
SPAGHETTI WITH SUMMER VEGETABLES

03 Thomas
RATATOUILLE

08 Thibaud
ZUCCHINI GRATIN

09 Hermeline
CRAB BISQUE

10 Ulrich
BREAM TARTARE

15 Donald
VACHERIN WITH SEASONAL FRUITS

16 Carmel
EGGPLANT CAVIAR

17 Charlotte
EASY THAI SALAD

22 Madeleine
APPLE AND TOMATO GAZPACHO

23 Brigitte
CHICKEN IN A ROSEMARY CRUST

24 Christine
RATATOUILLE AND FRESH GOAT'S CHEESE VERRINES

29 Marthe
NECTARINE CAKE

30 Juliette
PANCETTA-ROASTED RABBIT

31 Ignace
FISH TERRINE

04
Elisabeth

TOMATO SALAD

05
Antoine

PEACHES IN MUSCAT

06
Mariette

MOZZARELLA AND
SLOW-COOKED TOMATOES

07
Ralph

ZANDER WITH ZUCCHINI

11
Benoît

CHOUCHOUKA

12
Olivier

GREEN TABOULEH

13
Henri

FISHERMAN'S ROUILLE

14
Camille

PAN-BAGNAT

18
Frédéric

SOUPE DE POISSON

19
Arsène

FRIED RED MULLET

20
Marina

SPINACH-RICOTTA LASAGNE

21
Victor

CURRIED PORK TENDERLOIN

25
Jacques

PENNE AND BASIL SALAD

26
Anne

GRILLED BASS WITH HERBS

27
Nathalie

CLASSIC QUICHE

28
Samson

PIPERADE

01 02 03 04

01 july

Duck with honey

Serves 6

PREPARATION TIME 15 MINUTES
MARINATING TIME 24 HOURS
COOKING TIME 10 MINUTES

3 tablespoons honey
200 ml (7 fl oz) Sauternes
1 tablespoon Armagnac
3 duck breasts
1 tablespoon herbes de Provence (Provençal herb mix)
6 apricots
3 peaches
1 eggplant (aubergine)
50 g (1¾ oz/⅓ cup) whole almonds
50 g (1¾ oz/⅓ cup) hazelnuts
salt and pepper

Combine the honey with the Sauternes and Armagnac. Slash the duck skin in a criss-cross pattern*, dip in the marinade, sprinkle with the *herbes de Provence*, roll in plastic wrap and chill overnight. Halve the apricots, quarter the peaches and cube the eggplant. Cook the eggplant and duck, skin side down, in a dry frying pan, for 5–7 minutes. Drain the fat, return the duck to the pan, cook for 1 minute, flesh side down. Add the rest of the marinade, fruit and nuts and cook for 2 minutes. Season.

WHY SLASH THE DUCK BREASTS? That way the marinade can reach the flesh, to give it more flavour.

02 july

Spaghetti with summer vegetables*

Serves 6

PREPARATION TIME 10 MINUTES
COOKING TIME 10 MINUTES

400 g (14 oz) spaghetti
4 garlic cloves, peeled
1 bunch of basil, leaves picked
olive oil
fleur de sel
300 g (10½ oz) ratatouille (see opposite)

Cook the spaghetti, keeping it *al dente*. Chop the garlic and basil. Sauté both in some olive oil, add the spaghetti, and season with the *fleur de sel*. Reheat the ratatouille, serve a plate of spaghetti with the ratatouille.

CAN THIS RECIPE BE RUINED? HOW? Add the spaghetti to lukewarm water, really crowding the pot, cook for 30 minutes on a low heat, and you'll get mush.

03 july

Ratatouille: 2 methods*

Serves 6

PREPARATION TIME 20 MINUTES
COOKING TIME 1 TO 3 HOURS

3 eggplants (aubergines)
3 zucchini (courgettes)
4 tomatoes
6 bulb spring onions (scallions)
6 garlic cloves, peeled
2 red capsicums (peppers)
2 green capsicums (peppers)
200 ml (7 fl oz) olive oil
1 bay leaf
salt and pepper

The separation method: Cut the eggplants, zucchini and tomatoes into cubes. Slice the spring onions, garlic and capsicums. Pan-fry the eggplant, garlic, spring onion and capsicum in olive oil with the bay leaf for 45 minutes until they are completely *confits***. Quickly sauté the zucchini in very hot oil, add the tomatoes, cook for 2 minutes, then mix all the vegetables together, reheat quickly and season. This ratatouille offers you different textures.

The « all together, all together … » method: Preheat the oven to 160°C (315°F/Gas 2–3). Cut the eggplants, zucchini and tomatoes into cubes. Slice the spring onions, garlic and capsicums. Combine all the vegetables, add the bay leaf, season. Put all the vegetables into a large dish, drizzle generously with olive oil, bake for 3 hours, stirring the ratatouille at regular intervals. In this second recipe, the vegetables will cook together, the texture is softer and there'll be less to chew.

AND WHAT WOULD THE PREFERRED METHOD OF MR REYNAUD BE? Mr Reynaud, for his part, enjoys the method where there are different textures, the eggplant very soft, the zucchini very crisp …

**HOW DO YOU CONFIT VEGETABLES? Start on a high heat then gradually lower the heat during the course of the cooking.*

TOMATO SALAD

04 july

Tomato varieties? There are more than a hundred varieties of tomato, so it's important to play on the different textures, colours and flavours of tomato to make your salad unforgettable. For example, use the very tasty marmande, some fleshy oxheart, some juicy noire de crimée and the acidic green zebra tomato … get your hands on any heirloom varieties you can find.

Tomato salad

Serves 6

PREPARATION TIME 10 MINUTES

800 g (1 lb 12 oz) heirloom tomatoes*
olive oil
balsamic vinegar
aromatic herbs
fleur de sel

This is a simple dish that doesn't deserve mediocrity. Tomato salads are eaten from 1st July, once the sun has penetrated the flesh and the fruit reaches maturity. We then realise that mother nature does things well and that it would be high time to listen to her. A tomato, ladies and gentlemen, is something that has flavour, you just have to eat it at the right time! Choose a mixture of tomatoes of different shapes, varieties and colours. A touch of olive oil, a dash of balsamic vinegar, some basil and any other herbs, a little *fleur de sel* … and there you have a starter that's 100% pleasure and 100% in season.

05 july

Peaches in muscat

Serves 6

PREPARATION TIME 20 MINUTES

COOKING TIME 10 MINUTES

CHILLING TIME 24 HOURS

6 white peaches
750 ml (26 fl oz/3 cups) muscat
   (Muscat de Rivesaltes is a good drop)
120 g (4¼ oz) sugar
juice of 2 limes
1 cinnamon stick
3 star anise

Make a small incision in the base of each peach. Plunge them into boiling water for 30 seconds, then remove the skin. Place in a saucepan, then add the muscat, sugar, lime juice, cinnamon stick and star anise. Bring to the boil, then reduce the heat and simmer for 10 minutes. Chill in the poaching liquid for 24 hours*.

How to serve? Serve well-chilled, glazed with the juices.

06 july

What varieties do I prefer? The green zebra and noire de crimée for their acidity, the colour, the difference in flavours.

What's special about buffalo mozzarella? It's the real mozzarella, made from buffalo milk, and is both creamy and tasty.

Mozzarella and slow-cooked tomatoes

Serves 6

PREPARATION TIME 15 MINUTES

COOKING TIME 3 HOURS

12 heirloom tomatoes*
8 garlic cloves
80 ml (2½ fl oz/⅓ cup) olive oil
fleur de sel
1 tablespoon herbes de Provence (Provençal herb mix)
6 balls buffalo mozzarella**
1 bunch of basil, leaves picked

Preheat the oven to 100°C (200°F/Gas ½). Place the tomatoes in a roasting tin. Peel and chop the garlic, scatter the garlic over the tomatoes, add the olive oil, the *fleur de sel* and the *herbes de Provence*. Bake for 3 hours. To serve, place 1 ball of mozzarella and 2 lukewarm tomatoes in each serving bowl and add some cooking juices and basil leaves.

07 july

Zander with zucchini

Serves 6

PREPARATION TIME 20 MINUTES
COOKING TIME 10 MINUTES

6 zander (pike-perch) or perch
3 zucchini (courgettes)
3 onions
2 tablespoons plain (all-purpose) flour
150 ml (5 fl oz) olive oil
salt and pepper
1 handful of rocket (arugula) leaves

Clean and rinse the fish. Cut the zucchini into thin sticks. Peel and slice the onions. Flour the zanders. Pan-fry them in 3 tablespoons of olive oil for 5 minutes each side, then season. In another frying pan, sauté the onions in the remaining oil for 5 minutes, add the zucchini and cook for a further 5 minutes, then add the rocket* and season.

*You add the rocket during cooking? *Careful! When you stop cooking and the rocket may wilt from the heat.*

08 july

Zucchini gratin

Serves 6

PREPARATION TIME 20 MINUTES
COOKING TIME 15 MINUTES

3 onions
1 kg (2 lb 4 oz) young zucchini (courgettes)
1 bunch of lemon thyme
6 sprigs of rosemary
100 ml (3½ fl oz) olive oil
fleur de sel and pepper

Preheat the oven to 150°C (300°F/Gas 2). Slice the onions and zucchini into rounds. Intersperse slices of onion* and zucchini in a gratin dish, packing them together tightly**. Add the lemon thyme and rosemary. Drizzle generously with olive oil, season with *fleur de sel* and pepper. Bake for 15 minutes (the zucchini and onions should stay *al dente*).

*Why so many onions? *Because they're good!*

**Funny technique? *You intersperse them vertically — the top part browns and the bottom part stays soft.*

09 july

Crab bisque

Serves 6

PREPARATION TIME 15 MINUTES
COOKING TIME 1 HOUR 50 MINUTES

2 kg (4 lb 8 oz) fresh velvet or blue swimmer crabs
3 carrots
50 g (1¾ oz) fresh ginger
4 onions
3 celery stalks
100 ml (3½ fl oz) olive oil
100 ml (3½ fl oz) Cognac
1 bouquet garni
1 tablespoon tomato paste (concentrated purée)
300 ml (10½ fl oz) pouring (whipping) cream
salt and pepper

*Why crush them with a rolling pin? *To get out all the crab meat, it's what will give the bisque its flavour.*

**Why use the blender when it has already been strained? *The blender will emulsify the bisque and give it a uniform texture.*

Rinse the crabs. Peel the carrots, ginger and onions, slice them thinly. Chop the celery. Heat the olive oil in a large saucepan and sauté the vegetables and crabs for 5 minutes (the crabs should redden with pleasure). Add the Cognac and flambé. Crush the crabs with a rolling pin*, add 2 litres (70 fl oz) water, the bouquet garni and the tomato paste, simmer for 75 minutes, strain the soup through a chinois. Add the cream and cook for 30 minutes. Season. Whizz with a stick-blender** before serving.

10 july

Bream tartare

Serves 6

PREPARATION TIME 20 MINUTES

600 g (1 lb 5 oz) sea bream fillets

½ teaspoon grated horseradish

1 tablespoon saké

3 tablespoons olive oil + plus extra for drizzling

2 bulb spring onions (scallions)

juice of 2 lemons

3 granny smith apples

salt and pepper

*1 bunch of fresh herbs**

Remove the skin** from the bream fillets, remove the bones and cut the fillets into small cubes. Combine the bream cubes with the horseradish, sake, olive oil, spring onion and half of the lemon juice, then season. Cut the apples into thin matchsticks, combine them with the remaining lemon juice. Pick off the leaves from the fresh herbs, combine them with the extra olive oil and season. Make a mound of apple matchsticks inside a cooking ring, then top with some bream tartare and add a few tufts of herbs.

✱WHAT CAN YOU USE FOR THE BUNCH OF HERBS? *For example, basil, dill, tarragon.*

✱✱THERE'S STILL SKIN ON THE FILLETS? *Well no, not if you remove it!*

11 july

Chouchouka*

Serves 6

PREPARATION TIME 10 MINUTES

COOKING TIME 15 MINUTES

1 large onion

1 red capsicum (pepper)

1 green capsicum (pepper)

olive oil

300 g (10½ oz) ratatouille (see page 284)

8 eggs

salt and pepper

Peel the onion, slice it thinly. Cut the capsicums into thin strips. In an ovenproof frying pan, sauté the onions and capsicums in the olive oil, then add the ratatouille. Break the eggs, beat them, season, pour into the pan, cook for 3–4 minutes, then put under a hot grill (broiler) for 7–8 minutes. Serve.

✱CHOUCHOUKA? WHAT DOES THAT MEAN? *The literal translation of chouchouka is: « oulala, your omelette is so good with all these leftover vegetables from the ratatouille you made yesterday, how right you were to make this dish rather than let it go to waste, what a good idea you had there! »*

12 july

Green* tabouleh

Serves 6

PREPARATION TIME 10 MINUTES

CHILLING TIME 30 MINUTES

200 g (7 oz) medium-grain semolina

olive oil

juice of 4 lemons

2 tomatoes

2 bulb spring onions (scallions)

3 bunches of flat-leaf (Italian) parsley

salt and pepper

Combine the semolina with the olive oil** and lemon juice, chill for 30 minutes. Dice the tomato flesh, thinly slice the spring onions and parsley. Combine all the ingredients, then season***.

✱WHY GREEN? *Since there's lots of parsley, it's coloured green!*

✱✱HOW IS THE SEMOLINA COOKED? *The semolina will soak up the olive oil and lemon juice.*

✱✱✱WILL IT KEEP IN THE REFRIGERATOR? *You can keep the tabouleh in the refrigerator, but mind that the lemon juice will tend to cook the parsley.*

MARIE & LÉON

gaarrgghlic
...

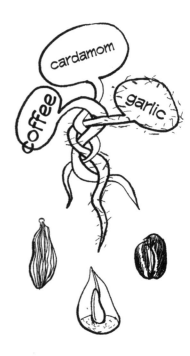

$\mathcal{G}$arlic is a great friend of cooking but a great enemy of the mouth. It permeates the body like a colony of ants in a packet of sugar — you breathe it, you sweat it and it clings to your skin.

What can I do, I hear you say, so that the pleasure of the palate doesn't turn you into a walking garlic clove?

1) Find a special friend who, like you, adores garlic, good conversation, maybe even more ... it could become a true tale of Marseille, *putainnn con!*

2) Stop eating it. Unbearable.

3) Remove the indigestible sprout inside, eat a coffee bean or a cardamom pod to offset some of the odours.

4) Stop talking for six hours, what's more, that'll give us a break!

13 july

**✱Why is it
called rouille?**
*It's a typical
Camargue dish which
gets its name from its
colour: rouille = rust.*

Fisherman's rouille*

Serves 6

PREPARATION TIME 20 MINUTES
COOKING TIME 1 HOUR 30 MINUTES

1 kg (2 lb 4 oz) cuttlefish hoods or octopus, cleaned
3 onions
200 ml (7 fl oz) olive oil
750 ml (26 fl oz/3 cups) white wine
800 g (1 lb 12 oz) potatoes
3 garlic cloves
1 egg yolk
1 tablespoon mustard
150 ml (5 fl oz) sunflower oil
salt and pepper
1 pinch of saffron threads

Cut the cuttlefish into wide strips. Peel and slice the onions. Sauté the onions with a little olive oil in a flameproof casserole dish, add the cuttlefish, moisten with white wine, cook, covered, over low heat for 1 hour, then uncover to allow the wine to completely evaporate. Peel the potatoes, cut them into large cubes, cook them for 15 minutes in boiling water. Peel and chop the garlic, combine it with the egg yolk and mustard, add the sunflower oil to make a mayonnaise, season, then add the saffron threads. Combine the potatoes with the cuttlefish, dress with the garlic mayonnaise in the dish. No more vampires!

MARIE & LÉON

oh Champs-Élysées

The Champs-Élysées as the field of play, a footstool for height, it's *le quatorze Juillet* (14th July) and in the Vachecrot household, it's sacred.

They arrive the night before at their Paris cousin's place (Georges has made it, he works in a Paris office!!!). The boot of the car is full: Auntie Marinette's eggs, cousin Jacques' pâté, Fernand's *caillettes* (meatballs), vegetables from the garden, the garlic sausage, it's all unloaded straight away, the fridge immediately fills to overflowing. The basket of zucchini slides into a corner of the balcony, the box of eggplants finds a home under the table and the six litres of *vin de noix* (nut wine) joins the seven litres left over from last year. Santa Claus is a resident of the countryside: he's generous but tends to overestimate the size of Parisian apartments. Cousin Georges' apartment becomes a walk-in pantry. Marie and Léon feel right at home. They take the knives out of their pockets, open a can of tuna, mayonnaise, onions, tomatoes, they cut the *miche* loaf in two, it's a day for things on bread. The backpack is ready, the *pan-bagnat* is in the fridge (under the *caillettes*, between the garlic sausage and the eggs), we can have a snooze with the newspaper, 14th July awaits us and we're ready. As for cousin Georges, he has lots of work to do, he's at the movies, a double cheeseburger in the right hand, a double-coated chocolate Magnum in the left ...

Luckily *le quatorze Juillet* only happens on 14th July.

14 july

Pan-bagnat
Serves 6
PREPARATION TIME 15 MINUTES
some sun
some sand
some sunscreen
400 g (14 oz) tinned tuna in brine
120 g (4¼ oz/½ cup) mayonnaise
1 cucumber
2 bulb spring onions (scallions)
a good assortment of tomatoes
6 hard-boiled eggs
6 pan-bagnat rolls*
a few lettuce leaves
salt and pepper

Flake the tuna, combine with the mayonnaise, season. Cut up the cucumber, spring onions and tomatoes. Slice the eggs into rounds. Cut the bread rolls in half and fill generously with tuna, vegetables, egg, lettuce, more tuna, then put the lid on. Eat dressed in your swimsuit. Point out the bit of tuna that's landed on your neighbour's nostril, poke gentle fun at him, quench your thirst (avoid drinking straight from the bottle, laughing fit could be fatal for the clarity of the water!!!). Since the sun takes malicious pleasure in turning a quality sandwich into a bacteriological minefield that will keep you on the toilet for the rest of the day, finish off your pan-bagnat once and for all before going for a dip (very important for cleaning out the bits of tuna stuck in your nostril — ah yes, we're poking gentle fun at you too!). A nice siesta and then to bed.

*WHAT KIND OF ROLL FOR THE PAN-BAGNAT? *Large pain-au-lait rolls.*

MARIE & LÉON

the legend of the vacherin

*I*n Norman mythology, Léon Vachecrot, *vacherin* (dairyman) by trade, is considered to be the god of chantilly cream and his marriage to Marie, rigged out like a real meringue, was an occasion for the whole forest to feast for three days and three nights. In order to immortalise the sacred union of the god Léon, the wedding gave rise to a real classic, meringue and chantilly cream, the *vacherin*, which thus became immortal and accessible to the common run of mortals.

15 july

Vacherin with seasonal fruit

Serves 6
PREPARATION TIME 10 MINUTES
800 g (1 lb 12 oz) fresh fruit
juice of 1 lime
fruit liqueur*
3 store-bought meringues
300 ml (10½ fl oz) pouring (whipping) cream
100 g (3½ oz) sugar
fruit sorbet

Cut all of the fresh fruit into cubes, purée half of it with the lime juice and a little fruit liqueur. Crush the meringues, whip the cream into a chantilly with the sugar. In glasses, arrange layers of fruit, coulis, meringue, chantilly and finish with a scoop of sorbet.

*LIQUEUR
SUGGESTIONS:
Use a liqueur that is the same as the fresh fruit being used.

16 july

Eggplant caviar
Serves 6

PREPARATION TIME 10 MINUTES
COOKING TIME 30 MINUTES

6 eggplants (aubergines)
2 garlic cloves
2 oranges
1 tablespoon herbes de Provence *(Provençal herb mix)*
80 ml (2½ fl oz/⅓ cup) olive oil
salt and pepper
baguette
1 lemon, cut into wedges

Preheat the oven to 160°C (315°F/Gas 2–3). Cut the eggplants in half, slash the flesh side in a criss-cross pattern*. Peel and chop the garlic, then zest and juice the oranges. Scatter the flesh of the eggplants with garlic, *herbes de Provence* and orange zest, drizzle with some olive oil and bake for about 10 minutes. Scrape out the eggplant flesh with a spoon, purée with the orange juice and olive oil, then season. Toast some slices of baguette and serve the eggplant caviar with lemon wedges.

*WHY SLASH THE EGGPLANTS BEFORE COOKING THEM? *So they cook evenly.*

17 july

Easy Thai salad
Serves 6

PREPARATION TIME 30 MINUTES
COOKING TIME 5 MINUTES

200 g (7 oz) chicken breast fillet
2 carrots
2 bulb spring onions (scallions)
1 celery stalk
3 garlic cloves
1 red bird's eye chilli
300 g (10½ oz) rice vermicelli
1 tablespoon sugar
3 tablespoons fish sauce
3 tablespoons sunflower oil
1 tablespoon lemon juice
200 g (7 oz) shelled prawns (shrimp) in brine*
*   or fresh small shelled prawns*

Chop the chicken breast into small cubes, cook it in boiling water for 5 minutes. Peel the carrots, shred them finely. Slice the spring onions and celery, peel and finely chop the garlic and chilli. Cook the vermicelli according to the instructions on the packet. Combine the sugar, fish sauce, sunflower oil, lemon juice, garlic and chilli. Mix all of the ingredients together with the prawns.

*WHAT ARE PRAWNS IN BRINE? *They're prawns that are preserved with salt.*

18 july

Soupe de poisson
Serves 6

PREPARATION TIME 30 MINUTES
COOKING TIME 1 HOUR 30 MINUTES

For the soup:
2 kg (4 lb 8 oz) rock fish*
3 onions
6 garlic cloves
olive oil
50 ml (1¾ fl oz) pastis
200 ml (7 fl oz) white wine
500 g (1 lb 2 oz) potatoes, cubed
1 tablespoon tomato paste (concentrated purée)
3 good pinches of saffron threads
salt and pepper
For the rouille:
50 g (1¾ oz) cooked potato
3 garlic cloves, peeled
1 egg yolk
1 teaspoon Dijon mustard
1 pinch of saffron threads
200 ml (7 fl oz) olive oil
Equipment:
mortar and pestle

*WHAT ARE ROCK FISH? *They're small fish that live in the rocks around the coast — their flavour is quite pronounced.*

**AND THAT'S DONE HOW, IN CONCRETE TERMS? *Once the fish is cooked, the main bones come out easily and any left will be captured by the chinois.*

Clean and rinse the rock fish. Peel and slice the onions and garlic. Sauté the onion and garlic in olive oil in a large saucepan, add the rock fish, flambé with the pastis. Moisten with the white wine. Add the potato, tomato paste, saffron and 2 litres (70 fl oz) water. Cook for 1 hour, remove the fish bones**, cook for a further 30 minutes, purée the whole mixture, pass through a chinois (cone-shaped strainer), then season. For the *rouille*, crush the potato with the garlic using a mortar and pestle, add the egg yolk, mustard and saffron, gradually add the olive oil to bring the sauce together. Season. Serve the fish soup with the *rouille*, some croûton toasts and grated Gruyère cheese.

19 july

Fried red mullet

Serves 6

PREPARATION TIME 20 MINUTES
COOKING TIME 10 MINUTES

18 small red mullet (rouget barbet)
2 tablespoons herbes de Provence (*Provençal herb mix*)
18 tinned anchovies in oil
3 onions, peeled
4 lemons
200 ml (7 fl oz) olive oil
salt and pepper

Clean the red mullet and set aside the livers*. Process the *herbes de Provence* with the livers and anchovies, then spread the inside of the fish with this mixture. Slice the onions and lemons into rounds. Heat the olive oil in a non-stick frying pan, add the onions, lemon and the mullets, cook for 2–3 minutes each side, lay on some paper towels to remove the excess oil. Season.

✱ How do you tell which is the liver? *It's easily spotted by its orange colour.*

20 july

Spinach-ricotta lasagne

Serves 6

PREPARATION TIME 20 MINUTES
COOKING TIME 35 MINUTES

80 g (2¾ oz) butter
80 g (2¾ oz) plain (all-purpose) flour
1 litre (35 fl oz/4 cups) full-cream (whole) milk
1 dash ground nutmeg
salt and pepper
3 onions
olive oil
800 g (1 lb 12 oz) fresh English spinach
200 g (7 oz) ricotta cheese
200 g (7 oz) store-bought lasagne sheets

Preheat the oven to 180°C (350°F/Gas 4). Melt the butter in a large saucepan, add the flour, cook for 5 minutes, add the cold milk*, bring to just barely simmering, stirring well, then add the nutmeg and season. Peel and slice the onions, soften them in olive oil and add the fresh spinach, allow all the moisture to evaporate, add the ricotta and combine well. In a gratin dish make layers of lasagne sheets, spinach and ricotta mixture, béchamel sauce, then repeat and finish with the béchamel. Bake for 30 minutes.

✱ Why add cold milk for the béchamel sauce? *The reaction between the hot roux and the cold milk will prevent lumps from forming.*

21 july

Curried pork tenderloin

Serves 6

PREPARATION TIME 20 MINUTES
COOKING TIME 20 MINUTES

3 carrots
6 French shallots (eschalots)
1 bunch of coriander (cilantro), picked
sunflower oil
50 g (1¾ oz) sultanas (golden raisins)
6 dried apricots
50 g (1¾ oz/⅓ cup) almonds
6 dried prunes
50 g (1¾ oz/⅓ cup) pistachio nuts
1 teaspoon curry powder
1 teaspoon tandoori spice
200 ml (7 fl oz) white wine
100 ml (3½ fl oz) pouring (whipping) cream
salt and pepper
2 pork tenderloins
50 g (1¾ oz) butter

Peel the carrots and shallots, cut the carrots into sticks and halve the shallots. Roughly chop the coriander. Sauté the shallots in sunflower oil, add the carrots, sultanas, apricots, almonds, prunes, pistachios, curry powder and tandoori spice, moisten with white wine, cook for 5 minutes, lower the heat and add the cream, cook for a further 5 minutes and season. Sear the tenderloins in the butter*. Cut the tenderloins into chunks, add them to the curry sauce and cook for a further 5 minutes.

✱ How to sear the tenderloins? *You just have to pan-fry them for 2–3 minutes in the butter, turning them regularly so they brown on all sides.*

22 july

Apple and tomato gazpacho

Serves 6

PREPARATION TIME 20 MINUTES

6 tomatoes
3 granny smith apples
juice of 1 lemon
2 bulb spring onions (scallions)
100 ml (3½ fl oz) cider vinegar
100 ml (3½ fl oz) olive oil
salt and pepper

Cut a cross in the base of the tomatoes and plunge into boiling water for 30 seconds, then remove the skins. Peel two of the apples*, cut them into cubes, then cut the third into thin matchsticks and combine with the lemon juice. Finely slice the spring onions. Purée the tomatoes with the apple cubes, add the cider vinegar, olive oil and the spring onion and season. Serve garnished with the apple matchsticks and drizzle with olive oil.

✳ WHY KEEP THE APPLE SKINS? *The skin of the granny smith apple has a firm texture that's very pleasant to chew on.*

23 july

✳ WHY RAISED IN THE OPEN AIR? *You're going to tell me that we don't eat the lungs, so why the open air bit ... but at least our chicken will be able to root around for small insects, worms and other adorable creatures that colonise our fields ... but « insect-raised chicken » doesn't have the same appeal!*

Chicken in a rosemary crust

Serves 6

PREPARATION TIME 15 MINUTES
COOKING TIME 1 HOUR

2 garlic cloves
2 French shallots (eschalots)
80 g (2¾ oz) lightly salted butter
2 sprigs of rosemary
1 teaspoon coarsely ground black pepper
150 g (5½ oz) dry bread
*1 good chicken raised in the open air**

Preheat the oven to 160°C (315°F/Gas 2–3). Peel and finely chop the garlic and shallots. Process the butter, rosemary, pepper, bread, garlic and shallots. Carefully cover the chicken with this paste. Bake for 1 hour. The crispy crust will keep the chicken tender — what a beautiful contrast!

24 july

Ratatouille and fresh goat's cheese verrines

Serves 6

PREPARATION TIME 15 MINUTES

1 French shallot (eschalot)
1 bunch of mint
6 chives
200 g (7 oz) fresh goat's cheese
100 ml (3½ fl oz) olive oil
salt and pepper
2 celery stalks
400 g (14 oz) ratatouille (see page 284)
Equipment:
6 verrine glasses or jars

Peel and finely chop the shallot. Chop the mint and snip the chives. Using a fork, mix the goat's cheese with the shallot, mint and chives, add the olive oil, and season. Cut the celery into thin sticks. In small glasses, make a mound of ratatouille, cover with goat's cheese and plant a stick of celery in each one.

25 july

Penne and basil salad

Serves 6

PREPARATION TIME 10 MINUTES
COOKING TIME 10 MINUTES

1 French shallot (eschalot)
400 g (14 oz) penne rigate
1 bunch of basil, leaves picked
juice of 1 lemon
150 ml (5 fl oz) olive oil
50 g (1¾ oz) parmesan cheese, shaved
fleur de sel and pepper

Peel and finely chop the shallot. Cook the penne rigate in boiling salted water until *al dente*, refresh immediately. Purée the basil leaves, lemon juice and olive oil, dress the pasta with the basil vinaigrette, add the shallot and the parmesan shavings*, then season with *fleur de sel* and pepper.

❋ How do you make parmesan shavings? Peeling the parmesan with a vegetable peeler is the simplest technique.

26 july

Grilled bass with herbs

Serves 6

PREPARATION TIME 15 MINUTES
CHILLING TIME 24 HOURS
COOKING TIME 15 MINUTES

1 bunch of basil
1 bunch of tarragon or flat-leaf (Italian) parsley
200 ml (7 fl oz) olive oil
1.5 kg (3 lb 5 oz) whole sea bass
1 tablespoon whole aniseed
1 tablespoon fennel seeds
2 sprigs of wild fennel or dill
3 sprigs of fresh thyme
2 tablespoons pastis
coarse salt

❋ How do you avoid the grill stripping the skin off the fish? The skin needs to be well browned in order not to stick to the grill, and then you can carefully turn the fish without ripping it to shreds.

Pick about ten leaves of basil and tarragon and purée them with the olive oil until smooth. Fill the cavity of the bass with the aniseed and fennel seeds, all of the remaining herbs and the pastis, wrap in plastic wrap and chill for 24 hours. Light the barbecue coals, brush the bass with the herbed olive oil, place it on a clean grill, cook for 7–8 minutes*, turn the bass, cook for a further 7 minutes. Serve with coarse salt and the herb oil.

27 july

Classic quiche

Serves 6

PREPARATION TIME 20 MINUTES
COOKING TIME 30 MINUTES

1 sheet store-bought shortcrust pastry
3 eggs
200 ml (7 fl oz) full-cream (whole) milk
200 ml (7 fl oz) pouring (whipping) cream
salt and pepper
200 g (7 oz) slices of ham
150 g (5½ oz) grated Gruyère cheese

❋ Suggestions of ingredients to add to this classic quiche? Dried fruit and nuts, other cheeses, herbs ...

Preheat the oven to 180°C (350°F/Gas 4). Lay the pastry in a round tart tin. Whisk the eggs with the milk and cream. Season. Dice the ham, scatter over the pastry base, cover with the egg mixture, sprinkle with the Gruyère and bake in the oven for 30 minutes.

28 july

Piperade*

Serves 6
PREPARATION TIME 30 MINUTES
COOKING TIME 20 MINUTES

6 onions
4 garlic cloves
100 ml (3½ fl oz) olive oil
1 kg (2 lb 4 oz) capsicums (peppers) (choose a variety)
1 tablespoon soft brown sugar
salt and pepper

Peel and slice the onions and garlic, then sauté them in the olive oil. Remove the skin** and the seeds of the capsicums and slice. Add the strips of capsicum and the sugar to the onions and garlic, sauté for a further 10 minutes, and season before serving.

* Do we know where the name comes from? *The name comes from the Greek* pípus radum, *which means to be mean with the pipe, but from that to a connection with red capsicums …?*

** To remove the skin of the capsicums: *Put them whole into a 200°C (400°F/ Gas 6) oven for 10 minutes until they brown, then enclose them in a plastic bag and the skin will easily peel off.*

29 july

Nectarine cake

Serves 6
PREPARATION TIME 20 MINUTES
COOKING TIME 30 MINUTES

6 nectarines
4 eggs
250 g (9 oz) sugar
150 g (5½ oz) butter
150 g (5½ oz/1 cup) plain (all-purpose) flour
100 g (3½ oz/½ cup) medium-grain semolina
5 g (⅛) baking powder

Preheat the oven to 180°C (350°F/Gas 4). Cut the nectarines into segments. Purée two of the nectarines. Beat the eggs with the sugar. Melt the butter, add the egg mixture, puréed nectarines, flour, semolina and baking powder. Arrange the nectarine segments in a tin, cover with the cake mixture, bake in the oven for 30 minutes.

* How to serve? *It will be best cold.*

30 july

Pancetta-roasted rabbit

Serves 6
PREPARATION TIME 10 MINUTES
COOKING TIME 45 MINUTES

1 tablespoon mixed peppercorns
1 good-quality rabbit
2 sprigs of rosemary
6 French shallots (eschalots)
1 garlic bulb
1 tablespoon herbes de Provence (Provençal herb mix)
1 tablespoon fennel seeds
6 slices rolled pancetta
250 ml (9 fl oz/1 cup) sweet wine
   (Muscat de Rivesalte works well)
50 g (1¾ oz) butter
salt

Preheat the oven to 180°C (350°F/Gas 4). Toast the peppercorns in a dry frying pan* and crush them. Cut the rabbit into pieces and sauté in a flameproof roasting tin with the rosemary, shallots with the skins left on, and garlic bulb cut in half, scatter over the pepper, *herbes de Provence* and fennel seeds. Bake for 30 minutes. Take the roasting tin out of the oven. Reduce the oven temperature to 150°C (300°F/Gas 2). Cover the rabbit with slices of pancetta, bake for 15 minutes. Remove the rabbit from the pan and keep warm. Deglaze the pan with the sweet wine and whisk in the butter using a fork to scrape up the bits on the base of the tin, Season. Pour over the rabbit and serve.

* Why toast the pepper? *It brings out the flavours.*

MARIE & LÉON

Grand Terrine Contest, Place de la Mairie, 4 pm

A Grand Terrine Contest will be taking place in the village square on 31st July with a judging panel of esteemed professionals to reward the most delicious creation. The winning terrine will feature on the cover of a food magazine and the winner will receive a cheque for €20 to spend in one of the village shops.

That's how it all started for Marie Vachecrot, a very ordinary cook married to Léon, a fine food lover. A contest like that is not to be missed, it's the moment to prove to all of these fine gourmets that her reputation is based on mere hearsay and that the truth is much more delicious. White fish as the base, eggs to bind, cream because it's good ... and then? Léon suggests adding some anchovies (why not?). And Kevin, some ginger (ah, adolescence!). Cousin Georges some kaffir lime, « *A variety of lime is used in Thai cuisine, very much in vogue right now in the capital.* » Marinette and Fernand, a touch of pastis, just to get out the bottle and have a glass. But no matter, Marie's terrine is meant to be a family affair, and will thus reflect the choices of all its members. The terrine is mixed, moulded, cooked and presented to the judging panel ...

First prize, after some fierce discussion, is awarded to ... oh, the suspense ... Geneviève Plomb (the mayor's wife) for her *terrine de Campagne*. Disappointment is the order of the day in the Vachecrot household, the next time they'll ask independent observers to take part in the deliberations — the contest smells of bias. The terrines are served as *amuses-bouches* for the gala dinner and Marie's terrine is a sensation. The village cries scandal, the €20 changes hands.

And that is how Marie, destined to the anonymity of her kitchen, became the Marie who went down in history.

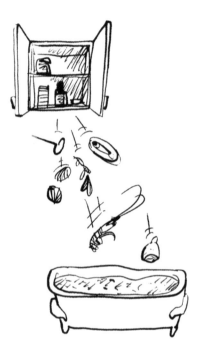

31 july

Fish terrine

Serves 6

PREPARATION TIME 20 MINUTES
COOKING TIME 1 HOUR

600 g (1 lb 5 oz) white fish fillets, such as whiting, cod or blue-eye trevalla

4 eggs

200 ml (7 fl oz) pouring (whipping) cream

salt and pepper

you decide what comes next!

✳ *A FEW SUGGESTIONS, EVEN SO? You can add herbs, citrus, shellfish, crustaceans, vegetables, spices ... some from the back of the cupboard, a touch of what's in the fridge, nothing is impossible.*

Preheat the oven to 160°C (315°F/Gas 2–3). Purée the fish with the eggs and cream, then season. Shape in a terrine dish, and cook in a bain-marie for 1 hour. Now comes the drama ... what should you add to make it your own? Imagine the possibilities — once you've mastered the base, you've mastered the terrine.✳

This month

August

the greengrocer

EGGPLANTS (AUBERGINES)
ZUCCHINI (COURGETTES)
GREEN BEANS
RADISHES
TOMATOES AND CUCUMBERS
CAULIFLOWER
CELERY
ASPARAGUS
BROAD (FAVA) BEANS
FENNEL
ROCKET (ARUGULA) LEAVES
BEETROOT (BEET) LEAVES
HERBS AND SPICES
APRICOTS
PURPLE FIGS
REDCURRANTS

the fishmonger

BREAM AND SMALL SOLE
PRAWNS (SHRIMP)
COD
RAZOR CLAMS AND OCTOPUS
COCKLES AND MUSSELS
DOG COCKLES
AND CLAMS (VONGOLES)
COOKED WHELKS
SPIDER CRABS AND EDIBLE
CRABS
SARDINES IN OIL
ANCHOVIES IN OIL

the butcher-deli

ROASTING BEEF
LAMB LEG
MORTEAU SAUSAGES
COOKED ROAST VEAL
BEEF PALERON
(SHOULDER-BLADE)
PANCETTA
DUCKLINGS

the cheese-seller

PARMESAN CHEESE
MOZZARELLA CHEESE

the grocer

LASAGNE SHEETS

01 Alphonse	**02** Julien	**03** Lydie
BEEF CARPACCIO WITH PARMESAN	PRAWN CURRY	STUFFED ZUCCHINI
08 Dominique	**09** Bénédicte	**10** Laure
SPIDER CRAB BISQUE	ROCKET QUICHE	BARBECUED APRICOTS
15 Marie	**16** Armel	**17** Hyacinthe
SPICED BREAM	CRAB TOASTS	PRAWN KEBABS
22 Fabrice	**23** Rose	**24** Barthélemy
SALMON CARPACCIO WITH CHERVIL	YOUNG SOLE MEUNIÈRE	SHELLFISH HOT-POT
29 Sabine	**30** Fiacre	**31** Aristide
DUCKLING WITH RHUBARB	WARM OCTOPUS	FROGS' LEGS

04
Vianney

SPICED BEEF

05
Abel

FLAKY FIG TART

06
Marlène

LE GRAND AÏOLI

07
Gaétan

LAMB AND BASIL KEBABS

11
Claire

CHICHIS

12
Clarisse

VEGETABLE DIP

13
Hippolyte

SALADE NIÇOISE

14
Evrard

FISH RILLETTES

18
Hélène

MOZZARELLA TART

19
Eudes

BOTTLED TOMATO PASSATA

20
Bernard

SEMI-DRIED TOMATOES

21
Ombeline

PENNE AND SLOW-COOKED
TOMATO SALAD

25
Louis

HERB LASAGNE

26
Césaire

EASY SORBET

27
Monique

ROAST CHICKEN AND
PANCETTA VEGETABLES

28
Augustin

MILLE-FEUILLE

01 02 03 04

01 aug

Beef carpaccio with parmesan

Serves 6

PREPARATION TIME 15 MINUTES
FREEZING TIME 30 MINUTES
COOKING TIME 5 MINUTES

600 g (1 lb 5 oz) roasting beef
50 g (1¾ oz) butter
1 tablespoon sunflower oil
200 g (7 oz) mushrooms
100 g (3½ oz) parmesan cheese
2 tablespoons truffle oil*
50 g (1¾ oz/⅓ cup) pine nuts
rocket (arugula) leaves
2 tablespoons olive oil
fleur de sel and pepper

✱DIY TRUFFLE OIL? *Place a truffle or some truffle peelings in some olive oil, leave for 1 week before using. Top up when the oil level gets low.*

Sear the beef in the butter and sunflower oil, keeping the middle raw, then freeze for 30 minutes. Slice the mushrooms, shave the parmesan. Slice the roast beef very thinly. Arrange the slices on a plate, drizzle with truffle oil, scatter over the mushrooms, parmesan and pine nuts. Combine the rocket and olive oil, place it on top of the carpaccio, season.

02 aug

Prawn curry

Serves 6

PREPARATION TIME 20 MINUTES
COOKING TIME 20 MINUTES

4 garlic cloves
50 g (1¾ oz) fresh ginger
4 French shallots (eschalots)
1 eggplant (aubergine)
1 red capsicum (pepper)
1 lemongrass stem, white part only
1 red bird's eye chilli
1 teaspoon tandoori spice*
1 teaspoon curry powder
100 ml (3½ fl oz) olive oil
18 large prawns (shrimp), shelled
250 ml (9 fl oz/1 cup) white wine
salt and pepper
200 ml (7 fl oz) coconut milk
6 sprigs of coriander (cilantro), leaves picked

✱WHAT IS TANDOORI SPICE? *It's a spice mix used in Indian cuisine, with an ochre colour and a subtle perfume, generally made up of chilli, paprika, garlic, thyme, ground coriander, cumin, pepper, celery, rosemary, cloves, bay, cinnamon and salt.*

Peel and slice the garlic, ginger and shallots. Cut the eggplant into large cubes and the capsicum into small cubes. Thinly slice the lemongrass and chilli. Sauté the spices and curry powder in olive oil with the vegetables for 10 minutes. Add the prawns, cook for 5 minutes, moisten with the wine, cover and cook for 5 minutes. Season, then add the coconut milk and coriander leaves.

03 aug

Stuffed zucchini

Serves 6

PREPARATION TIME 30 MINUTES
COOKING TIME 20 MINUTES

6 small zucchini (courgettes)
4 garlic cloves
50 g (1¾ oz) fresh ginger
3 French shallots (eschalots)
80 ml (2½ fl oz/⅓ cup) olive oil
400 g (14 oz) cooked roast veal
1 bunch of basil, leaves picked
1 teaspoon quatre-épices (four-spice mix)
200 ml (7 fl oz) pouring (whipping) cream
salt and pepper
300 ml (10½ fl oz) vegetable stock
Equipment:
melon-baller or apple-corer

✱WHY? *So it all stays moist and tender.*

Cut the zucchini into three sections and remove the end « caps ». Use a melon-baller to hollow out each section. Peel and slice the garlic, ginger and shallots. Preheat the oven to 160°C (315°F/Gas 2–3). Heat the olive oil in a frying pan and sauté the zucchini flesh, garlic, ginger and shallots. Process the veal with the basil, sautéed zucchini mixture, spices and cream, then season. Stuff each zucchini shell with this mixture. Top with the zucchini « caps ». Arrange in a gratin dish, moisten with the vegetable stock*, bake for 20 minutes.

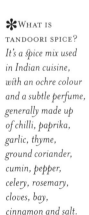

04
august

SPICED BEEF

04 aug

Spiced beef

Serves 6

PREPARATION TIME 30 MINUTES
MARINATING TIME 24 HOURS
COOKING TIME 5 MINUTES

6 garlic cloves
6 French shallots (eschalots)
2 lemongrass stems
3 red bird's eye chillies
1 red capsicum (pepper)
200 ml (7 fl oz) olive oil
juice of 2 lemons
250 ml (9 fl oz/1 cup) white wine
1 tablespoon honey
1 tablespoon of paprika
6 sprigs of thyme
salt and pepper
800 g (1 lb 12 oz) beef paleron*

Peel and slice the garlic and shallots. Chop the lemongrass and chillies** and thinly slice the capsicum. Combine with the olive oil, lemon juice, wine, honey, paprika and thyme and season. Thinly slice the beef and arrange it in a deep dish, coating each layer of beef with some marinade. Chill for 24 hours. Sear the meat on the barbecue, adding more marinade if needed.

✳ WHAT'S THE PALERON? *It's a part of the animal located near the shoulder blade, quite a muscly cut. It thus needs to be carved thinly and marinated for 24 hours.*

✳✳ A CAUTION REGARDING THE BIRD'S EYE CHILLI: *It is very strong. Rinse your hands well after handling it: one rub of the eyes and oh, the drama!*

05 aug

Flaky fig tart

Serves 6

PREPARATION TIME 10 MINUTES
COOKING TIME 35 MINUTES

30 g (1 oz) soft brown sugar
200 g (7 oz) store-bought butter puff pastry
80 g (2¾ oz) butter
1 egg
80 g (2¾ oz/⅓ cup) sugar
100 g (3½ oz/1 cup) ground almonds
1 tablespoon redcurrant jelly
6 purple figs
50 g (1¾ oz/½ cup) hazelnuts, skins removed
Equipment:
springform tart tin with a removable base*

Preheat the oven to 160°C (315°F/Gas 2–3). Scatter a sheet of baking paper with the brown sugar, lay the pastry on this sugar, lay the baking paper in the tin. Melt the butter, combine it with the egg, sugar, ground almonds and redcurrant jelly. Spread this mixture over the base of the tart, halve the figs and arrange them over the tart base, scatter with the hazelnuts. Bake in the oven for 30 minutes. You can brush the tart with some redcurrant jelly to give it some shine.

✳ WHY USE A TIN WITH A REMOVABLE BASE? *It's much easier to unmould. You can use one with a fluted edge or straight side.*

06 aug

Le grand aïoli

Serves 6

PREPARATION TIME 30 MINUTES
COOKING TIME 25 MINUTES

6 waxy, yellow-fleshed potatoes
12 Dutch carrots
3 zucchini (courgettes)
1 cucumber
1 cauliflower
1 bunch of radishes
6 bulb spring onions (scallions)
6 thick fillets of cod* or blue-eye trevalla
400 g (14 oz) cooked whelks (sea snails)**, optional
6 hard-boiled eggs
fleur de sel and pepper
For the aïoli:
2 eggs
1 tablespoon mustard
1 tablespoon wine vinegar
1 pinch of saffron threads
200 ml (7 fl oz) olive oil + extra for drizzling

Peel the potatoes and carrots. Cut the zucchini and cucumber into sticks. Cut the cauliflower into florets, scrape the radishes and cut the bulb spring onions into quarters. Cook the carrots and potatoes for 10 minutes in boiling water and the spring onion for 3 minutes. Place the cod fillets in a steamer, arrange the cooked carrots, potatoes, spring onion and zucchini around them, steam for 10 minutes.

To make the aïoli, combine the eggs, mustard, vinegar, saffron, and olive oil. Blend and season. Serve the cooked fish and vegetables with the whelks, radishes, cucumber, cauliflower and hard-boiled eggs. Dress with a drizzle of olive oil and the *fleur de sel*.

✳ COD AND NOT SALT COD? *I prefer to use fresh cod and season it to serve.*

✳✳ WHERE CAN I BUY COOKED WHELKS? *From your fishmonger.*

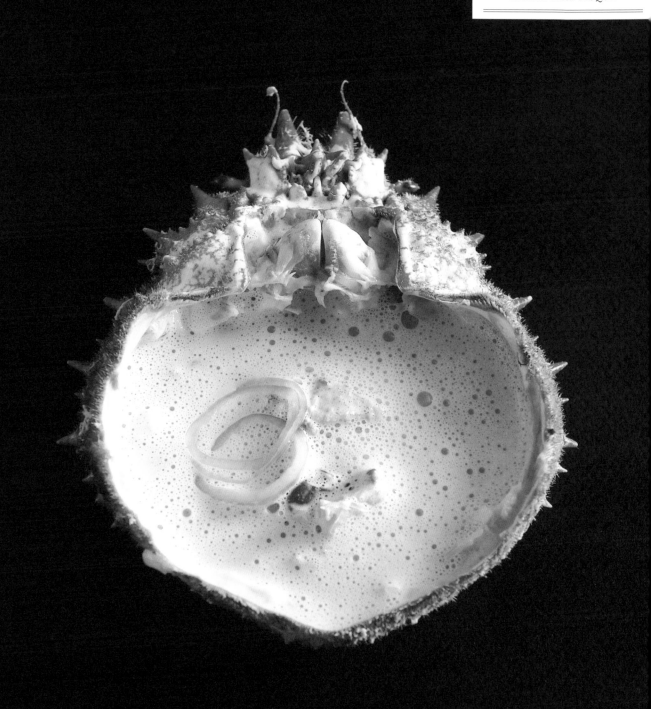

07 aug — Lamb and basil kebabs

Serves 6

PREPARATION TIME 30 MINUTES
CHILLING TIME 1 HOUR
COOKING TIME 10 MINUTES

1 kg (2 lb 4 oz) boneless lamb leg
1 bunch of basil
2 French shallots (eschalots)
150 g (5½ oz) dry bread
2 egg whites
2 tablespoons olive oil
salt and pepper

Cut the lamb into evenly sized 50 g (1¾ oz) pieces. Strip the basil leaves. Peel and chop the shallots and process them with the bread, egg whites, olive oil and half of the basil. Season. Thread the pieces of lamb onto skewers, interspersing them with the remaining basil leaves. Roll the kebabs in the basil breadcrumb mixture, pressing it on well. Chill for 1 hour before cooking. Light the barbecue coals. Cook the kebabs on the barbecue for 5 minutes each side (the embers need to be gentle*), or bake in a 160°C (315°F/Gas 2–3) oven for 10 minutes.

✱WHAT DOES GENTLE EMBERS MEAN? *The embers need to cook the meat tenderly and with love, not violently.*

08 aug — Spider crab bisque

Serves 6

PREPARATION TIME 1 HOUR
COOKING TIME 45 MINUTES

6 fresh spider or blue swimmer crabs
2 potatoes
2 carrots
2 French shallots (eschalots)
3 tablespoons olive oil
250 ml (9 fl oz/1 cup) white wine
2 very ripe tomatoes, diced
1 tablespoon tomato paste (concentrated purée)
200 ml (7 fl oz) pouring (whipping) cream
salt and pepper

Poach the spider crabs in a large volume of water for 15 minutes. Remove the meat from the shells* (this will take a little time). Clean out the body shells** They will be used, to our great delight, as tureens for the bisque. Ah, Brittany, the joys you bestow upon us! Peel the potatoes and carrots, cut them into cubes. Peel and slice the shallots. Sauté three-quarters of the shallots with the carrots and potatoes in the olive oil, moisten with the white wine. Add three-quarters of the crabmeat, the tomato and tomato paste, cook for 20 minutes. Add the cream, then purée and season. Serve the bisque in the crab shells, « Oh, it's so beautiful! » Add the rest of the crabmeat and a few shallot rings, « Really, too beautiful! ».

✱HOW SHOULD I GO ABOUT IT? *Using a lobster pick, you're going to empty out each of the spider crab claws and get the roe found in the body cavity.*

✱✱CLEAN THE SHELLS: *Simply rinse the shells of the crabs in water.*

09 aug — Rocket quiche

Serves 6

PREPARATION TIME 20 MINUTES
COOKING TIME 40 MINUTES

4 French shallots (eschalots)
1 Morteau or other smoked sausage
3 slices pancetta
olive oil
3 eggs
300 ml (10½ fl oz) full-cream (whole)milk
1 sheet store-bought butter puff pastry
1 handful of rocket (arugula) leaves
a few young beetroot (beet) leaves
salt and pepper

cooked salad

uncooked salad

Preheat the oven to 180°C (350°F/Gas 4). Cut the shallots in half. Cut the *Morteau* sausage into 5 mm (¼ inch) slices and the pancetta into four pieces. Sauté the shallot, sausage and pancetta in olive oil for about 7–8 minutes; allow to cool. Beat together the eggs and milk. Use the pastry to line a tart tin, then arrange the sausage mixture in the base of the tart and pour over the egg mixture. Bake for 30 minutes. Dress the rocket and beetroot leaves with olive oil and salt. Cover the quiche with the salad* before serving.

✱WHY? *Because a cooked salad isn't as good.*

10 aug

Barbecued apricots

Serves 6

PREPARATION TIME 10 MINUTES

COOKING TIME 10 MINUTES

18 ripe apricots
120 g (4¼ oz) butter
120 g (4¼ oz/⅓ cup) honey
6 sprigs of lemon thyme

Make six parcels out of foil. Halve the apricots and remove the kernel. Divide the apricots between the parcels, and add I tablespoon butter, I tablespoon honey and I sprig lemon thyme to each. Seal the parcels so they are airtight, place them on the barbecue* or in a preheated 180°C (350°F/Gas 4) oven for 10 minutes. Serve in the papillote parcels.

✳ IN THE EMBERS LIKE POTATOES? *Eh oui!*

11 aug

Chichis

Serves 6

PREPARATION TIME 10 MINUTES

RESTING TIME 1 HOUR 35 MINUTES

COOKING TIME 5 MINUTES

100 ml (3½ fl oz) full-cream (whole) milk
2 teaspoons dried yeast
250 g (9 oz/1⅔ cups) plain (all-purpose) flour
2 tablespoons orange flower water
100 g (3½ oz) sugar
1 egg
oil, for deep-frying

✳ HOW DO YOU DO THAT? *You can knead by hand, but a machine is great for this job!*

✳✳ HOW THICK? *About 1 cm (½ inch) is good.*

✳✳✳ DO THEY RISE A LOT? *They should double in size.*

Heat the milk to lukewarm, add the yeast, mix and set aside for 5 minutes. Knead* together the flour, milk, orange flower water, 50 g (1¾ oz) of the sugar and the egg for 5 minutes. Let the dough rest at room temperature for 45 minutes. Knead again and roll out the dough**, cut out doughnuts using a pastry cutter (or a glass dusted with flour). Place the doughnuts on baking paper, cover with a cloth, let them rise for 45 minutes***. Heat the oil in a deep-fryer to 180°C (350°F) and cook the doughnuts for 2 minutes each side. Drain on paper towel. Dust with the remaining sugar.

12 aug

Vegetable dip*

Serves 6

PREPARATION TIME 30 MINUTES

1 bunch thin asparagus
1 red capsicum (pepper)
1 green capsicum (pepper)
1 punnet cherry tomatoes
1 cucumber
1 cauliflower
3 carrots
1 bunch of radishes
2 witlof (chicory/Belgian endive) hearts

Cut all of the vegetables into sticks, rounds, florets ... serve them with:

FROMAGE BLANC AND CHIVE DIP

1 bulb spring onion (scallion)
1 bunch of chives
150 g (5½ oz) fromage blanc or mascarpone
150 ml (5 fl oz) olive oil
salt and pepper

Peel and thinly slice the spring onion and snip the chives. Mix everything together, season.

GARLIC AND OLIVE DIP

100 g (3½ oz/1 cup) sun-dried black olives, pitted
1 garlic clove
150 ml (5 fl oz) olive oil

Purée all of the ingredients together.

ANCHOVY DIP

100 g (3½ oz) tinned anchovies in oil
1 hard-boiled egg
150 ml (5 fl oz) olive oil
1 teaspoon Cognac

✳ CAN ALL THESE VEGETABLES REALLY BE EATEN RAW? *Yes indeed.*

Purée all of the ingredients together with 2 tablespoons water until smooth.

> **'A wet mid-August, the grapevine overdrinks.
> It's up to the good winemaker not to make it piss.'**

13 aug — Salade niçoise*

Serves 6

PREPARATION TIME 20 MINUTES
COOKING TIME 20 MINUTES

300 g (10½ oz) thin green beans
6 eggs
1 cucumber
2 bulb spring onions (scallions)
6 tomatoes
150 ml (5 fl oz) olive oil
1 tablespoon balsamic vinegar
18 tinned anchovies in oil
salt and pepper

Trim the beans, cook them in boiling salted water for 10 minutes, refresh immediately. Cook the eggs by immersing them in boiling water for 10 minutes, refresh in iced wate, remove the shells and querter the eggs lengthways. Cut the cucumber into sticks, peel and slice the spring onions, cut the tomatoes into wedges. Combine the olive oil and balsamic vinegar. Combine all of the ingredients with the anchovies, then dress them with the vinaigrette.

WHY DO SOME PEOPLE PUT RICE IN THIS SALAD? You can serve this salad as a main course, so add some rice or potatoes for more carbohydrates.

14 aug — Fish rillettes

Serves 6

PREPARATION TIME 10 MINUTES

300 g (10½ oz) tinned tuna in brine or sardines in oil
3 tablespoons mayonnaise
1 red onion, peeled
juice of 1 lime
1 bunch of chives
a few leaves of fresh herbs
2 tablespoons olive oil
croûton toasts

You've become firm mates with the Vachecrots, Marie and Léon, your camping neighbours, who invited you over for drinks the week before: crab sticks, salami, cocktail sausages, fluorescent pink *tarama* canapés, good times all round. It's high time the invitation was returned, the holidays are coming to an end, the aniseed *apéritif* is crying poor, the grass beneath the caravan awning has taken on the look of the Wimbledon final, it will be tonight. What an idea, at 5 pm on 14th August, to throw out an invitation, enthusiastically accepted by new friends, when the shops are in hibernation, curtains drawn and doors closed. A quick inventory of the caravan cupboard and there you are crushing some tuna with a fork with a little mayonnaise, a thinly sliced onion, add some lime juice, some chopped herbs* and olive oil, plus a few croûton toasts and you're ready for the Vachecrots! Ask your youngest to get a few ice cubes from the camping ground bar to make sweet music in your glass and the last-minute *apéritif* is transformed into a gala celebration ... or more if you're at *Cap d'Agde*.

WHAT KIND OF HERBS? For example basil, tarragon, mint ...

15 aug — Spiced bream

Serves 6

PREPARATION TIME 5 MINUTES
COOKING TIME 10 MINUTES

2 x 1 kg (2 lb 4 oz) sea bream or snapper
4 celery stalks
1 teaspoon black peppercorns*
1 teaspoon Sichuan peppercorns*
1 teaspoon juniper berries
6 star anise
100 ml (3½ fl oz) olive oil
salt
Equipment:
mortar and pestle

WHAT ARE THE SPECIAL CHARACTERISTICS OF THESE TWO PEPPERS? One brings freshness (the Sichuan pepper), the other strength.

Preheat the oven to 200°C (400°F/Gas 6). Scale and clean the bream. Thinly slice the celery stalks, set aside a few leaves. Toast the peppercorns, juniper berries and star anise in a dry frying pan. Crush half of the spices with a mortar and pestle, fill the cavities of the fish with the sliced celery and crushed spices. Lay the bream in a gratin dish, pour over the olive oil, add the whole spices and celery leaves. Bake for 10 minutes. Season**.

**TO SERVE WITH THE BREAM? A good mesclun salad with an excellent olive oil.*

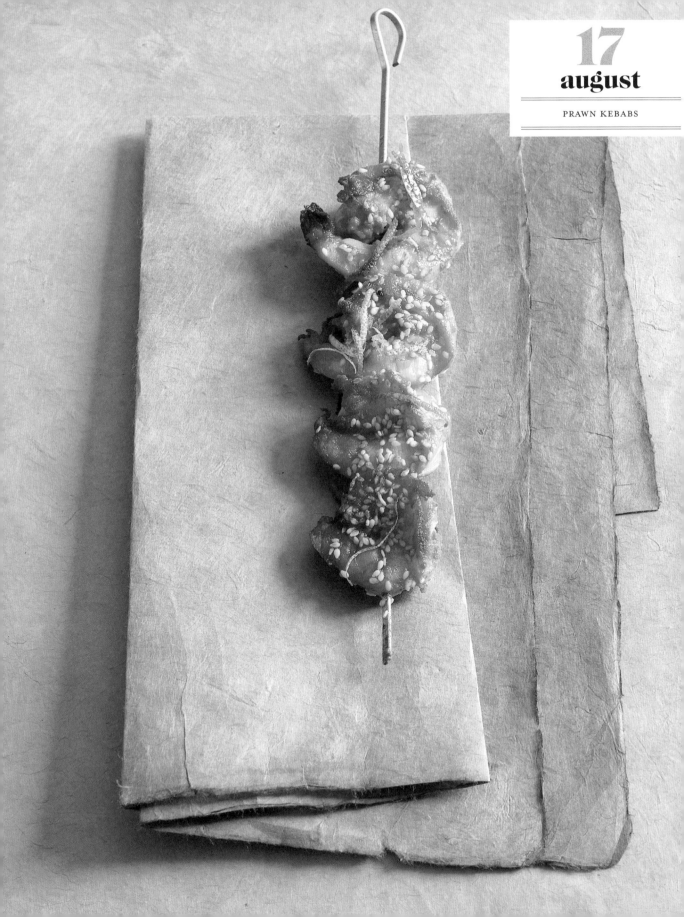

17 aug — Prawn kebabs

Serves 6

PREPARATION TIME 30 MINUTES
COOKING TIME 5 MINUTES

2 limes
1 teaspoon tomato sauce (ketchup)
1 tablespoon honey
24 large prawns (shrimp)*
50 g (1¾ oz/⅓ cup) sesame seeds
Equipment:
pastry brush

Zest and juice the limes. Combine the juice with the tomato sauce and honey. Peel** and devein the prawns, remove the heads so you don't have to make conversation. Skewer the prawns, glaze them with the lime juice mixture using the pastry brush, then sprinkle with sesame seeds. Cook them on a hot barbecue or under a grill (broiler) for 5 minutes. Serve with the remaining sauce and lime zest.

✳ How should I choose the prawns? *Choose large prawns (shrimp), not little pink school prawns that are waterlogged from sitting too long on the fishmonger's ice display in the middle of summer. You want real prawns, robust prawns, prawns with body … we can do without their soul!*

✳✳ I get that, but should I keep the tail? *Tail is the one true thing in life.*

16 aug — Crab toasts

Serves 6

PREPARATION TIME 45 MINUTES
COOKING TIME 20 MINUTES

2 live crabs
2 tablespoons mayonnaise
zest of 1 lemon
salt and pepper
150 g (5½ oz) broad (fava) beans
3 green asparagus spears
2 bulb spring onions (scallions)
1 loaf light brioche

Cook the crabs in boiling water for 20 minutes*. Remove all the meat and the roe from the shell**. Combine the crabmeat with the mayonnaise and lemon zest, then season. Boil the broad beans and remove the skins. Thinly slice the green asparagus and spring onions. Cut the loaf into thin toast slices, brown them under the grill (broiler) for 3 minutes. Top each toast with crabmeat, scatter over the asparagus, broad beans and spring onion.

✳ COOK THE CRABS: *The crab needs to be alive. The beast will imagine itself in a sauna in Tunisia's Hammamet, fall asleep waiting for his massage and disrobe on the plate without ever suspecting such a sort — or appetite — awaits him …*

✳✳ HOW TO REMOVE THE CRAB FLESH? *The same as for the spider crab (see page 338).*

18 aug — Mozzarella tart

Serves 6

PREPARATION TIME 20 MINUTES
COOKING TIME 30 MINUTES

6 tomatoes
150 g (5½ oz) mozzarella cheese
6 garlic cloves
2 tablespoons medium-grain semolina
200 g (7 oz) block store-bought butter puff pastry
2 sprigs of rosemary, leaves picked
fleur de sel
1 bunch of tarragon, leaves picked
olive oil

✳ WHAT A FUNNY IDEA … WHY SPRINKLE WITH SEMOLINA? *The semolina will absorb the juice of the tomatoes and thus prevent the tart from becoming soggy.*

Preheat the oven to 180°C (350°F/Gas 4). Cut the tomatoes into 5 mm (¼ inch) slices. Do the same with the mozzarella. Peel and slice the garlic cloves. Roll out the pastry and scatter the semolina over*. Arrange the tomato slices on the pastry so that they overlap, then add the garlic, rosemary leaves and mozzarella. Season, scatter over the tarragon and drizzle with olive oil. Bake for 30 minutes.

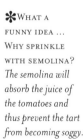

19 aug

Bottled tomato passata

Serves 6

PREPARATION TIME 10 MINUTES
COOKING TIME 2 HOURS 45 MINUTES

2 kg (4 lb 8 oz) well-ripened tomatoes
2 carrots
6 garlic cloves
6 onions
100 ml (3½ fl oz) olive oil
salt and pepper
1 bunch of basil

Cut a cross in the base of the tomatoes, plunge them into boiling water for 30 seconds, and remove their skins. Cut the tomatoes into wedges. Peel the carrots and cut them into thin rounds. Peel and slice the garlic and onions. In a very large saucepan, sauté the onions and garlic in the olive oil, add the tomato wedges and carrots, cook over a low heat for 45 minutes. Purée the whole mixture, pass through a chinois (cone-shaped strainer), and season. Pick off the leaves from the basil, mix the leaves into the tomato. Pour the purée into preserving jars and seal. Place them in a large saucepan, cover with water, place a weight on top of them* so they don't move, simmer very gently for 90 minutes. Store in a dry place**.

*WHY THIS PROCESS? *To sterilise the jars: this way they'll keep the whole year.*

**HOW LONG DOES THE HOME-MADE PASSATA KEEP: *One year.*

20 aug

Semi-dried tomatoes

Serves 6

PREPARATION TIME 10 MINUTES
COOKING TIME 6 HOURS

2 kg (4 lb 8 oz) roma (plum) tomatoes
10 garlic cloves
1 tablespoon herbes de Provence *(Provençal herb mix)*
fleur de sel and pepper
olive oil

Preheat the oven to 100°C (200°F/Gas ½). Halve the tomatoes and arrange them on a sheet of baking paper, flesh side down. Peel and roughly chop the garlic. Scatter over the tomatoes with the *herbes de Provence*, *fleur de sel* and pepper, then drizzle over the oil. Bake in the oven for 6 hours. Store* the tomatoes in olive oil with the garlic and *herbes de Provence*.

*HOW TO STORE: *The tomatoes can be kept for 1–2 months in the refrigerator if they are well covered with oil.*

21 aug

Penne and slow-cooked tomato salad

Serves 6

PREPARATION TIME 15 MINUTES
COOKING TIME 10 MINUTES

300 g (10½ oz) penne rigate
1 French shallot (eschalot)
100 g (3½ oz/⅔ cup) semi-dried tomatoes in oil, drained
1 bunch of chervil
1 bunch of flat-leaf (Italian) parsley
1 bunch of tarragon
150 ml (5 fl oz) olive oil
juice of 1 lemon
fleur de sel
1 teaspoon coarsely ground black pepper

Cook the penne rigate in boiling water for 7–8 minutes or until *al dente*. Peel and slice the shallot and semi-dried tomatoes. Pick off the leaves from the fresh herbs*. Combine the olive oil with the lemon juice. Combine all the ingredients and season with *fleur de sel* and coarsely ground black pepper.

*SHOULD THE HERB LEAVES BE CHOPPED OR LEFT WHOLE? *I prefer them chopped, but it's as you like!*

22 aug

Salmon carpaccio with chervil

Serves 6

PREPARATION TIME 20 MINUTES
COOKING TIME 5 MINUTES

3 garlic cloves
100 ml (3½ fl oz) olive oil
600 g (1 lb 5 oz) salmon fillets
1 bunch of radishes
½ cauliflower head
1 bunch of chervil
fleur de sel

Peel and chop the garlic, sauté in the olive oil for 5 minutes. Thinly slice* the salmon (from the thicker end towards the tail), brush the slices of salmon with the sautéed garlic oil. Slice the radishes into matchsticks, coarsely grate the cauliflower, and pick off the chervil leaves. Arrange the slices of salmon on a plate, cover with radish matchsticks, grated cauliflower and chervil leaves. Season with *fleur de sel*.

✳HOW THICK?
The slices should be the thickness of smoked salmon slices: use a knife with a long, thin, sharp blade.

24 aug

Shellfish hot-pot

Serves 6

PREPARATION TIME 5 MINUTES
COOKING TIME 20 MINUTES

600 g (1 lb 5 oz) cockles
600 g (1 lb 5 oz) razor clams
300 g (10½ oz) clams (vongoles)
600 g (1 lb 5 oz) dog cockles or cockles
200 ml (7 fl oz) wine vinegar
3 garlic cloves
3 French shallots (eschalots)
olive oil
500 ml (17 fl oz/2 cups) white wine
600 g (1 lb 5 oz) mussels, cleaned
1 bunch of tarragon
3 tablespoons balsamic vinegar
200 g (7 oz) butter, cubed
½ bunch of tarragon
½ bunch of flat-leaf (Italian) parsley

Purge the cockles, razor clams, clams and dog cockles in some water with the wine vinegar for 1 hour. Peel and slice the garlic and the shallots, then sauté them in olive oil in a large flameproof casserole dish. Add the white wine, and reduce by half. Add all of the shellfish and cook for 5 minutes. Pick off the tarragon leaves, combine them with the balsamic vinegar, reduce *à sec** in a saucepan, add the butter and whisk over a low heat. Combine the vinegar butter with the shellfish. Pick off the parsley leaves and scatter over.

NB: The scallops are just there to look pretty. Avoid cooking them in August: their season has finished, so they'll come from far away!

23 aug

Young sole meunière

Serves 6

PREPARATION TIME 10 MINUTES
COOKING TIME 10 MINUTES

12 whole young sole or flounder
100 g (3½ oz/⅔ cup) plain (all-purpose) flour
100 g (3½ oz) butter
1 tablespoon olive oil
2 lemons
salt and pepper

Have your fishmonger prepare the fish so they're ready to cook*. Flour the fish and tap to remove the excess. In a non-stick frying pan, melt the butter, add the olive oil, cook the sole for 3 minutes on each side — they should be golden brown. At the end of the cooking time, add the lemon juice, then season. Serve the sole drizzled with the lemon butter.

✳CHOOSING THE FISH? *Sole is a fish whose main bone can be removed easily, so choose whole fish rather than fillets.*

✳WHAT DOES THAT MEAN? *Reduce until there's almost no vinegar left in the saucepan.*

25 aug

Herb lasagne

Serves 6

PREPARATION TIME 30 MINUTES
COOKING TIME 40 MINUTES

80 g (2¾ oz) butter
80 g (2¾ oz) plain (all-purpose) flour
600 ml (21 fl oz) full-cream (whole) milk
400 ml (14 fl oz) pouring (whipping) cream
2 bunches of basil
2 bunches of chervil
1 bunch of tarragon
1 bunch of flat-leaf (Italian) parsley
salt and pepper
200 g store-bought lasagne sheets

Preheat the oven to 160°C (315°F/Gas 2–3). Melt the butter in a saucepan, add the flour, cook for 3 minutes, then add the milk and cream. Cook for 5 minutes, stirring well with a wooden spoon (make sure you scrape the base of the saucepan well). Pick the leaves from the herbs, stir them into the béchamel sauce, season. In a gratin dish, make layers of lasagne, béchamel sauce, lasagne ... finishing with a layer of the béchamel*. Bake in the oven for 30 minutes. You can also add goat's cheese or Gruyère to the béchamel**.

✳ WHY FINISH WITH A LAYER OF BÉCHAMEL? *If you finish with a sheet of lasagne, it will dry out.*

✳✳ OH? YOU DON'T MAKE A LAYER OF CHEESE? *No.*

26 aug

Easy sorbet

Serves 6

PREPARATION TIME 5 MINUTES

300 g (10½ oz) frozen fruit pieces
50 g (1¾ oz/¼ cup) sugar
1 egg white

The ideal is to make one's own frozen fruit during their peak season. Peaches, raspberries, strawberries, figs, pineapple ... cut them into small cubes and freeze them on a tray so that each cube is separate. Purée the frozen fruit with the sugar and the egg white* until the texture is creamy. Serve immediately.

✳ WHAT'S THE EGG WHITE FOR? *To emulsify the sorbet and give it a very smooth texture.*

27 aug

Roast chicken and pancetta vegetables

Serves 6

PREPARATION TIME 20 MINUTES
COOKING TIME 1 HOUR 5 MINUTES

6 Dutch carrots
18 slices pancetta
6 young fennel bulbs
1 bunch of basil
100 g (3½ oz) bacon, cut into lardons
100 g (3½ oz) dry bread
200 ml (7 fl oz) pouring (whipping) cream
1 free-range chicken
1 garlic bulb
6 French shallots (eschalots), unpeeled

Preheat the oven to 160°C (315°F/Gas 2–3). Peel the carrots, keeping their tops on, then roll them in a slice of pancetta. Roll each young bulb of fennel in a slice of pancetta. Pick off the leaves from the basil and chop them. Boil the bacon *lardons* for 5 minutes*. Process the basil with the dry bread, add the cream and bacon, then stuff the chicken with this mixture. Cut the garlic bulb in half. Lay the remaining slices of pancetta on the chicken. Place the chicken in a roasting tin, surround it with the pancetta-wrapped vegetables, add the shallots and the garlic. Bake in the oven for 1 hour. The pancetta will season the chicken.

✳ WHY BOIL THE BACON PIECES? *They will thus lose some of their fat and be more digestible.*

28
august

MILLE-FEUILLE

'A *mille-feuille* is like the *Bottin Mondain*, it's heavy and the cream is found inside.'

28 aug

Mille-feuille

Serves 6

PREPARATION TIME 20 MINUTES
COOKING TIME 20 MINUTES

200 g (7 oz) block store-bought butter puff pastry
100 g (3½ oz) icing (confectioners') sugar
crème pâtissière (see page 200)

Preheat the oven to 180°C (350°F/Gas 4). Generously dust the bench with icing sugar. Place the pastry on top and cover with icing sugar. Roll out to make a rectangular strip. Place the pastry on a sheet of baking paper, cover with another sheet of baking paper. Place a rack I cm (½ inch) above the mille-feuille* and bake in the oven for 20 minutes. Let the pastry cool. Trim the edges**, cut into three equal parts. Spread two parts with crème pâtissière***, assemble the mille-feuille and dust with icing sugar. Eat quickly while the pastry is still crisp.

*WHAT DOES THE RACK ABOVE THE MILLE-FEUILLE DO? This ensures the pastry rises evenly and is the same thickness all over.

**WHY TRIM THE EDGES? So you have a presentable mille-feuille, trim with a knife.

***IDEAS TO FLAVOUR YOUR MILLE-FEUILLES: You can add to the crème pâtissière (at the beginning) cocoa, liqueurs, or even pistachio paste …

29 aug

Duckling with rhubarb

Serves 6

PREPARATION TIME 15 MINUTES
COOKING TIME 10 MINUTES

800 g (1 lb 12 oz) fresh rhubarb
50 g (1¾ oz) butter
6 duckling breast fillets (Challans* are the best)
3 tablespoons maple syrup
2 tablespoons mixed peppercorns
salt
200 ml (7 fl oz) Muscat wine

Peel the rhubarb, cut it into short lengths. Cook it in a little water, keeping it firm (3–4 minutes), then sauté it in the butter. Slash the skin of the duckling fillets in a criss-cross pattern, cook, skin side down, for 5 minutes** then drain the fat. Dip the duckling fillets in a little of the maple syrup, then in the pepper and salt. Cook the duckling fillets, flesh side down, for 3 minutes. Remove the duckling from the pan, add the muscat, reduce by half, then add the remaining maple syrup. Finish the duckling under a hot grill (broiler), skin side up. Serve on the rhubarb, then pour over the maple sauce.

*WHAT'S SPECIAL ABOUT THE CHALLANS DUCK? It's an excellent product, very flavoursome.

**ARE THE DUCKLING FILLETS COOKED IN A FRYING PAN? WITH OR WITHOUT FAT? Yes, but the fat from the duckling is enough.

30 aug

Warm octopus

Serves 6

PREPARATION TIME 15 MINUTES
COOKING TIME 1 HOUR 45 MINUTES

2 kg (4 lb 8 oz) octopus
1 bouquet garni
100 ml (3½ fl oz) soy sauce
100 ml (3½ fl oz) olive oil
3 French shallots (eschalots)
juice of 1 lemon
fleur de sel

Have your fishmonger clean the octopus*. Cook in a large volume of water for 90 minutes with the bouquet garni — the cooking time for the octopus depends on the texture you prefer (some, like me, enjoy a firmer octopus and will thus reduce the cooking time). Remove the octopus from the water, brush it with soy sauce and olive oil, place it in a gratin dish and put it under a hot grill (broiler) for 5 minutes. Peel and slice the shallots, mix them into the octopus' cooking juices with the lemon juice. Finely slice the octopus, pour over the shallot juices, season with *fleur de sel*.

*HOW DO YOU CLEAN AN OCTOPUS? Remove the beak then rinse the head.

MARIE & LÉON

light rain or cats and dogs it is the feast of the frogs ... or of Léon

*O*de to the Frog sung by Léon Vachecrot for his sweet Marie, one August evening, a few minutes before a storm ... You can work out the relationships of cause and effect!

Ah! they're so pretty the legs of my frogs,
la-ee, la-ee, la-ee, la-ee, la-ee, la-ee, la-ee, la-ee.

Yes, they're so pretty the legs of my frogs,
la-ee, la-ee, la-ee, la-ee, la-ee, la-ee, la-ee, la-ee.

There's a racket in the pond,
When evening comes along,
It's the big sundown party,
With the naked frog throng,
The toad's all smiles,
The least delight,
The least of trials,
Makes their hearts beat tonight.

Ah! they're so pretty the legs of my frogs,
la-ee, la-ee, la-ee, la-ee, la-ee, la-ee, la-ee, la-ee.
Yes, they're so pretty the legs of my frogs,
la-ee, la-ee, la-ee, la-ee, la-ee, la-ee, la-ee, la-ee.

The fisherman in green clothes,
Smiles stupidly,
The bait dressed in red clothes,
Strikes calmly,
Butter by the kilo,
Garlic — not too much,
Well-chopped parsley,
Frogs for lunch!

Ah! they're so pretty the legs of my frogs,
la-ee, la-ee, la-ee, la-ee, la-ee, la-ee, la-ee, la-ee.
Yes, they're so pretty the legs of my frogs,
la-ee, la-ee, la-ee, la-ee, la-ee, la-ee, la-ee, la-ee ...

31 aug
Frogs' legs
Serves 6
PREPARATION TIME 10 MINUTES
COOKING TIME 10 MINUTES

36 fresh or frozen frogs' legs
100 g (3½ oz/⅔ cup) plain (all-purpose) flour
8 garlic cloves
1 bunch of flat-leaf (Italian) parsley
200 g (7 oz) butter
salt and pepper

✱ FOAMY BUTTER: *When you cook butter, it passes through different stages, including a foamy one (just before the brown butter or noisette stage), and that's the moment the frogs' legs are added. A foam party for frogs!*

If required, thaw out the frogs' legs, then blot them dry on paper towels and flour them. Peel and roughly cut up the garlic. Pick the parsley leaves and chop. Melt the butter in a frying pan over high heat until it foams up*, add the garlic and the frogs' legs, and cook for about 10 minutes (they should be well browned). Season generously, scatter over the chopped parsley, then serve from the cooking pan. Warning! It's better to cook the legs in a few batches than to overcrowd the pan, which will prevent the legs from cooking evenly.

September

the greengrocer

CAPSICUMS (PEPPERS)
ZUCCHINI (COURGETTES)
EGGPLANTS (AUBERGINES)
CELERY
RED ONIONS
POTATOES
GREEN BEANS
TOMATOES
CORN
LETTUCE
BABY SPINACH LEAVES
HERBS AND SPICES
CHANTERELLE MUSHROOMS
CEP (PORCINI) MUSHROOMS
OYSTER MUSHROOMS
PURPLE FIGS
GREEN FIGS
CONFERENCE PEARS

the fishmonger

SCHOOL PRAWNS (SHRIMP)
SALT COD
BREAM

the butcher-deli

CHICKEN
HAMBURGER STEAK
VEAL ESCALOPE
DUCK BREAST
SPECK
HAM ON THE BONE
PROSCIUTTO

the cheese-seller

COMTÉ CHEESE
RACLETTE CHEESE

the grocer

SHORT-GRAIN RICE
LASAGNE SHEETS
SWEETENED CHESTNUT PURÉE
CHESTNUTS

01 Gilles
PENNE AND PRAWN SALAD

02 Ingrid
SAUTÉED CHICKEN WITH CHANTERELLE MUSHROOMS

03 Grégoire
PROVENÇALE-STYLE GREEN BEANS

08 Adrian
MACARONI CHEESE

09 Alain
CHICKEN NUGGETS

10 Inès
FRENCHBURGER

15 Augustin
DUCK BREAST WITH FIGS

16 Édith
CEP MUSHROOM TART

17 Lubin
WILD MUSHROOM OMELETT

22 Maurice
CHICKEN WITH OYSTER MUSHROOMS

23 Automne
GNOCCHI WITH MUSHROOMS

24 Mercedes
PEARS IN WINE

29 Gabriel
MEAT (AND VEGETABLE) LOAF

30 Jérôme
PEAR FLAN

01

04
Rosalie

SALT COD BRANDADE

05
Raïssa

VEGETABLE TEMPURA

06
Bertrand

LEEK FLAMICHE

07
Reine

ROAST FIGS

11
Adelphe

CORDON BLEU

12
Apollinaire

CROQUE-MONSIEUR

13
Amy

RICE PUDDING

14
Materne

VEGETABLE CROQUETTES

18
Espérance

CHANTERELLE MUSHROOM
PIE

19
Marie-Émilie

CREAM OF
CEP MUSHROOM SOUP

20
Davy

PICKLED CEP MUSHROOMS

21
Levi

BREAM IN A SALT CRUST

25
Hermann

VEAL AND CAPSICUM LASAGNE

26
Damien

MONT BLANC

27
Vincent

CORN WITH BACON

28
Venceslas

CHESTNUT SOUP

02 03 04 05

01 sept

Penne and prawn salad

Serves 6
PREPARATION TIME 30 MINUTES
COOKING TIME 15 MINUTES

400 g (14 oz) penne rigate
30 small school prawns (shrimp)
1 bunch of tarragon
1 egg yolk
1 tablespoon Savora (honey mustard) sauce
1 tablespoon wine vinegar
zest and juice of 1 lemon
100 ml (3½ fl oz) olive oil
150 ml (5 fl oz) sunflower oil
salt and pepper

Cook the penne in a large quantity of boiling salted water for about 10 minutes: they should be al dente. Refresh immediately. Shell the prawns. Pick off the tarragon leaves. Combine the egg yolk with the Savora sauce, vinegar, lemon zest and juice, add both the oils and blend*. Season. Combine the ingredients, then add the tarragon.

*How should I blend it? *Plunge a stick blender into the combined ingredients, et hop, you're off.*

02 sept

Sautéed chicken with chanterelle mushrooms

Serves 6
PREPARATION TIME 15 MINUTES
COOKING TIME 15 MINUTES

3 garlic cloves
2 red onions
6 free-range chicken breast fillets
3 red capsicums (peppers)
300 g (10½ oz) fresh chanterelle mushrooms*
50 g (1¾ oz) butter
1 bunch of coriander (cilantro), leaves picked
salt and pepper

Peel and thinly slice the garlic and onions. Slice the chicken fillets into thin strips, as well as the capsicums. Clean the mushrooms** in fresh water, dry them with a cloth. Sauté the chicken in the butter with the capsicums, onions and garlic for 10 minutes. Add the mushrooms and coriander leaves, cook for a further 5 minutes. Season.

*Other mushrooms? *Choose good-looking pine or chestnut mushrooms.*

** Can the chanterelles be rinsed without getting water-logged? *They are often very dirty. Ideally, wipe them with a damp cloth.*

03 sept

Provençale-style green beans

Serves 6
PREPARATION TIME 10 MINUTES
COOKING TIME 20 MINUTES

800 g (1 lb 12 oz) combined green beans and flat beans
4 tomatoes
olive oil
1 onion, sliced
2 garlic cloves, sliced
1 teaspoon herbes de Provence (Provençal herb mix)
½ bunch of flat-leaf (Italian) parsley
salt and pepper

Cook the green beans in boiling salted water for about 10 minutes. Refresh immediately*. Cut a cross in the base of the tomatoes and plunge into boiling water for 30 seconds, then remove their skin, cut into cubes. Heat the oil in a frying pan and sauté the onion, garlic, tomatoes and *herbes de Provence*, compoter**, stew together for 5 minutes. Reheat the green beans, combine all of the ingredients, then season.

*Why refresh the beans? *Refreshing sets the chlorophyll in the beans, so they will keep their green colour.*

**Compoter: *Cook until it has the texture of a compote.*

04 sept

Salt cod brandade

Serves 6

PREPARATION TIME 24 HOURS
COOKING TIME 30 MINUTES

800 g (1 lb 12 oz) dried salt cod
800 g (1 lb 12 oz) potatoes
10 garlic cloves
1 litre (35 fl oz/4 cups) full-cream (whole) milk
200 ml (7 fl oz) olive oil
salt and pepper
rocket (arugula) leaves

The day before, de-salt the cod by placing it in fresh water to soak, changing the water regularly and rinsing the cod. Peel the potatoes and garlic. Cook the potatoes in a large volume of water for 20–30 minutes. Cook the salt cod and garlic in the milk diluted with 1 litre (35 fl oz/4 cups) water (watch the milk on the stove!) for 20 minutes. Remove the skin and bones from the cod. Combine the cooked garlic and potatoes, roughly crush with the olive oil, and season*. Make a circle of the potato purée on a plate, scatter with pieces of salt cod and serve with a rocket salad.

✳ ADD ANY SALT APART FROM THE SALT COD? *Before seasoning the purée, taste the salt cod, if it is still quite salty, there's no need.*

05 sept

Vegetable tempura

Serves 6

PREPARATION TIME 15 MINUTES
COOKING TIME 5 MINUTES

Assortment of vegetables:
capsicum (pepper)
zucchini (courgette)
eggplant (aubergine)
celery
onion
fresh herbs, such as shiso (perilla)
tempura flour
2 eggs
oil, for deep-frying
salt and pepper

It's back-to-school (or work) time, the sun-soaked vegetables are still being shown off at the market, so we'll make the most of it. Cut the vegetables into rounds or strips. Prepare the tempura batter (follow the instructions on the flour packet). Heat the oil to 180°C (350°F), dip the vegetables in the batter, plunge the vegetable fritters in the oil for 3–4 minutes, then drain on paper towels. Season and serve immediately.

06 sept

Leek flamiche

Serves 6

PREPARATION TIME 30 MINUTES
CHILLING TIME 30 MINUTES
COOKING TIME 30 MINUTES

For the pastry:
1 French shallot (eschalot)
100 g (3½ oz) butter
200 g (7 oz/1⅓ cups) plain (all-purpose) flour
1 bunch of coriander (cilantro), leaves picked
fleur de sel and pepper
1 egg
For the filling:
3 leeks, white part only
3 tablespoons olive oil
300 ml (10½ fl oz) pouring (whipping) cream
1 tablespoon ground cumin + extra for garnish
Equipment:
tartlet tins

Preheat the oven to 160°C (315°F/Gas 2–3). For the pastry, peel and finely chop the shallot. Process the butter with the flour, coriander and shallot. Season, then add the egg. Wrap* and chill the pastry for 30 minutes. Roll it out and use it to line tartlet tins. Bake in the oven for 10 minutes.

For the filling, thinly slice the leeks, wash them well in plenty of water. Sauté the leeks over low heat in the olive oil for 15 minutes (they should soften without colouring). Add the cream and cumin, cook for a further 15 minutes (the cream should be completely absorbed by the leek). Season. Place a tablespoon of leek in each tart base, then sprinkle with ground cumin. Serve lukewarm.

✳ WHY CHILL THE PASTRY IN PLASTIC? *So it becomes firmer and easier to roll out.*

07 sept

Roast figs

Serves 6

PREPARATION TIME 15 MINUTES
COOKING TIME 20 MINUTES

1 vanilla bean
500 ml (17 fl oz/2 cups) fresh apple juice
100 g (3½ oz) butter
100 g (3½ oz) soft brown sugar
100 g (3½ oz) desiccated coconut
1 egg + 1 egg yolk
12 ripe purple figs*
fig sorbet

❋Why purple ones? They are more flavoursome with a less herbaceous quality than green figs.

❋❋Is the incision enough to make room for the cream? It's enough.

Preheat the oven to 160°C (315°F/Gas 2–3). Split the vanilla bean lengthways, scrape out the seeds and mix them into the apple juice. Melt the butter, combine with the sugar, desiccated coconut, egg and egg yolk. Make a cross-shaped incision in the top of each fig**, fill with the coconut cream. Arrange the figs in a gratin dish, pour the vanilla mixture around the figs (to one-third of their height). Bake for 20 minutes. Serve with a fig sorbet.

08 sept

Macaroni cheese

For 6 children and a few adults

PREPARATION TIME 15 MINUTES
COOKING TIME 30 MINUTES

1 bunch of basil (some greens for our little darlings!)
300 g (10½ oz/2⅓ cups) grated Gruyère cheese
300 ml (10½ fl oz) pouring (whipping) cream
300 g (10½ oz) elbow macaroni
8 slices leg ham off the bone (no skimping on quality!)
salt and pepper

❋We know about those parents who, on the pretext of feeding their children, devour the meal that was intended for the children themselves, saying: « Let me help you, you won't finish that, you ate too many chips before dinner again! » Nice work!

Preheat the oven to 160°C (315°F/Gas 2–3). Pick off the basil leaves and slice them. Combine the Gruyère cheese with the cream and basil. Cook the macaroni in boiling water for about 10 minutes, keeping them *al dente*. Combine the macaroni with two-thirds of the cheese mixture and season. Make a layer of macaroni in a gratin dish, cover with ham, WE SAID LEG HAM, OFF THE BONE, cover with more macaroni, more ham AH! COME ON NOW, OFF THE BONE, macaroni … finish with the rest of the cheese mixture. Bake for 20 minutes. Serve the children first, keep the parents back* (a drop of red in the next room should do it), then release the parents to scrape the plates clean and finish the dish.

09 sept

Chicken nuggets, specially for Basilou (or how to please the littlest one)

Serves 6

PREPARATION TIME 30 MINUTES
COOKING TIME 10 MINUTES

6 FREE-RANGE chicken breast fillets, (otherwise, just buy pre-made nuggets!)
200 ml (7 fl oz) pouring (whipping) cream
salt and pepper
4 eggs
150 g (5½ oz) dry bread
50 g (1¾ oz) butter
2 tablespoons sunflower oil
tomato sauce (ketchup)

❋You can add all sorts of ingredients to your nuggets, such as onions, garlic, vegetables, spices … But my Basilou likes his nuggets plain, so plain is how I make them!

Cut the chicken into small cubes, process, add the cream and season. Beat the eggs until just combined. Process the bread into fine breadcrumbs. Use your hands to shape the chicken into nuggets, dip them in the beaten egg, then in the breadcrumbs*. Cook on a low heat in a non-stick frying pan with some butter and a little sunflower oil for 3–4 minutes each side. Serve with tomato sauce (ketchup) … if you're aiming to please, you might as well go all out!

10 sept

Frenchburger

Serves 6

PREPARATION TIME 15 MINUTES
COOKING TIME 20 MINUTES

1–2 baguettes
6 slices speck
6 hamburger steaks from your butcher
1 tablespoon Savora (honey mustard) sauce
1 tablespoon wholegrain mustard
1 tablespoon tomato sauce (ketchup)
1 red onion
3 tomatoes
180 g (6¼ oz) Comté cheese
your choice of salad leaves

✳ How can one retain one's dignity while eating such a dish? *Raise your head, look into the distance, push out your chin, take committed bites without shifting your gaze from the horizon, pretend not to see the large blob of tomato sauce that has just appeared on your new T-shirt … et voilà!*

Cut 1 baguette into six pieces or 2 baguettes into thirds, split them open. Cook the slices of speck for 3 minutes on a low heat. Cook the hamburger steaks in the same frying pan: keep them rare. Rest the hamburgers for 5 minutes, take them out of the pan, add the Savora sauce, mustard and tomato sauce to the pan, scrape the base of the pan with a spatula. Peel and slice the onion into rings along with the tomatoes. Cut the Comté cheese into thin slices. Spread the opened baguettes with the tomato-mustard sauce, lay over the speck, hamburger, cheese, tomato and onion, then pass under a hot grill (broiler) for 5 minutes. Add the lettuce and close the baguettes back up* and serve.

11 sept

Cordon bleu (this one's for my Jean)

Serves 6

PREPARATION TIME 15 MINUTES
COOKING TIME 15 MINUTES

6 free-range chicken breast fillets or 6 thin escalopes of veal
3 slices leg ham off the bone (it's back!)
120 g (4¼ oz) Raclette cheese, sliced
4 eggs
100 g (3½ oz) dry bread
100 g (3½ oz/1 cup) ground almonds
salt and pepper
40 g (1½ oz) butter

✳ Suggestions for ingredients to add to the chicken or breadcrumbs: *Once again, you can add herbs such as basil or tarragon, you can add pesto, tomato passata (puréed tomatoes) or tapenade to the filling. It's up to you to make your own cordon bleu.*

Use a rolling pin to pound the chicken fillets until thin. Cut the slices of ham in half. Lay a slice of ham over half of each chicken fillet, then a slice of cheese, fold over the escalope and flatten. Beat the eggs until they're just combined. Process the bread and ground almonds, season. Dip the escalopes into the eggs, then into the breadcrumbs, repeat this operation*. Cook in butter in a frying pan over low heat for 5–7 minutes each side.

12 sept

Croque-monsieur for Zounette (though she prefers frogs' legs and the cuisine of Michel Troigros)

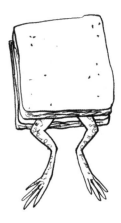

Serves 6

PREPARATION TIME 15 MINUTES
COOKING TIME 5 MINUTES

12 slices soft white sandwich bread
300 g (10½ oz/2⅓ cups) grated Gruyère cheese
250 ml (9 fl oz/1 cup) pouring (whipping) cream
3 slices leg ham, off the bone (again!)
3 slices prosciutto, finely shredded
200 g (7 oz/4 cups) baby spinach leaves
fried eggs, optional

✳ How do I make a croque-madame? *Make a croque-monsieur with an egg on top.*

Preheat the oven to 180°C (350°F/Gas 4). Lay the bread slices out on the work bench. Combine the grated Gruyère and cream. Spread the bread slices with half of this mixture. Distribute the slices of ham, shredded prosciutto and baby spinach leaves however you like on half the bread slices, cover with another slice of bread and the remaining cream mixture. Cook in the oven for 5 minutes. Top your *croques* with a fried egg if you like*.

13 sept

Rice pudding

Serves 6

PREPARATION TIME 15 MINUTES
COOKING TIME 25 MINUTES

1 vanilla bean
600 ml (21 fl oz) full-cream (whole) milk
350 g (12 oz) caster (superfine) sugar
200 g (7 oz) short-grain rice
350 ml (12 fl oz) pouring (whipping) cream
50 g (1¾ oz) lightly salted butter

Split the vanilla bean lengthways, scrape the seeds into the milk, add the bean to infuse. Add 150 g (5½ oz/⅔ cup) of the sugar and bring to the boil. Pour the rice into the milk, cook over low heat for 20 minutes, stirring regularly. Let the rice cool in the milk*. Whip 200 ml (7 fl oz) of the cream with 1 tablespoon of the sugar into a chantilly, fold into the rice. Make a caramel with the remaining sugar and 1 tablespoon water, then add the butter and remaining cream, cook for 3 minutes. Pour the caramel sauce over the rice pudding**.

❋WHY NOT MIX IN THE CREAM STRAIGHT AWAY? *If the rice is too hot, the cream will liquefy.*

❋❋HOW SHOULD IT BE SERVED? *In small ramekins, or big ones.*

14 sept

Vegetable croquettes

Serves 6

PREPARATION TIME 10 MINUTES
COOKING TIME 40 MINUTES

500 g (1 lb 2 oz) potatoes, peeled
200 g (7 oz/1⅓ cups) plain (all-purpose) flour
3 eggs
salt and pepper
sunflower oil

Cook the potatoes for 30 minutes in boiling water. Mash them, add the flour and the eggs and season. Then add your choice of:

3 carrots: Cooked in simmering water and puréed, then added to the potato purée.

200 g (7 oz) English spinach: Wilted in butter and puréed, then added to the potato purée.

200 g (7 oz) cauliflower: Cooked in simmering water and puréed, then added to the potato.

Using two spoons, make vegetable croquettes, cook them in a frying pan containing 5 mm (¼ inch) oil for 5 minutes on each side*. Drain on paper towels before serving.

❋MY CROQUETTES FALL APART IN THE OIL. WHAT CAN I DO? *Have pasta instead or, more seriously, add a little extra flour.*

15 sept

Duck breast with figs

Serves 6

PREPARATION TIME 15 MINUTES
COOKING TIME 15 MINUTES

1 French shallot (eschalot)
½ bunch of flat-leaf (Italian) parsley
12 green figs
3 duck breasts
150 ml (5 fl oz) ruby or tawny Port
2 tablespoons of crème de cassis (blackcurrant liqueur)
50 g (1¾ oz) butter
salt and pepper

Peel and slice the shallot, chop the parsley and halve the figs. Slash the duck breasts in a criss-cross pattern. Cook them skin side down in a frying pan for 7 minutes, drain the fat*, turn the duck over for 2 minutes, then remove to a plate. Deglaze the pan with the Port and the crème de cassis, add the figs, cook for 5 minutes. Add the butter, then season. Reheat the duck in the sauce with the figs, garnish with the shallot and chopped parsley.

❋WHY? *Otherwise you'll have a swimming pool of duck fat, hello arteries!*

15
september

DUCK BREAST WITH FIGS

'On Saint-Edith's Day, *piaffe* some mushrooms.'

16 sept

Cep mushroom tart

Serves 6

PREPARATION TIME 15 MINUTES
COOKING TIME 30 MINUTES

400 g (14 oz) fresh cep (porcini) mushrooms*
3 French shallots (eschalots)
100 g (3½ oz) air-dried duck breast
100 g (3½ oz) speck, cut into lardons
1 tablespoon Armagnac
50 g (1¾ oz/½ cup) walnut kernels
2 slices soft white sandwich bread, cubed
150 ml (5 fl oz) pouring (whipping) cream
3 garlic cloves
80 g (2¾ oz) butter
200 g (7 oz) block store-bought butter puff pastry

Preheat the oven to 180°C (350°F/Gas 4). Clean the ceps with a damp cloth. Peel and slice the shallots, dice the duck breast. Sauté the shallot and duck with the speck for about 5 minutes. Flambé with the Armagnac. Add the walnuts, bread cubes and cream. Process the duck and walnut mixtures together to make a stuffing. Peel and chop the garlic, sauté it in the butter. Roll out the pastry and cut into rounds, spread with the filling, cover with the cep mushrooms and dot generously with garlic butter. Bake for 30 minutes.

✳ CHOOSING GOOD CEP MUSHROOMS:
The cep is like Johnny Hallyday in French music, it's the boss, the all-round champion. You only buy cep mushrooms in season: they should be hard like pebbles. You get down on your genoux to find them, watch out for your joujoux, your head in the choux, without waking the hiboux, often full of poux ... and what's more, you get to brush up on your French ...

17 sept

Wild mushroom omelette

Serves 6

PREPARATION TIME 10 MINUTES
COOKING TIME 10 MINUTES

12 eggs
100 ml (3½ fl oz) pouring (whipping) cream
1 bunch of flat-leaf (Italian) parsley
10 chives
salt and pepper
200 g (7 oz) fresh wild mushrooms*
3 French shallots (eschalots)
50 g (1¾ oz) butter
2 tablespoons sunflower oil
50 g (1¾ oz/½ cup) walnut kernels
½ bunch of tarragon, leaves picked

Beat the eggs and cream. Pick and chop the parsley leaves, snip the chives and add to the egg mixture. Season. Clean the mushrooms and dry with a cloth. Slice the shallots, sauté them with the mushrooms** in the butter and oil (if they are extra-fresh, cook them quickly over high heat). Pour in the omelette mixture, add the walnuts and finish cooking. Garnish with tarragon.

✳ WHICH MUSHROOMS, FOR EXAMPLE?
Black trumpets, hedgehog mushrooms, chanterelles, ceps (porcini), St George's mushrooms ...

✳✳ HOW LONG TO COOK THE MUSHROOMS?
Cook them in a hot pan for 5 minutes.

18 sept

Chanterelle mushroom pie

Serves 6

PREPARATION TIME 20 MINUTES
COOKING TIME 35 MINUTES

6 garlic cloves
6 French shallots (eschalots)
olive oil
400 g (14 oz) cooked rice
salt and pepper
3 eggs
300 ml (10½ fl oz) pouring (whipping) cream
2 sheets store-bought butter puff pastry
400 g (14 oz) fresh chanterelle mushrooms
1 egg yolk
Equipment:
pie tin

Preheat the oven to 180°C (350°F/Gas 4). Chop the garlic and shallots, sauté them over high heat in olive oil, combine with the rice, season. Combine the eggs and cream, then add to the rice. Lay one sheet of pastry in a pie tin, fill with the mushrooms and add the rice mixture, then moisten the edges of the pie with water. Cover with the other sheet of pastry and seal the edges. Make a hole in the top*, use a knife to score the pastry in a crescent pattern, brush with the egg yolk** then bake for 30 minutes.

✳ WHY MAKE A HOLE IN THE TOP?
So the steam from cooking can escape from the pie.

✳✳ WHAT DOES BRUSHING IT WITH EGG YOLK DO? *It makes the pastry nice and golden.*

19 sept

Cream of cep mushroom soup

Serves 6

PREPARATION TIME 15 MINUTES
COOKING TIME 40 MINUTES

400 g (14 oz) cep (porcini) mushrooms
200 g (7 oz) potatoes, peeled
6 French shallots (eschalots)
olive oil
1 dash ground nutmeg
250 ml (9 fl oz/1 cup) white wine
300 ml (10½ fl oz) pouring (whipping) cream
salt and pepper

before   *after*

Cut 300 g (10½ oz) of the ceps into cubes*, slice the remaining ceps. Cut the potatoes into cubes. Peel and slice the shallots, set aside the equivalent of one shallot. Heat some olive oil and sauté the cubed ceps with the bulk of the shallot in a saucepan, add the nutmeg, pour in the white wine, add the potatoes. Cover with water, then with a lid, and cook over low heat for 30 minutes. Purée, add the cream, season, then cook for a further 5 minutes. Pan-fry the remaining sliced ceps and shallot over high heat** in olive oil. Serve the soup in shallow bowls and top with a tablespoon of sautéed ceps.

✳In cubes? *It's about giving you a bit more work to do.*

✳✳For how long? *Give them 5 minutes.*

20 sept

Pickled cep mushrooms

Makes 4 x 300 g (10½ oz) jars

PREPARATION TIME 10 MINUTES
RESTING TIME 2 HOURS
FURTHER RESTING TIME 1 WEEK

*1 kg (2 lb 4 oz) cep (porcini) mushrooms**
1 tablespoon juniper berries
1 tablespoon mixed peppercorns
4 sprigs of rosemary
4 bay leaves
12 garlic cloves
1 litre (35 fl oz/4 cups) white vinegar
Equipment:
4 x preserving jars

Clean the cep mushrooms with a damp cloth, plunge them into boiling water for 30 seconds, let them drain for 2 hours. Roughly crush the juniper berries and peppercorns. Fill the jars with ceps without packing them down, along with 1 sprig of rosemary, 1 bay leaf, 3 unpeeled garlic cloves, a little juniper berry and pepper in each, then cover completely with vinegar. Seal the jars and keep in the refrigerator for 1 week before using**.

✳What's a bouchon cep mushroom? *A small cep mushroom the size of a Champagne bouchon — a Champagne cork.*

✳✳How can they be used? *The pickled ceps go wonderfully with charcuterie products.*

21 sept

Bream (or other scale fish) in a salt crust

Serves 6

PREPARATION TIME 15 MINUTES
COOKING TIME 10 MINUTES

4 kg (9 lb) coarse salt
2 x 600 g (1 lb 5 oz) bream
olive oil

Preheat the oven to 200°C (400°F/Gas 6). Spread 1 kg (2 lb 4 oz) coarse salt in a baking dish, then place the cleaned bream on top. Moisten the remaining salt* and cover the bream completely with the moistened salt. Bake in the oven: allow 10 minutes per 1 kg (2 lb 4 oz) of fish. Break the salt crust** (avoid doing this over the carpet), take out the fish. Serve as simply as possible. Drizzle with the olive oil.

✳What proportion of water? *Use 250 ml (9 fl oz/1 cup) water per 1 kg (2 lb 4 oz).*

✳✳How should the salt crust be broken? *With a serrated knife, such as a bread knife.*

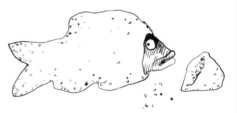

22 sept

Chicken with oyster mushrooms

Serves 6

PREPARATION TIME 20 MINUTES
COOKING TIME 1 HOUR

6 garlic cloves
4 French shallots (eschalots)
1 kg (2 lb 4 oz) oyster (pleurotus) mushrooms
1 tablespoon herbes de Provence (Provençal herb mix)
salt and pepper
1 egg white
3 tablespoons olive oil
1 free-range chicken
50 g (1¾ oz) butter

Preheat the oven to 160°C (315°F/Gas 2–3). Peel and chop the garlic and shallots. Chop 150 g (5½ oz) of the oyster mushrooms, combine with the garlic and shallots, add the *herbes de Provence* and season. Combine with the egg white and olive oil. Spread this mixture over the chicken, bake in the oven for 1 hour. Sauté the remaining mushrooms in the butter over high heat for 10 minutes, and season. Combine with the cooking juices to serve.

23 sept

Gnocchi with mushrooms

Serves 6

PREPARATION TIME 25 MINUTES
CHILLING TIME 2 HOURS
COOKING TIME 30 MINUTES

300 g (10½ oz) potatoes
200 g (7 oz/1⅓ cups) plain (all-purpose) flour
1 bunch of basil, leaves picked
3 eggs
salt and pepper
200 g (7 oz) mushrooms
2 French shallots (eschalots), peeled and sliced
250 ml (9 fl oz/1 cup) dry white wine
300 ml (10½ fl oz) pouring (whipping) cream
6 chives, snipped

Peel and cook the potatoes in a large volume of water for 20 minutes and make a mash. Process the flour, basil and eggs together, combine with the potato and season. Make « sausages », roll in plastic wrap and chill for 2 hours. Cut the sausages into gnocchi*, ridge them with the back of a fork. Sauté the mushrooms with the shallots, add the white wine and reduce. Add the cream and the gnocchi, season, cook for 5 minutes on a gentle heat. Serve with the chives.

✱HOW BIG SHOULD THE GNOCCHI BE? *1 cm (½ inch).*

24 sept

Pears in wine

Serves 6

PREPARATION TIME 10 MINUTES
COOKING TIME 45 MINUTES
RESTING TIME 24 HOURS

6 Conference pears
1 vanilla bean
1 litre (35 fl oz/4 cups) red wine
150 g (5½ oz) soft brown sugar
1 teaspoon black peppercorns
4 star anise
1 teaspoon quatre-épices (four-spice mix)

Peel the pears, keep the stem attached. Split the vanilla bean lengthways, scrape out the seeds and add them to the red wine with the bean*. Place the pears in a saucepan, cover with the vanilla-wine, add the sugar, peppercorns, star anise and spices. Cook, uncovered, over gentle heat for 45 minutes. Allow the pears to infuse for 24 hours in the refrigerator before serving.

✱WHY ADD THE BEAN AS WELL? *It will infuse the wine and add flavour.*

MARIE & LÉON

lasciatemi cantare

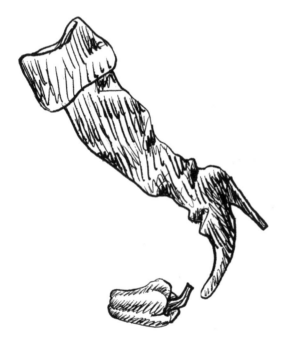

Lasciatemi cantare ... about weddings ... *con la chitarra in mano* ... some *Chianti* ... *lasciatemi cantare* ... everything in litres of Barolo ... *sono un Italiano* ... from Piedmont to Apulia, the lovers ... *Buongiorno Italia gli spaghetti al dente* ... trouble waking up, unforeseen curiosity ... *e un partigiano com presidente* ... pasta with truffles, wagon-loads of penne ... *con l'autoradio sempre nelle mano destra* ... and still more *Moscato di Pantelleria,* parmesan cheese ... *e un canarino sopra la finestra* ... and lasagne.

And that is how Marie ... *buongiorno Italia con i tuoi artisti* ... went down in history.

25 sept

Veal and capsicum lasagne

Serves 6

PREPARATION TIME 30 MINUTES
COOKING TIME 50 MINUTES

4 veal escalopes
2 red capsicums (peppers)
2 green capsicums (peppers)
3 onions
3 tomatoes
olive oil
salt and pepper
50 g (1¾ oz) butter
50 g (1¾ oz/⅓ cup) plain (all-purpose) flour
600 ml (21 fl oz) full-cream (whole) milk
1 dash ground nutmeg
200 g (7 oz) store-bought lasagne sheets
200 g (7 oz) aged sheep's cheese good for grating
  (such as Ossau-Iraty)

Preheat the oven to 180°C (350°F/Gas 4). Cut the escalopes and capsicums into small cubes. Peel and slice the onions. Cut the tomatoes into wedges. Sauté the veal with the onions in the olive oil, add the capsicums and tomatoes, let them stew for 20 minutes, then season. Melt the butter in a saucepan, add the flour, cook for 3 minutes, stirring well. Add the milk and nutmeg, and cook for 5 minutes. In a gratin dish, make a layer of meat, a layer of béchamel sauce, a layer of cheese and a layer of lasagne, repeat, finish with the grated sheep's cheese. Bake in the oven for 30 minutes.

> 'The chestnut tree is sometimes called the « sausage tree », but when the chestnut is still in its prickly pod, it's the « *Merguez* » tree!'

26 sept

Mont Blanc*
Serves 6
PREPARATION TIME 15 MINUTES
COOKING TIME 10 MINUTES

200 g (7 oz) block store-bought shortcrust pastry
  (or see Strawberry tart recipe, page 200)
150 g (5½ oz) sweetened chestnut purée
50 g (1¾ oz) butter, softened
200 ml (7 fl oz) pouring (whipping) cream
1 tablespoon vanilla sugar

Preheat the oven to 160°C (315°F/Gas 2–3). Roll out the pastry and line individual tartlet tins, place a small spoonful of chestnut purée in each, bake for 10 minutes, allow to cool. Mix the butter into the remaining chestnut purée. Whip the cream and vanilla sugar into a chantilly, then combine with the chestnut mixture. Fill each tartlet with the creamy chestnut mixture**.

✳WHY IS IT CALLED MONT BLANC? *It's a mountain made from a molehill.*

✳✳PUT IT IN THE FRIDGE OR SERVE STRAIGHT AWAY? *Straight away is better!*

27 sept

Corn with bacon
Serves 6
PREPARATION TIME 10 MINUTES
COOKING TIME 30 MINUTES

6 corn cobs
1 bunch of flat-leaf (Italian) parsley, leaves picked
100 g (3½ oz) butter, softened
salt and pepper
6 thick slices smoked bacon

Cook the corn cobs in boiling salted water for 15 minutes. Finely chop the parsley, work it into the butter with a fork, then season. Cut 2 of the corn cobs into quarters*, set aside six quarters. Slice off the kernels from the rest of the corn with a knife. Pan-fry the slices of bacon. Serve with 1 cob quarter and the corn kernels, top with the parsley butter.

✳HOW CAN I CUT THE COBS WITHOUT CUTTING OFF MY HAND? *Pierce the cob with a carving fork, slide a long knife between the prongs of the fork, press down and the deed is done.*

28 sept

Chestnut soup
Serves 6
PREPARATION TIME 10 MINUTES
COOKING TIME 25 MINUTES

2 garlic cloves
2 French shallots (eschalots)
3 tablespoons olive oil
400 g (14 oz) peeled chestnuts
250 ml (9 fl oz/1 cup) white wine (from Ardèche of course)
1 bay leaf
300 ml (10½ fl oz) pouring (whipping) cream
salt and pepper

Peel and slice the garlic and shallots. Heat the olive oil in a saucepan and sauté them for 5 minutes until golden. Add 300 g (10½ oz) of the chestnuts, cook for 5 minutes, deglaze with the white wine, then add 250 ml (9 fl oz/ 1 cup) water and the bay leaf, cook for 10 minutes. Remove the bay leaf. Purée, add the cream, season, then bring to a simmer for another few minutes. Roughly crush the remaining chestnuts. Scatter over the soup.

MARIE & LÉON

alcohol? no. medicinal waters? yes!

*J*t's Sunday, it's 5.45 pm, Marie and Léon Vachecrot, cousins by marriage, have just spent Sunday lunch at the family home.

Marie, whose face increasingly resembles a field of poppies, is singing herself hoarse in an attempted solo performance of François Feldman's latest opus (no one knows his songs like she does). A couplet — a goblet, a song — a bottle. Given the album contains two songs and 10 remixes, we're well covered. As for Léon, he left the auditorium long ago to return to the couch. Peach *eau-de-vie*, apple, pear, apricot, there's never too many for Léon, who is determined to conduct a comparative test worthy of *50 Millions de Consommateurs* on the quality of the alcohols served. « *Five serves of fruit and vegetables a day, they say, jus' need one more and m'good.* » It's too early to expect our cousins to leave, dinner is clearly on the menu ...

29 sept

Meat (and vegetable) loaf

Serves 6

PREPARATION TIME 15 MINUTES
COOKING TIME 45 MINUTES

500 g (1 lb 2 oz) leftover cooked meat
200 g (7 oz) cooked vegetables
3 onions, peeled and sliced
200 ml (7 fl oz) pouring (whipping) cream
4 eggs
1 tablespoon coriander seeds
1 bunch of chives, snipped
salt and pepper

Preheat the oven to 160°C (315°F/Gas 2–3). The leg of lamb hasn't quite given up the ghost, the vegetables are still there, it's all processed with some onions, cream, eggs, coriander seeds to give it pep, and some chives. You put it in the oven for 45 minutes, with François Feldman as your soundtrack, Léon for the bass notes (the fourth serving of fruit got the better of him) — the cousins will be dining here, the beds are made up.

MARIE & LÉON

Russian roulette in the woods

The month of September is harvesting time in the Vachecrot household. The whole kitchen stands on alert to make the jams, the quince pastes, prepare the *crème de marrons* (sweetened chestnut purée), clean the mushrooms …

It is true that September is the pantry for the rest of the year: it marks the transition between abundance and calm. Nature has provided, now she will nap. There's no question of our family missing this annual rendezvous, the surrounding woods, fields and forests are expecting them. Marie equips herself with a wicker basket, Kevin with a milk canister, Léon a plastic bag, each has their own method, each their own habits.

Wearing their rubber boots, the Vachecrots set out on their crusade — the mushrooms had better watch out! « *Oh look how beautiful that one is, all red with white spots, just like Kevin at the peak of his adolescence … and that one, you'd think it was a cep but it's all Bordeaux red, like a bordello cushion under its cap … look at this mushroom, it's just got married with its big ring on its stem … that said, it doesn't look all that healthy with its greenish tinge … »*The hunt for mushrooms quickly takes on elements of a game of Russian roulette, the slim pickings have an air of danger about them. You can't cut corners with a mushroom, it must be respected. After a visit to the local pharmacy, the mushrooms are in the bin, Marie still has her basketful of pears: « *We'll make a cake, that's good too.* » Kevin and his canister on his arm: « *Marcel's milk is the best after all.* » Léon and his plastic bag: « *I love* L'Équipe du Dimanche, *I also bought* Chromes et Flammes. » The Vachecrots are back home, alive, the pear flan is cooking in the kitchen, phew, they're saved.

30 sept

Pear flan

Serves 6

PREPARATION TIME 10 MINUTES
COOKING TIME 40 MINUTES

4 Conference, Beurre bosc or William pears
1 tablespoon cornflour (cornstarch)
300 ml (10½ fl oz) full-cream (whole) milk
4 eggs
150 g (5½ oz) sugar
300 ml (10½ fl oz) pouring (whipping) cream
1 tablespoon sultanas (golden raisins)
1 tablespoon flaked almonds

Preheat the oven to 160°C (315°F/Gas 2–3). Peel the pears, cut them into wedges, remove the core. Blend the cornflour in a little of the milk. Beat the eggs with the sugar, add the remaining milk, the cream and cornflour paste. Pour the mixture into a round cake tin, arrange the pears in a rosetta pattern, scatter with the sultanas and flaked almonds. Bake in the oven for 40 minutes.

October

the greengrocer

PUMPKINS (WINTER SQUASH)
CARROTS
CELERY
LEEKS
ONIONS
CEP (PORCINI) MUSHROOMS
MUSHROOMS
HERBS AND SPICES
REINETTE APPLES
DRIED FRUIT AND NUTS
BANANAS
DRIED FIGS

the fishmonger

COCKLES
ALBACORE TUNA LOIN
BREAM

the butcher-deli

BOAR
VENISON
PHEASANT
CHICKEN
LAMB SHOULDER
STEWING BEEF
BEEF CHEEKS
SHIN OF VEAL
SMOKED PORK SHOULDER
RACK OF PORK
VEAL ROAST
FATTENED DUCK
SPICY CHORIZO
SMOKED PORK BELLY
AIR-DRIED DUCK BREAST

the cheese-seller

PARMESAN CHEESE

the grocer

SNAILS
ARBORIO RICE
TOMATO PASTE
(CONCENTRATED PURÉE)
SWEETENED CHESTNUT PURÉE

01 Rémi
BOAR IN WHITE WINE

02 Léger
PHEASANT SALMIS

03 Gérard
SHREDDED VENISON

08 Pélagie
TARTE TATIN

09 Denis
LAMB CURRY

10 Ghislain
PUMPKIN SOUP

15 Thérèse
CARAMEL FONDANT CAKE

16 Hedwige
SOUFFLÉ OMELETTE

17 Ignace
BŒUF BOURGUIGNONNE

22 Élodie
SNAILS IN TOMATO SAUCE

23 Arnould
SMOKED PORK SHOULDER
WITH LEEKS

24 Florentin
HOKKAIDO PUMPKIN RISOTTO

29 Narcisse
LAST OF THE
CHEESE PLATTER QUICHE

30 Bienvenue
VEAL STEAKS
WITH ANCHOVIES

31 Quentin
DIY DUCK CONFIT

04
Fanny

PENNE AND DUCK SALAD

05
Faustine

COCKLES WITH
BROWN BUTTER

06
Bruno

CEP MUSHROOM RISOTTO

07
Serge

CHICKEN IN CREAM AND
SHALLOT SAUCE

11
Firmin

BEEF WITH CARROTS

12
Wilfried

SEARED TUNA

13
Géraud

BAKED APPLES

14
Céleste

OSSO BUCO

18
Luc

PARIS-BREST

19
Renée

ROAST TUNA

20
Adeline

VEAL WITH PUMPKIN

21
Céline

CHESTNUT CRÈME BRÛLÉE

25
Daria

RACK OF PORK

26
Dimitri

BREAM CARPACCIO WITH LIME

27
Émeline

FRENCH APPLE TART

28
Simon

CAESAR SALAD

01 02 03 04

MARIE & LÉON

bang!

*J*n October, animals of all colours watch their backs as the hunting season begins.

It's in the South-West that our friends the Vachecrots are invited into a *palombière* — a pigeon hide — at Pierrette and Claude's place, in order to study the region's hunting know-how.

They approach stealthily through the forest. Silence is an ally of the hunter, a light hidden in a tree gives the go-ahead, the hide and its bracken corridors opens its doors. It's a giant cubby for big children, the rifle has replaced the cork gun, the cordial has a higher proof. The atmosphere, with the stove bubbling and boar simmering, promises a special day. A little Bordeaux to relax and help along with the assimilation process, some boar sausage by way of an *amuse-bouche*, muzzles all around and they're open for business.

« *Go on Marie, go up to the lookout, so you understand what hunting means round here.* »

Settled into a tawny moleskin seat, a brand-new camouflage bucket hat on her head, Marie listens attentively to today's lesson, provided by the most local of the group. « *So, you pull the strrrhing, rhourhou, that brrrhings them over, rhourhou, the rrhed one is forrh the top pine, the plank moves, the pigeon flaps its wings, it attrrracts the others and then, crrrhac!! The blue one forrh the bottom one, shhh, rrhouurhou …* » The pigeon impression is as enjoyable as a Jacques Audiard dialogue, it's a real performance, cinemascope-style.

Sausage, Bordeaux, game stew, songs, the silence has given in to the atmosphere, the only cadavers are the dead bottles, the pigeon is laughing, the rifle is clean.

01 oct

Boar in white wine

Serves 6

PREPARATION TIME 30 MINUTES
MARINATING TIME 24 HOURS
COOKING TIME 1 HOUR 50 MINUTES

*1.2 kg (2 lb 10 oz) boneless boar shoulder**
6 carrots
6 onions
4 garlic cloves
1 litre (35 fl oz/4 cups) white wine
2 tablespoons rum
1 tablespoon juniper berries
1 bouquet garni
3 tablespoons balsamic vinegar
200 g (7 oz) speck, cut into lardons
1 tablespoon plain (all-purpose) flour
300 ml (10½ fl oz) veal stock
50 g (1¾ oz) butter

Preheat the oven to 180°C (350°F/Gas 4). Cut the boar into 50 g (1¾ oz) pieces. Slice the carrots into rounds, peel and slice the onions and crush the garlic. Place all these ingredients into a large pot, add the white wine, rum, crushed juniper berries, bouquet garni and balsamic vinegar. Keep in the refrigerator for 24 hours. Remove the meat from the marinade. Sauté the speck in a large frying pan for 5 minutes. Add the pieces of boar, sauté them for 5 minutes. Place the boar and speck in a flameproof casserole dish, heat again, add the flour and cook for 5 minutes. Finally add the marinade and the veal stock, season. Cover, cook in the oven for about 90 minutes**. Take the casserole dish out of the oven, add the butter to the sauce and bring to the boil.

✽WHAT DOES BOAR TASTE LIKE? *Boar has quite a strong flavour, it's flesh is firm and dark red.*

✽✽HOW DO YOU KNOW WHEN THE MEAT IS COOKED? *Insert a knife into the meat, it shouldn't meet any resistance.*

02 oct

Pheasant salmis*

Serves 6

PREPARATION TIME 20 MINUTES
COOKING TIME 1 HOUR

2 pheasants (real ones, who have been
  flying since birth)
150 g (5½ oz) butter
salt and pepper
2 carrots
4 onions
3 leeks, white part only
1 tablespoon plain (all-purpose) flour
300 ml (10½ fl oz) red wine
2 tablespoons Cognac
200 ml (7 fl oz) chicken stock
1 bouquet garni

✱WHAT DOES
SALMIS MEAN?
*A salmis is a dish
of poultry or game
served with a red
wine sauce.*

Preheat the oven to 180°C (350°F/Gas 4).
Clean the pheasants**, set aside the liver and
heart. Rub the flesh with 20 g (¾ oz) of the
butter and season. Bake in a flameproof
casserole dish for 20 minutes. Peel and finely
dice the carrot and onion. Cut the leeks in
half, rinse. Detach the thighs, wings and breast
of the pheasants, crush the carcasses***. Melt
50 g (1¾ oz) of the butter in the casserole dish,
then add the flour and cook for 2 minutes.
Deglaze with the wine, Cognac and stock. Add
the carcasses, livers and hearts, vegetables and
bouquet garni. Let this simmer for 30 minutes
over low heat and season. Add the remaining
pieces of pheasant and remaining butter, then
bring to the boil.

✱✱CLEAN
THE PHEASANT:
*Reach right inside
to pull out the lungs.*

✱✱✱
How? *By pounding
them with a rolling
pin.*

03 oct

Shredded venison

Serves 6

PREPARATION TIME 1 HOUR
COOKING TIME 2 HOURS 15 MINUTES

6 carrots
3 celery stalks
4 garlic cloves
4 French shallots (eschalots)
*1 kg (2 lb 4 oz) boneless venison shoulder**
50 g (1¾ oz) butter
100 g (3½ oz) slices bacon, chopped
100 ml (3½ fl oz) Cognac
1 tablespoon plain (all-purpose) flour
1 bay leaf
500 ml (17 fl oz/2 cups) veal stock
mashed potato

✱WHERE CAN
I GET VENISON
IF I DON'T HAVE A
HUNTING PERMIT?
*All good butchers
carry game in season.
Ideally, acquire a
hunting friend and
offer him dinner in
exchange for a piece
of venison.*

Peel the carrots, slice them into rounds,
slice the celery with its leaves. Peel and
roughly chop the garlic and the shallots.
Cut the venison into small pieces. Sauté the
venison in the butter with the bacon, garlic
and shallots, and flambé with the cognac.
Add the flour, bay leaf and cook for a further
5 minutes. Moisten the venison with the
veal stock, add the carrots and celery, cook
over low heat for 2 hours, covered, stirring
regularly. At serving time, season and roughly
break up the pieces with a fork. Serve with
a mashed potato.

04 oct

Penne and duck salad

Serves 6

PREPARATION TIME 10 MINUTES
COOKING TIME 10 MINUTES

300 g (10½ oz) penne rigate
1 bulb spring onion (scallion)
1 bunch of radishes
150 g (5½ oz) air-dried duck breast
3 tablespoons Viandox or veal jus*
100 ml (3½ fl oz) olive oil
salt and pepper

✱ISN'T VIANDOX
A BIT OF A HAS-
BEEN INGREDIENT?
*This sauce, based on
meat extracts, was
commonly consumed
at pre-war counters.
It has moved out of
the bistro and into
the kitchen. It is
to gastronomy what
Raoul Vachecrot
is to French football!*

Cook the penne in a large volume of boiling
salted water for about 10 minutes; refresh.
Peel and thinly slice the spring onion,
including the green stem. Cut the radishes
into rounds. Cut the duck breast into cubes.
Combine the Viandox with the olive oil. Mix
all the ingredients together and season (careful,
as the Viandox is already salty).

05 oct

Cockles with brown butter

Serves 6

SOAKING TIME 1 NIGHT
PREPARATION TIME 20 MINUTES
COOKING TIME 5 MINUTES

1 kg (2 lb 4 oz) cockles* or baby clams (vongole)
1 French shallot (eschalot)
100 ml (3½ fl oz) white wine
juice of 1 lemon
100 g (3½ oz) cold butter

Rinse the cockles well so they release their water**. Peel and finely chop the shallot. Put the white wine, shallot and lemon juice in a saucepan. Bring to the boil, allow to cook until the liquid has completely evaporated. Add 2 tablespoons cold water, then whisk in the cold butter over a high heat: the texture should be smooth and creamy and the butter completely melted. Steam the cockles in another saucepan over gentle heat, turning them over regularly for about 5 minutes. Pour over the brown butter just before serving.

✱WHAT SEASON? *The cold period is best, but you can find them all year round.*

✱✱RINSE AND PURGE? *Cockles are often very sandy. Ideally, soak overnight in salted water.*

06 oct

Cep mushroom risotto

Serves 6

PREPARATION TIME 15 MINUTES
COOKING TIME 30 MINUTES

200 g (7 oz) fresh cep (porcini) mushrooms*
2 French shallots (eschalots)
80 ml (2½ fl oz/⅓ cup) olive oil
300 g (10½ oz) arborio rice**
200 ml (7 fl oz) white wine
300 ml (10½ fl oz) chicken stock
50 g (1¾ oz) parmesan cheese
salt and pepper
½ bunch of tarragon, leaves picked

brown cap

ivory stem

no   yes

Clean the cep mushrooms using a damp cloth, cut them into small cubes. Peel and slice the shallots. Sauté the mushrooms and shallots in a saucepan for 5 minutes in the olive oil, add the rice, sauté until pearly. Moisten with the white wine, cook on a low heat for 20 minutes, moistening regularly with the chicken stock. Add the roughly chopped parmesan when serving. Season and scatter with the tarragon leaves.

✱ HOW DO I FIND GOOD CEP MUSHROOMS? *They have an initial spurt in June and return in autumn. Choose them firm, small, with an ivory stem and a good brown cap.*

✱✱ARBORIO RICE? *It's a rice with large round grains. High in starch, it holds up perfectly in long cooking: perfect for risotto.*

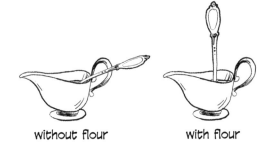

without flour   with flour

07 oct

Chicken in cream and shallot sauce

Serves 6

PREPARATION TIME 20 MINUTES
COOKING TIME 50 MINUTES

1 free-range chicken
6 garlic cloves
6 French shallots (eschalots)
50 g (1¾ oz) butter
1 tablespoon plain (all-purpose) flour
250 ml (9 fl oz/1 cup) white Port
1 bouquet garni
2 sprigs of rosemary
400 ml (14 fl oz) pouring (whipping) cream
12 cherry tomatoes
salt and pepper

Have the butcher cut the chicken into eight portions: thighs, drumsticks, breasts and wings. Peel the garlic and shallots, and cut them in half. Melt the butter in a flameproof casserole dish and sauté the chicken, shallots and garlic for 5 minutes, then add the flour*. Add the Port, bouquet garni and rosemary and cook, covered, for 30 minutes. Add the cream and cherry tomatoes, cook for a further 15 minutes, then season.

✱WHAT'S THE FLOUR FOR? *The flour will act to bind the sauce.*

MARIE & LÉON

upside down, right side up

In the beginning, Marie Vachecrot, a very ordinary cook married to Léon, a lover of fine food, spent her time experimenting with how her kitchen worked along with all the utensils that lived in it.

It was a strange world, this kitchen — for Marie, everything in it took on a strange and hostile air. The potato-masher had the look of a third-generation computer, the vegetable-cutter was transformed into a sophisticated combat weapon. « *You'd need at least a graduate degree in political science or business to run that sphere,* » she thought. Not put off by such ignorance, she threw herself into making an apple tart, her darling husband's favourite dessert.

But as things would have it, the recipe was read backwards and the pastry found itself on top of the apples ... Never mind, a session in the oven won't go to waste, it's turned out straight away – a matter of covering up the blunder — the apple's on top again, the tart is rather pretty, the error's corrected ... and it's with undisguised pride that Marie emerges from her kitchen, proclaiming, like a drumroll in battle mode, « *TA TA TATIN, here's dessert!* »

The tart was a hit with the crowd around the table, to the great surprise of all involved. A disreputable cousin appropriated the recipe (which Marie was obviously unable to reproduce) for herself, nicknamed it *Tatin* and thus a culinary legend was born. The truth has now been restored.

And that is how Marie, destined to the anonymity of her kitchen, became the Marie who went down in history.

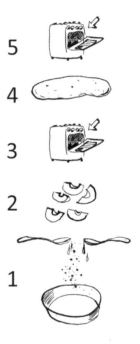

08 oct

Tarte Tatin
Serves 6

PREPARATION TIME 20 MINUTES
COOKING TIME 30 MINUTES

150 g (5½ oz) sugar
100 g (3½ oz) butter
1 kg (2 lb 4 oz) Reinette or Golden delicious apples, peeled and halved
200 g (7 oz) store-bought butter puff pastry

Preheat the oven to 180°C (350°F/Gas 4). Put the sugar in a flameproof round cake tin with 2 tablespoons water. Put the tin over gentle heat, add the butter and stir to make a light caramel*. Arrange the apple halves, round side down, on top of the caramel, packing them tightly as they tend to shrink during cooking. Bake for 15 minutes. Roll the pastry into a circle, about 5 cm (2 inches) wider than the tin. Cover the apples with the pastry, bake for a further 15 minutes. As soon as it comes out of the oven, turn the tart over to unstick the apples and turn out**.

 ✱MAKE A LIGHT CARAMEL? *Cook the sugar until it turns a beautiful light golden brown.*

✱✱IT WON'T STICK? *To avoid it sticking, turn out the tart before it cools down.*

09 oct

Lamb curry

Serves 6

PREPARATION TIME 20 MINUTES
COOKING TIME 1 HOUR 45 MINUTES

1.2 kg (2 lb 10 oz) boneless lamb shoulder
4 onions
6 garlic cloves
4 tomatoes
6 carrots
50 g (1¾ oz) butter
1 tablespoon plain (all-purpose) flour
2 tablespoons curry powder
1 bouquet garni
50 g (1¾ oz/⅓ cup) cashew nuts
50 g (1¾ oz/⅓ cup) almonds
50 g (1¾ oz/⅓ cup) pistachio nuts
6 dried figs
½ bunch of coriander (cilantro),
    leaves picked and roughly chopped
200 ml (7 fl oz) pouring (whipping) cream
200 ml (7 fl oz) coconut milk
salt and pepper
2 bananas

✳How? *Trim the fat from the shoulder with a knife.*

✳✳Curdles? *The cream can tend to split: a whizz with a hand-held blender et voilà, no one's the wiser.*

✳✳✳ WHY SLICE IT INTO ROUNDS? *It will present better on the plate.*

Trim the excess fat from the lamb*, cut into large cubes. Peel and roughly chop the onions and garlic. Dice the tomatoes. Peel the carrots, cut them into sticks. Sauté the pieces of lamb in the butter with the onions and garlic for 5 minutes, add the flour, cook for a further 5 minutes. Add 1 litre (35 fl oz/4 cups) water, the tomatoes, curry powder and bouquet garni, cover and cook over low heat for 1 hour. Add the nuts, dried figs, carrots, coriander, cream and coconut milk, and cook, uncovered, for 30 minutes. Season. If the sauce curdles**, take out the meat and dried fruit and nuts, and whizz with a stick blender. Just before serving add the banana, sliced into rounds***.

10 oct

Pumpkin soup

Serves 6

PREPARATION TIME 20 MINUTES
COOKING TIME 30 MINUTES

1.2 kg (2 lb 10 oz) pumpkin (winter squash)
3 onions
2 tablespoons sugar
100 g (3½ oz) butter, cubed
salt and pepper
125 g (4½ oz/½ cup) sour cream

Peel the pumpkin and cut it into large cubes. Peel and slice the onions. Place the pieces of pumpkin with the onions in a saucepan, cover with water, add the sugar, cook, covered, for 30 minutes. Add the butter, purée and season. Serve with a spoonful of sour cream.

11 oct

Beef with carrots

Serves 6

PREPARATION TIME 20 MINUTES
COOKING TIME 3 HOURS

1.2 kg (2 lb 10 oz) beef cheeks
3 onions
3 celery stalks
1 kg (2 lb 4 oz) carrots
50 g (1¾ oz) butter
1 teaspoon ground cumin
1 tablespoon plain (all-purpose) flour
500 ml (17 fl oz/2 cups) white wine
500 ml (17 fl oz/2 cups) beef stock
1 bouquet garni
salt and pepper

✳WHAT'S SPECIAL ABOUT THE CHEEK? *The cheek is a very fibrous cut of beef, it is very tender and has the perfect amount of fat.*

✳✳WHY ADD THE CARROTS AFTER 2 HOURS? *They'll only cook for an hour and won't turn into mush.*

Trim the excess fat from the beef cheeks* and cut them in half. Peel and slice the onions. Finely slice the celery. Peel the carrots and cut them into sticks. Sauté the beef cheeks in butter in a flameproof casserole dish with the onions, celery and cumin for 10 minutes. Add the flour, cook for a further 5 minutes, pour over the white wine and beef stock, add the bouquet garni and cover. Cook for 2 hours over a gentle heat. Next add the carrot sticks**, cook for a further 1 hour, then season.

'Only the fisherman is proud to reel in a tuna, the others will never mention it.'

12 oct

Seared tuna

Serves 6

PREPARATION TIME 20 MINUTES
COOKING TIME 5 MINUTES

4 garlic cloves
1 tablespoon almonds
50 g (1¾ oz) spicy chorizo
2 tomatoes
3 bulb spring onions (scallions)
600 g (1 lb 5 oz) albacore tuna loin
100 ml (3½ fl oz) olive oil
salt and pepper

✱How SHOULD THE TUNA BE WHEN IT IS COOKED CORRECTLY? *Tuna becomes dry as it cooks. The most suitable is to cook it bleu (still raw in the middle).*

Peel the garlic, slice it with the almonds. Cut the chorizo and tomatoes into cubes, slice the spring onions. Brown the tuna in olive oil on all sides, 1 minute per side*. Remove the tuna from the pan, sauté the chorizo in the same pan with the spring onions, garlic and almonds, add the diced tomato at the end, season. Slice the tuna and place a spoonful of the chorizo mixture on top of the tuna.

13 oct

Baked apples

Serves 6

PREPARATION TIME 10 MINUTES
COOKING TIME 30 MINUTES

6 Reinette*, Golden delicious or Granny smith apples
80 g (2¾ oz) butter
3 tablespoons honey
2 tablespoons Calvados (apple brandy)
2 tablespoons black cherry jam
100 g (3½ oz/1 cup) flaked almonds

✱WHY REINETTES IN PARTICULAR? *It's a variety of apple with lots of flavour which holds up well to cooking.*

Preheat the oven to 180°C (350°F/Gas 4). Peel the apples, remove the core using an apple-corer. Cut the butter into six pieces and fill each apple with a piece. Combine the honey with the Calvados, pour this mixture over the apples, bake for 20 minutes, basting the apples regularly with the cooking juices. Spread the apples with the cherry jam and scatter over the flaked almonds. Bake for another 10 minutes.

14 oct

Osso buco

Serves 6

PREPARATION TIME 20 MINUTES
COOKING TIME 1 HOUR 10 MINUTES

6 onions
2 garlic cloves
6 good slices veal shin (osso buco)
olive oil
500 ml (17 fl oz/2 cups) white wine
3 carrots
6 tomatoes
1 bay leaf
2 tablespoons tomato sauce (ketchup)
1 teaspoon ground cumin
1 tablespoon tomato paste (concentrated purée)
salt and pepper
1 bunch of flat-leaf (Italian) parsley,
   leaves picked and chopped

✱ THE TECHNIQUE: *Crush the garlic with the flat side of a knife.*

✱✱ HOW DO I KNOW WHEN IT'S WELL COOKED? *The meat is properly cooked when it comes away from the bone.*

Peel and slice the onions and crush the garlic*. In a large flameproof casserole dish, sauté the veal in olive oil, add the onions and garlic, deglaze with the white wine. Slice the carrots into rounds, cut the tomatoes into wedges, add these to the casserole dish with the bay leaf, tomato sauce, cumin and tomato paste, then season. Cover, simmer for 1 hour over low heat, check the meat for doneness**. Cook a bit longer if necessary. Serve scattered with the chopped parsley leaves.

> **'Bœuf Bourguignonne is the extra gene of French cuisine, it is something one is born with.'**

without flour   with flour

15 oct

Caramel fondant cake

Serves 6

PREPARATION TIME 10 MINUTES
COOKING TIME 15 MINUTES

150 g (5½ oz) sugar
100 g (3½ oz) lightly salted butter
80 ml (2½ fl oz/⅓ cup) pouring (whipping) cream
4 eggs, beaten
140 g (5 oz) plain (all-purpose) flour
Equipment:
6 small ramekins

Preheat the oven to 180°C (350°F/Gas 4). Place the sugar in a saucepan with 60 ml (2 fl oz/¼ cup) water, caramelise it while stirring. Add the butter and cream, cook for 5 minutes. Cool to lukewarm, add the egg and the sifted flour. Butter and flour the ramekins, fill them with the caramel mixture. Bake for 7 minutes*, then unmould immediately.

✱THE IDEAL SEMI-COOKED STATE? *The top should barely resist when touched.*

16 oct

Soufflé omelette

Serves 6

PREPARATION TIME 10 MINUTES
COOKING TIME 10 MINUTES

1 bunch of chives
8 eggs
1 dash ground nutmeg
salt and pepper
olive oil

Preheat the oven to 180°C (350°F/Gas 4). Snip the chives. Break the eggs, whip them with a beater* for about 10 minutes, add the chives and nutmeg, then season. Heat the olive oil in a frying pan, and pour in the omelette. Put the pan in the oven** for 5–7 minutes. Serve immediately.

✱WHY WHIP THE EGGS? *The omelette will puff up in the oven.*

✱✱ PUT THE FRYING PAN IN THE OVEN? *Only if it's a cast-iron one! Otherwise you can use a tart tin.*

17 oct

Bœuf Bourguignonne

Serves 6

PREPARATION TIME 20 MINUTES
COOKING TIME 3 HOURS 10 MINUTES

200 g (7 oz) speck
3 onions
4 garlic cloves
1.2 kg (2 lb 10 oz) boneless beef shoulder
50 g (1¾ oz) butter
1 tablespoon plain (all-purpose) flour
500 ml (17 fl oz/2 cups) Rhône wine or other red wine
500 ml (17 fl oz/2 cups) veal stock
1 bouquet garni
1 sprig of rosemary
300 g (10½ oz) fresh mushrooms
salt and pepper

Preheat the oven to 160°C (315°F/Gas 2–3). Cut the speck into chunks. Peel and slice the onions. Peel and crush the garlic. Cut the beef into 60 g (2¼ oz) pieces. In a flameproof casserole dish, braise the pieces of beef in butter with the speck, garlic and onions for 5 minutes. Add the flour* cook for a further 5 minutes, pour in the wine and the veal stock, add the bouquet garni and rosemary. Cover and cook in the oven for 2 hours. Next, add the mushrooms, cover again, return to the oven for 1 hour: the meat should be very tender. Season before serving.

✱WHY IS FLOUR ADDED? *It will act to bind the sauce.*

MARIE & LÉON

Paris to Brest, 580 km

In the beginning, Marie Vachecrot, a very ordinary cook not yet married to Léon, lover of fine food, spent her time dreaming of her handsome Apollo.

It is true that Marie, a Parisian by adoption, saw her Léon, a confirmed native of Brest, only too little. The postal service of the time was slow to deliver the two suitors' impassioned letters. They wished each other a Happy New Year at Easter, they told their tales of summer at Christmas. Their news was as fresh as a fishmonger's stall at closing time on 15th August.

Marie could bear it no longer, love gnawed at her soul, Léon was her truth, Brest her destiny.

A bicycle, calves that would put the planet's support hose to shame, three spare inner tubes, and Marie is ready to pedal and be reunited with the object of her desire. « *Watch out, Léon, I'm coming!!* » A few pumps of the pedals later and Brest held out its arms to her, the object of her desire became the object of her pleasure, Paris–Brest had got the better of her impatience.

The union of the two lovers was consecrated with a pastry in the shape of a wreath (a worthy homage to the state of Marie's bicycle's wheels after her mad adventure), and baptised a *Paris-Brest*.

And that is how Marie, destined to the anonymity of her kitchen, became the Marie who went down in history.

✱ How do I know when the sugar is ready? *The sugar is ready when it forms threads on the end of a fork.*

18 oct

Paris-Brest

Serves 6

PREPARATION TIME 30 MINUTES
COOKING TIME 20 MINUTES

400 g (14 oz) choux pastry (see page 210, 14 May)
1 egg yolk
50 g (1¾ oz/½ cup) flaked almonds
icing (confectioners') sugar
For the nougatine:
100 g (3½ oz) sugar
50 g (1¾ oz/½ cup) flaked almonds
For the praline crème pâtissière:
150 g (5½ oz/⅔ cup) sugar
8 egg yolks
150 g (5½ oz) butter, softened
100 g (3½ oz) praline paste
Equipment:
piping (icing) bag

Preheat the oven to 180°C (350°F/Gas 4). Using a piping (icing) bag, make a ring of the choux pastry on a baking tray lined with baking paper. Brush with egg yolk, scatter over the flaked almonds, bake for 20 minutes. Take the pastry ring out of the oven and allow to cool. Cut the ring in half horizontally.
For the nougatine, make a caramel with the sugar and 2 teaspoons water, then add the flaked almonds. Oil a sheet of baking paper. Pour the nougatine onto the paper and cool. To make the crème pâtissière, cook the sugar with 3 tablespoons water*. Whisk the egg yolks, adding the cooked sugar little by little and keep whisking until it has completely cooled. Add the softened butter and praline paste.
Pipe the praline cream on one half of the pastry ring using a piping bag, arrange pieces of nougatine on top, top with the other half of the pastry ring and dust with icing sugar.

19
october

ROAST TUNA

19 oct

Roast tuna

Serves 6

PREPARATION TIME 20 MINUTES
CHILLING TIME 12 HOURS
COOKING TIME 25 MINUTES

1 orange
1 teaspoon ground cardamom
800 g (1 lb 12 oz) yellowfin tuna fillet
  (it's a species that's less endangered than bluefin!!)
300 g (10½ oz) celery
3 onions
100 ml (3½ fl oz) olive oil
300 g (10½ oz) peeled chestnuts
salt and pepper

The day before, juice and zest the orange, mix both with the cardamom and rub the tuna fillet with this mixture, wrap in plastic wrap and chill for 12 hours. Preheat the oven to 180°C (350°F/Gas 4). Remove the celery fibres*, cut into short lengths. Peel and slice the onions. Sauté them in the olive oil for 5 minutes, add the celery and chestnuts and cook for about 5 minutes. Place the tuna in a baking dish, surround with the vegetables and chestnuts, bake in the oven for 10–15 minutes, then season.

✳ REMOVE THE CELERY FIBRES?
Using a knife, pull away the fibres, that way the celery will be more tender.

21 oct

Chestnut crème brûlée

Serves 6

PREPARATION TIME 10 MINUTES
COOKING TIME 45 MINUTES

8 egg yolks
150 g (5½ oz/firmly packed ⅔ cup) soft brown sugar
800 ml (28 fl oz) pouring (whipping) cream
150 g (5½ oz) sweetened chestnut purée
Equipment:
6 small ramekins

Preheat the oven to 120°C (235°F/Gas ½). Whisk the yolks with 100 g (3½ oz/½ cup) of the sugar*, then add the cream and chestnut purée. Pour this custard into the ramekins, cook in a bain-marie for 45 minutes. Allow to cool and sprinkle with the remaining sugar. Scorch the top with a kitchen blowtorch and serve immediately.

✳ WHY SOFT BROWN SUGAR?
For its quite particular taste.

20 oct

Veal with pumpkin

Serves 6

PREPARATION TIME 20 MINUTES
COOKING TIME 1 HOUR 10 MINUTES

4 onions
1.2 kg (2 lb 10 oz) veal roast
120 g (4¼ oz) butter
1 tablespoon herbes de Provence *(Provençal herb mix)*
1 teaspoon coriander seeds
1 bay leaf
250 ml (9 fl oz/1 cup) white wine
salt and pepper
400 g (14 oz) Hokkaido or Jap pumpkin (winter squash)

Preheat the oven to 180°C (350°F/Gas 4). Peel and slice the onions. Brown the veal roast in 40 g (1½ oz) of the butter in a flameproof casserole dish. Add the onion, *herbes de Provence*, coriander seeds and bay leaf. Moisten with a little of the white wine, cover and cook in the oven for 30 minutes, basting regularly with the rest of the wine. Season. Cut the pumpkin into wedges, keeping the skin. Arrange them around the roast, cover again and return to the oven for 30 minutes, basting frequently. Transfer the roast to a serving dish, cover with foil and set aside for 5 minutes to rest. Arrange the pumpkin and onions around the veal. Add the remaining butter to the cooking juices and bring to the boil, whisking well*.

✳ BRING TO THE BOIL AND WHISK?
To emulsify the sauce with the butter: it will take on a creamy consistency.

'The snail is nature's Narcissus. Wherever it goes it can't help leaving its mark.'

22 oct

Snails in tomato sauce

Serves 6
PREPARATION TIME 10 MINUTES
COOKING TIME 10 MINUTES

3 tomatoes
3 onions
6 garlic cloves
1 bunch of tarragon
1 leek
100 g (3½ oz) butter
36 large tinned Burgundy snails (Helix pomatia)
250 ml (9 fl oz/1 cup) white wine
1 tablespoon of pastis
salt and pepper

Blanch and peel the tomatoes, chop the flesh. Peel and slice the onions and garlic. Pick off the tarragon leaves, slice the white part and a third of the green part* of the leek. Gently sauté the onion, leek and garlic in 50 g (1¾ oz) of the butter. Add the snails, moisten with the white wine and pastis. Cook gently for 10 minutes, add the diced tomatoes, the remaining butter and tarragon leaves, bring to the boil, then season.

✳ WHAT DOES THE GREEN PART ADD? *The green part adds colour and texture because it is tougher than the white part.*

23 oct

Smoked pork shoulder with leeks

Serves 6
PREPARATION TIME 20 MINUTES
COOKING TIME 1 HOUR 35 MINUTES

6 leeks
1 smoked pork shoulder (butt-end)
1 onion studded with 3 cloves
1 bouquet garni
50 g (1¾ oz) butter
50 g (1¾ oz/⅓ cup) plain (all-purpose) flour
200 ml (7 fl oz) pouring (whipping) cream
1 tablespoon grated horseradish
salt and pepper
breadcrumbs

horseradish

Preheat the oven to 180°C (350°F/Gas 4). Cut the leeks in half, rinse them well in plenty of water. Cook the smoked pork shoulder in a large volume of water* with the clove-studded onion and the bouquet garni. Add the leeks and cook for 75 minutes. Remove the meat from the broth, cut it into slices, lay the slices in a gratin dish. Melt the butter in a saucepan, add the flour. Cook for 2 minutes, then add 300 ml (10½ fl oz) of the cooking liquid, reduce for 5 minutes, add the cream and the horseradish, then season. Cover the slices of pork with cooked leeks, pour over the horseradish cream, sprinkle with breadcrumbs. Bake in the oven for 10 minutes.

✳ WHAT IS THE ADVANTAGE OF COOKING THIS WAY? *The pork will stay very moist and tender.*

24 oct

Hokkaido pumpkin risotto

Serves 6
PREPARATION TIME 10 MINUTES
COOKING TIME 25 MINUTES

3 French shallots (eschalots)
200 g (7 oz) Hokkaido or Jap pumpkin (winter squash)
80 ml (2½ fl oz/⅓ cup) olive oil
300 g (10½ oz/1⅓ cups) arborio rice
200 ml (7 fl oz) white wine
300 ml (10½ fl oz) vegetable stock
50 g (1¾ oz) parmesan cheese
salt and pepper

Peel and finely slice the shallots. Cut the pumpkin into small cubes*. Sauté the pumpkin and shallots in a saucepan in the olive oil for 5 minutes. Add the rice, sauté until it becomes pearly, then moisten with the white wine. Cook on a low heat for 20 minutes, moistening with the vegetable stock, add the parmesan, roughly chopped, then season.

✳ DO I NEED TO PEEL THE PUMPKIN? *No need to peel it, the skin becomes very tender when cooked.*

'A pig sleeps within every man, you can see it when he wakes up.'

25 oct — Rack of pork

Serves 6

PREPARATION TIME 10 MINUTES
COOKING TIME 2 HOURS 10 MINUTES

3 French shallots (eschalots)
1 rack of pork*
100 ml (3½ fl oz) olive oil
1 bunch of thyme
1 bunch of Dutch carrots
3 slightly thick slices speck
salt and pepper

Preheat the oven to 150°C (300°F/Gas 2). Peel the shallots, cut them in half. In a flameproof roasting tin, sauté the rack of pork* in the olive oil to brown it on all sides, then cook in the oven for 1 hour, covered in foil**, basting the rack and adding a little water as needed. Add the shallots, thyme, carrots and speck, cover again, and cook for a further 1 hour, basting regularly, season.

* WHAT IS A RACK OF PORK? *Four pork chops joined together.*

** WHY COVER IT? *It will cook more evenly.*

26 oct — Bream carpaccio with lime

Serves 6

PREPARATION TIME 20 MINUTES

6 whole bream, filleted
2 limes
3 tablespoons soy sauce
1 tablespoon fish sauce
3 tablespoons olive oil
2 bulb spring onions (scallions), sliced
12 mint leaves
fleur de sel and pepper

Remove the bones from the fish using a pair of tweezers. Slide the blade of a knife between the skin and the flesh of the fish. Slice the bream fillets as you would smoked salmon*, lay them on a plate. Zest 1 of the limes and juice both. Combine the lime juice with the soy sauce, fish sauce and olive oil, pour this dressing over the fillets. Scatter with spring onion rings, add some young mint leaves and lime zest, then season**.

* WHICH IS TO SAY? *In thin slices starting from the head end towards the tail.*

** WHEN SHOULD IT BE EATEN? *According to tastes, it can be eaten immediately or left to marinate.*

27 oct — French apple tart

Serves 6

PREPARATION TIME 20 MINUTES
COOKING TIME 20 MINUTES

100 g (3½ oz/lightly packed ½ cup) soft brown sugar
1 sheet store-bought butter puff pastry
6 granny smith apples
50 g (1¾ oz) medium-grain semolina
50 g (1¾ oz/½ cup) ground almonds
50 g (1¾ oz) butter

Preheat the oven to 180°C (350°F/Gas 4). Scatter 50 g (1¾ oz/¼ cup) of the brown sugar* over the pastry and cut into a round. Peel the apples, halve and core them. Slice the apples. Prick the pastry with a fork, sprinkle over the semolina** and ground almonds. Arrange the apples in a rosetta pattern. Melt the butter and brush it over the tart, sprinkle with the remaining sugar. Bake for 15 minutes, then brown under a hot grill (broiler) for a further 5 minutes. Allow the tart to cool so the caramel hardens.

* TO WHAT END? *To add a touch of caramel to the pastry.*

** WHAT'S THE SEMOLINA FOR? *For soaking up the excess apple juice, that way the pastry won't get soggy.*

28 oct

Cæsar salad

Serves 6

PREPARATION TIME 15 MINUTES

3 garlic cloves
3 free-range chicken breast fillets
250 ml (9 fl oz/1 cup) milk
⅓ baguette
125 ml (4 fl oz/½ cup) olive oil
24 tinned anchovies in oil
80 g (2¾ oz) shaved parmesan cheese
1 good-looking romaine (cos) lettuce (a Romaine
is generally always good-looking!), leaves separated

Peel and finely chop the garlic. Cut the chicken into thin strips. Poach the chicken* for 5 minutes in a saucepan with a glass of milk and 300 ml (10½ fl oz) water. Cut the baguette into small cubes, combine it with the chopped garlic and 2 tablespoons of the olive oil. Put under the grill (broiler) for 5 minutes to toast the croûtons to a golden brown. Process half of the anchovies with half of the parmesan, the remaining olive oil and 3 tablespoons water. Dress the lettuce leaves with the vinaigrette. Top the salad with the croûtons, chicken, remaining parmesan and the anchovies.

✱WHY? *This way it will stay very white with a creamy texture.*

29 oct

Last of the cheese platter quiche

Serves 6

PREPARATION TIME 15 MINUTES
COOKING TIME 20 MINUTES

*200 g (7 oz) leftover cheese**
2 eggs
200 ml (7 fl oz) pouring (whipping) cream
1 dash ground nutmeg
1 sheet store-bought shortcrust pastry
50 g (1¾ oz/½ cup) walnut kernels

Preheat the oven to 180°C (350°F/Gas 4). Chop up the leftovers from the Sunday lunch cheese platter, the one that spent the afternoon on the table while you were sleeping peacefully in front of the television. Combine the eggs with the cream and nutmeg. Lay the shortcrust pastry in a tin, scatter with the cheese and walnuts, pour over the custard. Bake for 20 minutes.

✱WHAT COMBINATION OF CHEESES? *Combine different sorts: blue cheese with both hard and soft-rind cheeses.*

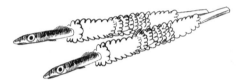

30 oct

Veal steaks with anchovies

Serves 6

PREPARATION TIME 20 MINUTES
COOKING TIME 15 MINUTES

6 x 185 g (6½ oz) veal steaks
24 tinned anchovies in oil
6 bulb spring onions (scallions)
6 garlic cloves, peeled
4 tomatoes
50 g (1¾ oz) chorizo
80 ml (2½ fl oz/⅓ cup) olive oil
1 handful of rocket (arugula) leaves
50 g (1¾ oz) butter
pepper

Using the point of a knife, stud the veal steaks with anchovies in three places*. Cut the spring onions into quarters, slice the garlic, and dice the tomatoes and chorizo. Heat the olive oil and sauté the spring onion, then add the garlic, chorizo, remaining anchovies and tomato. Cook for 5 minutes, then add the rocket, cook for a further 5 minutes. In a separate frying pan, fry the veal steaks in butter, keeping them rare, about 7–8 minutes. Serve the steaks surrounded by the vegetables. Don't season: the anchovies will already provide salt. Let people further season or not according to their own taste.

✱HOW DO YOU STUD VEAL WITH ANCHOVIES? *Use the point of a knife to make an incision, then insert the anchovy, pushing it well inside.*

MARIE & LÉON

there is a corner of France where happiness blooms

The South-West is putting on its show. *Magret* (duck) every which way and a trip to Auntie Louise's farm in Périgueux for the Vachecrots.

There's already something to eat for the littlest ones. « *They're too cute those baby ducklings waddling around in groups, she's like a killer whale moving through a school of fish.* » A nice metaphor for Auntie Louise! « *Look at the one that's all white with the black feathers in his tail, he's soooo cute, you could just pick him up and hug him, I love the country, it's so ... what's the word ... green ...* » Their older brothers have set themselves up a bit further away, near the pond. « *Look at it dive, all you can see are its flippers on the surface of the water, it's incredible, he comes up again straight away, it's so funny. Quick, take a photo, didn't I tell you we'd be in a different world here?* » The oldest ones are kept inside small enclosed spaces. « *Ah, they're not allowed to go out for three weeks ... and that long tube, Auntie Louise, that's to fatten them, you push it down into ... Don't stay here Kevin, go and play with the ducklings.* » A trip to the lab, white like an operating theatre. « *It's super clean Auntie, but what are you doing? Why are you putting the duck's head into that funnel, and what's that knife in your hand. Stop! Quick, close the door Léon, Kevin could come back. Poor animal, sniff! Do you think it suffered? Take a few feathers for Kevin, as a souvenir ...* »

Two hours later.

« *Your confit is so good Tata, and the stuffed neck, a pure joy, the magret was perfectly cooked, rare to perfection. Ah! The country, when you taste it, it's really something else!* »

31 oct

DIY duck confit
Serves 6

PREPARATION TIME 30 MINUTES
MARINATING TIME 24 HOURS
COOKING TIME 2 HOURS

✳ A DETACHED DUCK? *Cut up the duck to separate the thigh with the drumstick and the breast with the wing.*

✳✳ HOW SHOULD IT BE STORED? *In its fat and in the refrigerator, the duck pieces will keep for several months.*

1 fine fattened duck (or 6 duck thighs)
2 tablespoons coarse salt
2 tablespoons coarsely ground black pepper
2 tablespoons herbes de Provence (*Provençal herb mix*)
500 g (1 lb 2 oz) duck fat

Detach* the duck thighs and breasts, cover with coarse salt, pepper and *herbes de Provence*. Cover with plastic wrap and keep in the fridge for 24 hours. The next day, rinse the pieces of duck and wipe them dry with some paper towels. Heat the duck fat in a large saucepan, add the duck pieces, cook over gentle heat for 2 hours. Store the duck in its fat**.

This month

the greengrocer

HOKKAIDO PUMPKINS (WINTER SQUASH)

BEETROOT (BEETS)

CAULIFLOWER

POTATOES

APPLES

TOMATOES

CELERY

DILL

CARROTS

MUSHROOMS

TURNIPS

FENNEL

the fishmonger

SKATE

SALMON

SMALL CUTTLEFISH

the butcher-deli

CHICKEN

VEAL KIDNEYS

VEAL HEAD

ROASTING BEEF

PORK CHOPS

ROASTING PORK

GUINEA FOWL

PIGEON

BOUDIN NOIR (BLOOD SAUSAGE)

PORK SPARE-RIBS

PORK KNUCKLE

TOULOUSE SAUSAGES

MORTEAU SAUSAGES

DUCK CONFIT

MINCED BEEF

LAMB KNUCKLE

PROSCIUTTO

BEEF BLANKET TRIPE

LAMB NECK

the cheese-seller

COMTÉ CHEESE

the grocer

JUNIPER BERRIES

PUY (BLUE-GREEN) LENTILS

TARBAIS (WHITE) BEANS

November

01 Cassandre — PUMPKIN GRATIN

02 Solenn — CUTTLEFISH IN INK

03 Hubert — FAR BRETON

08 Geoffroy — BOUDIN NOIR WITH APPLES

09 Théodore — CARAMELISED SPARE-RIBS

10 Léon — CASSOULET

15 Albert — PROSCIUTTO BITES

16 Marguerite — SEMI-COOKED SALMON

17 Elisabeth — NEW TRIPE

22 Cécile — LACQUERED PORK KNUCKLES

23 Clément — CALF'S HEAD

24 Flora — WHOLE VEAL KIDNEYS

29 Saturnin — SALMON POT-AU-FEU

30 André — DIY RAVIOLI

01

04
Charles
ROAST BEEF WITH BEETROOT

05
Sylvie
PORK CHOPS IN
MUSTARD SAUCE

06
Bertille
GUINEA FOWL WITH
CAULIFLOWER

07
Karine
PIGEON TOASTS

11
Martin
BEEF TAGINE

12
Christian
CARROT SOUP

13
Brice
ŒUFS À LA NEIGE

14
Sidoine
LAMB KNUCKLES

18
Aude
ROAST PORK

19
Tanguy
EGGS MEURETTE

20
Edmond
MUTTON STEW

21
Gélase
SALT PORK WITH LENTILS

25
Catherine
CHICKEN POT-AU-FEU

26
Delphine
FRITAS PATATAS

27
Séverin
GRAVLAX

28
Jacquy
SKATE WITH CAPERBERRIES

02 03 04 05

MARIE & LÉON

allô, ouiiiii ...

*I*n the beginning, Marie Vachecrot, a very ordinary cook married to Léon, a lover of fine food, couldn't bear the period of the year around October–November, sad months when nothing happens.

The sunny weather is already long gone, Christmas is still far away. Time went past, she in front of her little screen watching film after film, he almost the same. What to do to cheer up this time of year? Television: it's habit-forming!

A fancy-dress party, now there's an idea for transforming the autumnal gloom. « *We need some colour, some dress-ups. We need some jokes, some laughs, some high spirits.* » « *You're off your gourd, my darling, how will you organise such a party, you'll have to turn off the TV!* » Regardless, motivated as if for a grand final *Belote* game, Marie rushed around decorating the house — pumpkins turned into lanterns, Marie dresses up as a witch. The invitations are sent out, the telephone starts ringing immediately, « *Allô oui, yes, the party is definitely on ... Allô oui, of course, I'd be glad to ... Allô oui, oh great, you're coming ...* » Léon got into the swing of it, the party was a success and the food was top quality — a choice of *tripe ou truite* (tripe or trout). To avoid wasting the leftover pumpkins, the next day they made gratin. Cousin Georges, who was there that evening, exported the event to America, where it really took off!

Halloween was born, with each year « *trick or treat!* »

And that is how Marie, destined to the anonymity of her kitchen, became the Marie who went down in history.

01 nov Pumpkin gratin

Serves 6
PREPARATION TIME 20 MINUTES
COOKING TIME 50 MINUTES

1.2 kg (2 lb 10 oz) Hokkaido or Jap pumpkin
  (winter squash)
3 onions
4 eggs
200 ml (7 fl oz) pouring (whipping) cream
1 teaspoon ground nutmeg
salt and pepper
1 tablespoon soft brown sugar

Preheat the oven to 180°C (350°F/Gas 4). Remove the pumpkin seeds*, cut it into small cubes. Peel and slice the onions, cook the pumpkin with the onions in a saucepan, covered with boiling water, for 30 minutes. Drain the pumpkin, purée it with the eggs and cream, add the nutmeg and season. Pour the pumpkin into a gratin dish, sprinkle with brown sugar. Bake for 20 minutes.

✱ PEEL IT? *The skin of the Hokkaido pumpkin gives the chestnut flavour of this variety, so above all, do not peel it.*

01
november

PUMPKIN GRATIN

02 nov

Cuttlefish in ink

Serves 6

PREPARATION TIME 30 MINUTES
COOKING TIME 45 MINUTES

1 kg (2 lb 4 oz) small cuttlefish
12 garlic cloves
3 tablespoons olive oil
500 ml (17 fl oz/2 cups) white wine
3 tablespoons cuttlefish ink*
300 ml (10½ fl oz) pouring (whipping) cream
pepper

✻ IS IT EASY TO FIND CUTTLEFISH INK? WHAT DOES IT ADD TO THE DISH? *You can easily find cuttlefish ink at the fishmonger's. It gives a dark colour and iodine flavour.*

Remove the beaks from the cuttlefish, keep the body and the tentacles. Peel and roughly chop the garlic cloves. Sauté the garlic in the olive oil for 5 minutes, add the cuttlefish, cook for 20 minutes. Deglaze with the white wine, add the ink, cook for a further 10 minutes. Add the cream and simmer for another 10 minutes. Season with the pepper.

03 nov

Far* Breton

Serves 6

PREPARATION TIME 10 MINUTES
SOAKING TIME 1 HOUR
COOKING TIME 1 HOUR

200 g (7 oz) pitted prunes
100 ml (3½ fl oz) rum
200 g (7 oz) sugar
5 eggs
250 g (9 oz/1⅔ cups) plain (all-purpose) flour
500 ml (17 fl oz/2 cups) full-cream (whole) milk
300 ml (10½ fl oz) pouring (whipping) cream

✻ WHERE DOES THE NAME FAR COME FROM? *Originally the far was a sort of porridge made from buckwheat flour, a typically Breton dish. Today the far is associated with a cake containing prunes or raisins.*

Preheat the oven to 180°C (350°F/Gas 4). Soak the prunes in hot water mixed with the rum for 1 hour. Combine the sugar with the eggs, add the sifted flour, then the milk and cream to obtain a smooth batter. Pour the batter into a lined loaf (bar) tin. Drain the prunes and arrange over the batter. Cook for about 1 hour (the cooking time will depend on what size tin you use). Serve cold.

04 nov

Roast beef with beetroot

Serves 6

PREPARATION TIME 20 MINUTES
COOKING TIME 20 MINUTES

6 beetroot (beets)
6 bulb spring onions (scallions)
1 bunch of flat-leaf (Italian) parsley, leaves picked
1.2 kg (2 lb 10 oz) boneless beef roast,
    tied with kitchen string
80 ml (2½ fl oz/⅓ cup) sunflower oil
80 g (2¾ oz) butter
1 tablespoon fennel seeds
salt and pepper

✻ CAN YOU PUT A BAKING DISH DIRECTLY ON THE STOVETOP? *If it's a metal baking dish it can go directly from the stovetop to the oven.*

Preheat the oven to 160°C (315°F/Gas 2–3). Peel the beetroot, cut into thin wedges. Halve the spring onions. Roughly chop the parsley. Brown the roast beef in a baking dish* in 2 tablespoons of the oil and 40 g (1½ oz) of the butter. Bake the beef for 15 minutes for rare. Pan-fry the beetroot and spring onions with the fennel seeds in the remaining butter and oil for about 10 minutes. Take the roast beef out of the oven and rest for 5 minutes. Combine the vegetables with the cooking juices of the roast beef, add the parsley, season.

05 nov

Pork chops in mustard sauce

Serves 6
PREPARATION TIME 20 MINUTES
COOKING TIME 25 MINUTES

6 pork rib chops
3 onions
sunflower oil
50 g (1¾ oz) butter
1 tablespoon plain (all-purpose) flour
200 ml (7 fl oz) white wine
300 ml (10½ fl oz) pouring (whipping) cream
2 tablespoons wholegrain mustard
salt
6 sprigs flat-leaf (Italian) parsley, leaves picked

Preheat the oven to 180°C (350°F/Gas 4). Pan-fry the chops in a little oil for 3 minutes each side, arrange them in a baking dish. Peel and slice the onions, cover the chops with them. Melt the butter in a saucepan, add the flour, cook for 2 minutes. Add the white wine and the cream, bring to the boil*, then add the mustard, and salt to taste. Pour the mustard sauce over the ingredients in the baking dish, bake for 15 minutes. Scatter over the parsley.

✳ WHY BRING THE CREAM TO THE BOIL? To combine the cream and white wine well with the flour; boiling will thicken the sauce, to create a béchamel.

06 nov

Guinea fowl with cauliflower

Serves 6
PREPARATION TIME 20 MINUTES
COOKING TIME 45 MINUTES

1 or 2 guinea fowls
100 ml (3½ fl oz) olive oil
salt and pepper
1 cauliflower
3 onions
200 g (7 oz) speck, cut into lardons
1 tablespoon juniper berries
1 teaspoon ground cumin

Preheat the oven to 180°C (350°F/Gas 4). Cut the guinea fowls into six pieces: thighs, drumsticks, wings. Brush with oil and season. Cut the cauliflower into florets*. Peel and slice the onions. Combine the cauliflower with the onions and speck, add 2 tablespoons of the oil. Crush the juniper berries. Arrange the guinea fowl in a baking dish, surround with the cauliflower mixture, sprinkle over the cumin and juniper berries. Bake for 45 minutes. Stir the cauliflower regularly so that it soaks up all the cooking juices.

✳ WHAT DOES THAT MEAN? Cut up the cauliflower into small bouquets.

07 nov

Pigeon toasts

Serves 6
PREPARATION TIME 20 MINUTES
COOKING TIME 20 MINUTES

3 pigeons*
100 g (3½ oz) cold butter, cubed
2 tablespoons Cognac
2 French shallots (eschalots), peeled and sliced
200 ml (7 fl oz) Banyuls (fortified wine from the Pyrenées)
1 tablespoon balsamic vinegar
salt and pepper
12 small toasted baguette slices

✳ CAN YOU GET PIGEON AT THE BUTCHER'S? It is readily available, but order it in advance so you're sure to have it on the day.

✳✳ IS THAT EASY? HOW DO YOU DO IT? You use exactly the same technique as for a chicken, you start by removing the thigh and drumstick, then you remove the breasts with the wing.

Preheat the oven to 180°C (350°F/Gas 4). Clean the pigeons, finely chop the livers and hearts. Melt 50 g (1¾ oz) of the butter in a deep ovenproof frying pan, brown the pigeons on each side. Bake for 5 minutes. Add the Cognac to the pan and flambé. Joint the pigeons**, return the carcasses, crushed, to the frying pan, add the shallots, livers and hearts, moisten with the Banyuls, add the vinegar and reduce by half. Remove the carcasses, whisk in the remaining butter, and season. Gently reheat the pigeons in a warm oven, place some of the chopped giblets and shallots on each toast, topped with a piece of pigeon and pour over the sauce.

07
november

PIGEON TOASTS

'When the weather is sanguine, the next day there's boudin!'

08 nov

Boudin noir with apples

Serves 6

PREPARATION TIME 15 MINUTES
COOKING TIME 20 MINUTES

6 waxy potatoes
3 granny smith apples
2 French shallots (eschalots)
2 tablespoons sunflower oil
80 g (2¾ oz) butter
100 g (3½ oz) peeled chestnuts
1 teaspoon ground cinnamon
salt and pepper
1 kg (2 lb 4 oz) boudin noir (blood sausage)

Peel the potatoes and apples and cut them into wedges, remove the apple cores. Peel and slice the shallots. In a non-stick frying pan, sauté the potatoes and the shallots in the sunflower oil and 40 g (1½ oz) of the butter for 10 minutes. Add the apples and the chestnuts and cook for 5 minutes, sprinkle with cinnamon, and season. Gently heat the *boudin* in the frying-pan* in the remaining butter. Serve immediately.

✳ How can I prevent the skin from splitting and how do I know when the boudin is cooked? *The boudin is already cooked when you buy it, you just need to reheat it: use a gentle heat so that the skin doesn't split (that said, you don't eat the skin of a boudin, so don't panic, it's what's inside that counts!).*

09 nov

Caramelised spare-ribs

Serves 6

PREPARATION TIME 20 MINUTES
COOKING TIME 1 HOUR

1.2 kg (2 lb 10 oz) rack of pork spare-ribs
1 bouquet garni
2 tablespoons honey
2 tablespoons white Port
1 teaspoon fennel seeds
1 teaspoon ground cumin
1 teaspoon coarsely ground black pepper
salt

Preheat the oven to 180°C (350°F/Gas 4). Cook the rack of ribs in boiling water with the bouquet garni for 45 minutes*, then drain. Score the fatty side in a criss-cross pattern. Combine the honey with the Port, fennel seeds and cumin, then add the coarsely ground black pepper. Spread this mixture generously over the fatty side of the ribs. Bake for about 15 minutes, basting the ribs regularly with the marinade.

✳ Why cook the spare-ribs beforehand? *The meat takes a while to cook, preparing the meat will make the job of baking it easier: the ribs will stay moist and tender.*

10 nov

Cassoulet*

Serves 6

PREPARATION TIME 20 MINUTES
SOAKING TIME 24 HOURS
COOKING TIME 3 HOURS

600 g (1 lb 5 oz) dried Tarbais beans (white beans)
6 onions
6 garlic cloves
3 tablespoons duck fat
4 tomatoes, diced
2 tablespoons tomato paste (concentrated purée)
6 Toulouse sausages, chopped
6 slices smoked bacon, chopped
salt and pepper
6 confit duck wings

The day before, soak the beans in a large volume of water. Peel and slice the onions, peel and crush the garlic. Melt the duck fat in a large flameproof casserole dish, add the garlic, onions and beans, cover with water (twice the volume), add the diced tomato, tomato paste, sausages and bacon, simmer over a low heat for 2–3 hours: the beans should be soft and tender. Season. Heat the confit duck wings in the oven, push them into the cassoulet. Serve immediately.

✳ Cassoulet Preconceptions? *There are some preconceptions about cassoulet ... prout ... which are ... pffuut ... absolutely true ... (if you get my meaning). It is the ideal dish for a big table of friends, a one-course meal that you can prepare the day before. You raise your glasses, you sing (a reprise of Nougaro's Toulouse is in order) without spending the evening in the kitchen.*

MARIE & LÉON

desert desserts

*I*n the beginning, Marie Vachecrot, a very ordinary cook married to Léon, a lover of fine food, spent her time dreaming of exotic countries, grandiose landscapes and different cultures.

Léon, a man as brave as good bread (I don't really understand this French metaphor either, but anyway, we're short on time, so it will do), decided, to Marie's great joy, to take her on a tour of Morocco (via a session on the MaximiniPrix bargain-finding website). What a change of scene it was for Marie: the sights, the sounds, the smells, the smiles, all of it was different. Benevolence floated like a soft silk shawl around her delicate shoulders, in front of a sunset over the Draa valley (ah, poetry, take me away!). Marie's bus companions (of misfortune) distinguished themselves as genuine world champions of the rude song, the art of haggling (without buying, of course!), and bucket-hat logos — in short, real-world champions of the finer things in life. Marie cared not a fig, she was living her dream, her hand was curled up inside Léon's, she delighted in everything around her (outside of the bus, of course).

On the last evening there was a dinner beneath a Berber tent, the Boulaouane was on tap, the bus reprised all of its classics ... Marie has a lump in her throat, her everyday life is so close at hand, but even so it's nicer to lend a hand in the kitchen. On her return to the table, her hands laden with a quality tagine, Marie found herself faced with a group ruddy with the spirit of « It's-free-so-I'll-drink-up. » She was applauded for the quality of the dish. « Go on Marie, show us your ... » this dish became her dish, it was all they talked about on the return charter flight.

And that is how Marie, destined to the anonymity of her kitchen, became the Marie who went down in history.

11 nov

Beef tagine
Serves 6
PREPARATION TIME 20 MINUTES
COOKING TIME 50 MINUTES

4 onions
6 garlic cloves
4 celery stalks
6 ripe tomatoes
80 ml (2½ fl oz/⅓ cup) olive oil
800 g (1 lb 12 oz) minced (ground) beef
1 tablespoon soft brown sugar
250 ml (9 fl oz/1 cup) white Port
1 tablespoon tomato paste (concentrated purée)
1 teaspoon harissa
1 sprig of thyme
salt and pepper
Equipment:
tagine dish

Peel and slice the onions. Peel the garlic. Finely slice the celery stalks. Finely dice the tomatoes. Heat the oil in a tagine dish and sauté the mince with the onion, garlic, celery and sugar for 5 minutes. Deglaze with the Port. Add the tomato paste, tomato, harissa and thyme, cover, and cook over a low heat for 45 minutes. Season, before serving.

12
november

CARROT SOUP

12 nov

Carrot soup

Serves 6

PREPARATION TIME 20 MINUTES
COOKING TIME 45 MINUTES

1 kg (2 lb 4 oz) carrots
2 onions
1 tablespoon sugar
1 tablespoon ground cumin
300 ml (10½ fl oz) pouring (whipping) cream
a few celery leaves
salt and pepper

Peel the carrots, slice them into rounds, peel and slice the onions. Cook these with the sugar and cumin in a saucepan with twice their volume of water for 30 minutes*. Purée the mixture, add the cream and cook for a further 15 minutes, then add the roughly sliced celery leaves, season.

✻ COOK HOW? *Cook gently, at a bare simmer, covered.*

13 nov

Œufs à la neige

Serves 6

PREPARATION TIME 20 MINUTES
COOKING TIME 15 MINUTES

1 vanilla bean
8 eggs, separated
1 litre (35 fl oz/4 cups) full-cream (whole) milk
450 g (1 lb/2 cups) sugar
80 g (2¾ oz/⅔ cup) crushed hazelnuts

Split the vanilla bean lengthways, scrape out the seeds and mix them into the milk. Whisk the yolks with 150 g (5½ oz) of the sugar until the mixture becomes pale and frothy. Bring the milk to the boil, pour it over the yolk mixture, cook on a gentle heat, stirring constantly, for 7–8 minutes (the *crème Anglaise* should coat the back of a spoon). Careful, this is a delicate operation, the temperature of the custard mustn't go over 85°C (185°F) or else the yolks will coagulate* and then, oh, the drama! Beat the egg whites to very stiff peaks, add 150 g (5½ oz) of the sugar, beat for 3 more minutes. You then have two ways of making the « floating islands ». Either make quenelles of beaten egg white and poach them for 3–4 minutes in boiling milk**, or fill ramekins with beaten egg white and cook them in a microwave for about 1 minute (they should be firm to the touch)***. Next, make a caramel with the remaining sugar and 2 tablespoons water, and add the hazelnuts. Coat the « floating islands » with this caramel. Serve chilled with the *crème Anglaise*.

✻ AND IF THE EGG YOLKS DO COAGULATE? *Blend the failed* crème Anglaise *with 200 ml (7 fl oz) cold pouring (whipping) cream and* voilà, *no one's the wiser!*

✻✻ WHY? *The boiling milk will cook the egg white.*

✻✻✻ AGAIN, WHY? *It's another cooking method, quicker, but not as tasty.*

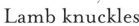

14 nov

Lamb knuckles

Serves 6

PREPARATION TIME 20 MINUTES
COOKING TIME 3 HOURS

4 onions
6 garlic cloves
1 bunch of chives
200 g (7 oz) mushrooms
6 lamb knuckles (hind shanks)
300 g (10½ oz) dried white beans
  (coco de Paimpol are a good choice)
2 bay leaves
500 ml (17 fl oz/2 cups) red wine
500 ml (17 fl oz/2 cups) chicken stock
salt and pepper

Preheat the oven to 160°C (315°F/Gas 2–3). Peel and slice the onions and garlic, snip the chives. Clean the mushrooms and cut them into quarters. Arrange the lamb knuckles in a flameproof casserole dish, add all of the other ingredients, then season. Cover and cook in the oven for about 3 hours*. Add water as needed to ensure the lamb is covered.

✻ A COOKING TIP? *You just need to monitor the cooking without turning the lamb knuckles.*

15
november

PROSCIUTTO BITES

15 NOV

Prosciutto bites

Serves 6

PREPARATION TIME 20 MINUTES

200 g (7 oz) Comté cheese slices
1 handful of seasonal salad leaves*
3 tablespoons olive oil
1 white onion
1 cooked Morteau *or other smoked sausage*
6 slices of prosciutto
a good film**
1 bottle of Arbois *or your favourite white wine*

Cut the slices of Comté into rectangles, dress the salad leaves with olive oil, then peel and slice the onion into rings, along with the *Morteau* sausage. Roll up a piece each of the Comté, onion, *Morteau* sausage and a salad leaf in a slice of prosciutto. Press « play » on the DVD player, press « stop » (you forgot to open the *Arbois*), press « play » again and off you go!

* **SUCH AS?** *Frisée lettuce, mâche, witlof (any of the winter greens).*

** **SUCH AS?** *A good film like* La Soupe aux Choux ...

ON   OFF

16 NOV

Semi-cooked salmon

Serves 6

PREPARATION TIME 30 MINUTES
COOKING TIME 15 MINUTES

2 French shallots (eschalots), peeled
100 g (3½ oz) dry bread
1 bunch of dill, leaves picked
2 teaspoons coriander seeds
50 g (1¾ oz) butter
salt and pepper
6 thick fillets of salmon
4 oranges
50 g (1¾ oz) walnuts

Preheat the oven to 100°C (200°F/Gas ½). Process the shallots with the bread, dill and 1 teaspoon of the coriander seeds. Add the butter and season. Spread each salmon fillet with this mixture. Turn off the oven and place the salmon in it for 15 minutes*. Zest 2 of the oranges, remove the skin and pith of all the oranges and chop the flesh. Combine the orange zest and flesh with the walnuts and remaining coriander seeds. Serve the salmon at room temperature with the orange salad.

* **WHY A TURNED-OFF OVEN?** *So that the salmon benefits from the heat of the oven without cooking completely and so it is semi-cooked!*

17 NOV

New* tripe

Serves 6

PREPARATION TIME 20 MINUTES
COOKING TIME 3 HOURS 5 MINUTES

1 kg (2 lb 4 oz) blanched beef blanket (rumen) tripe**
1 kg (2 lb 4 oz) carrots
3 onions
6 garlic cloves
3 tablespoons olive oil
50 ml (1¾ fl oz) Calvados
1 litre (35 fl oz/4 cups) cider
1 bouquet garni
salt
1 green chilli, sliced

Slice the blanket tripe into thin strips. Peel the carrots and cut them into large dice. Peel and slice the onions. Peel and crush the garlic. Heat the olive oil in a flameproof casserole dish, add the onions, garlic and tripe, sauté for 5 minutes. Moisten with the Calvados, flambé, then add the cider, carrots and bouquet garni. Cover and cook over low heat for 3 hours (adding a little water if necessary). Season with salt and chilli before serving.

* **WHY NEW?** *It is high time we made our own tripe, it freezes easily, so forget the bad trip of tinned and preserved tripe.*

** **CAN I USE OTHER TRIPE BESIDES BLANKET TRIPE?** *The bonnet (the reticulum or honeycomb tripe) and the bible (the omasum or book tripe) are other parts of the animal's stomach that will make a good tripe dish.*

cow bonnet   *donkey bonnet*

18 nov — Roast pork

Serves 6

PREPARATION TIME 20 MINUTES
COOKING TIME 1 HOUR 30 MINUTES

1.2 kg (2 lb 10 oz) pork roast (from the neck-blade)
sunflower oil
300 ml (10½ fl oz) veal stock
100 g (3½ oz) dried cep (porcini) mushrooms
4 onions
300 g (10½ oz) peeled chestnuts
50 g (1¾ oz) butter
1 teaspoon piment d'Espelette (Basque chilli powder)
*   or mild chilli powder*
1 tablespoon ground cumin
fleur de sel

Preheat the oven to 160°C (315°F/Gas 2–3). Brown the pork in oil on all sides, bake for 1 hour uncovered, baste it from time to time with the veal stock*. Rehydrate the dried ceps for 10 minutes in hot water. Peel and slice the onions. Sauté the onions, chestnuts and ceps in some butter, add the chilli powder and cumin, moisten with veal stock. Pour this preparation over the roast, bake for a further 30 minutes. Season with *fleur de sel*.

✳ Ah, my grandmother used lots of veal stock as well … It's not a bit of a has-been ingredient? Mais non! Veal stock is indispensable in cooking, it is the basis of many sauces …

MEUROT

19 nov — Eggs meurette*

Serves 6

PREPARATION TIME 15 MINUTES
COOKING TIME 35 MINUTES

12 mushrooms
200 g (7 oz) smoked bacon, cut into lardons
12 bulb spring onions (scallions)
1 tablespoon olive oil
1 teaspoon plain (all-purpose) flour
750 ml (26 fl oz/3 cups) Beaujolais Nouveau or merlot
salt and pepper
12 eggs
100 ml (3½ fl oz) wine vinegar
50 g (1¾ oz) cold butter, cubed
6 chives, snipped

✳ Where does this name come from? The word meurette comes from meurot, meaning the low wall or muret of the steps of the houses of the Burgundy vignerons. This muret, which was often sheltered, served as a summer kitchen.

✳✳ Why vinegar? It will help to set the egg whites without dispersing in the water.

It's the third Thursday in November, the *Beaujolais* is making its comeback. When you're talking *Beaujolais*, you're talking cooking with red wine: we'll celebrate *le bojo* with dignity, we've got the whole day to do it! We'll have poached eggs in red wine sauce – *oeufs meurette* (with all due respect to the natives of Burgundy). Cut the mushrooms into quarters. Sauté the bacon with the spring onions in the olive oil and add the mushrooms. Add the flour, let it cook for 2 minutes, pour in the wine and cook for 30 minutes, season. Poach the eggs in vinegared water** for 3–4 minutes. At serving time, add the cold butter to the sauce, bring to the boil while whisking. Pour the sauce over the eggs, scatter with chives.

20 nov — Mutton stew

Serves 6

PREPARATION TIME 20 MINUTES
COOKING TIME 2 HOURS 15 MINUTES

4 onions
4 garlic cloves
1 kg (2 lb 4 oz) waxy potatoes
1 kg (2 lb 4 oz) mutton neck
olive oil
1 tablespoon plain (all-purpose) flour
1 bouquet garni
salt and pepper

Peel the onions, garlic and potatoes. Cut the potatoes in half, and slice the garlic and onion. In a flameproof casserole dish, sauté the mutton, onion and garlic in olive oil for about 10 minutes. Add the flour, cook for a further 5 minutes. Cover with water (twice the volume of meat), cover the dish, and cook over low heat with the bouquet garni for 90 minutes. Add the potatoes*, cook for a further 30 minutes, then season.

✳ Why add the potato so late? The meat will become meltingly tender from cooking slowly for a long time and the potatoes won't fall apart.

21 nov

Salt pork with lentils*

Serves 6

PREPARATION TIME 20 MINUTES
COOKING TIME 1 HOUR 20 MINUTES

2 carrots
1 brown onion
1 kg (2 lb 4 oz) rack pork spare-ribs,
    brined (ask your butcher to do this)
1 Morteau *or other smoked sausage*
200 g (7 oz) smoked bacon
1 onion studded with 3 cloves
3 leeks, white part only, rinsed
1 bouquet garni
300 g (10½ oz) puy (blue-green) lentils
salt and pepper

Peel the carrots and cut them into fine dice. Peel and slice the onion. In a large saucepan filled with water, cook the meats with the clove-studded onion, leeks and bouquet garni for 1 hour. Add the lentils, cook for a further 20 minutes. Drain, reserving the liquid. Slice the meats. Place the lentils in a dish with a ladleful of the broth, season, add the meats and leeks. Scatter over the sliced onion.

✳ LENTILS:
Otherwise known as lens culinaris.

22 nov

Lacquered pork knuckles*

Serves 6

PREPARATION TIME 20 MINUTES
COOKING TIME 2 HOURS 30 MINUTES

1 red cabbage
3 onions
3 pork knuckles
1 bouquet garni
fleur de sel
2 tablespoons chestnut honey or your favourite
150 g (5½ oz) smoked bacon, cut into lardons
olive oil
80 g (2¾ oz) lightly salted butter, cubed

Slice the red cabbage. Peel and slice the onions. Put the pork knuckles in a large saucepan and add the bouquet garni and cabbage. Cook at a low simmer for 2 hours. Remove the cabbage, drain and set aside. Preheat the oven to 180°C (350°F/Gas 4). Drain the knuckles and place in a baking dish, scatter over some *fleur de sel* and spread over the honey. Bake for 20 minutes, coating regularly with honey. Sauté the bacon and onion in olive oil for 5 minutes, add the cooked cabbage and simmer for 10 minutes. Add the cold butter, then purée and season. Serve the lacquered knuckles with the red cabbage purée.

✳ IS IT REALLY THE SAME KIND OF LACQUER AS FOR LACQUERED DUCK? *No, for lacquered duck you also use soy sauce and an assortment of spices.*

23 nov

Calf's head

Serves 6

PREPARATION TIME 20 MINUTES
COOKING TIME 3 HOURS

3 leeks
1 ready-to-cook rolled calf's head with the tongue*
1 onion studded with 3 cloves
1 bouquet garni
6 carrots
6 turnips
6 potatoes
1 bunch of flat-leaf (Italian) parsley, leaves picked
3 hard-boiled eggs, mashed
fleur de sel

✳ WHAT EXACTLY IS IT? *Butchers adore customers who buy a calf's head, it's a bit like a Citroën customer going to Jaguar. It's a matter of cooking a calf's head with the tongue inside, all rolled up together. Purists eat it with the brains, but here I must confess that dining on the thoughts of a calf is too much for me!*

Cut the leeks in half lengthways, rinse them well in plenty of water. Cook the calf's head in a large volume of water with the clove-studded onion, leek and bouquet garni for 2 hours 30 minutes. Next, add the carrots, turnips and potatoes and continue cooking for 30 minutes. Chop the parsley. Cut the calf's head into slices, serve with the vegetables, a little of the cooking liquid, the egg and parsley. Season with *fleur de sel*.

24 nov — Whole veal kidneys

Serves 6

PREPARATION TIME 20 MINUTES

COOKING TIME 15 MINUTES

2 good pale veal kidneys

salt and pepper

2 onions

6 carrots

1 cucumber

1 bunch of radishes

1 teaspoon herbes de Provence *(Provençal herb mix)*

250 ml (9 fl oz/1 cup) veal stock

200 g (7 oz) cherry tomatoes

Preheat the oven to 180°C (350°F/Gas 4). Trim the fat from the kidneys, remove the thin membrane that covers them, devein and season. Pound the fat between two pieces of plastic wrap using a rolling pin until it's about about 1 cm (½ inch) thick, then wrap the kidneys in this fat and tie up with kitchen string*. Peel and slice the onions, then cut the carrots, cucumber and radishes into sticks. Sauté the kidneys in a flameproof roasting tin so they render some of their fat, add the vegetables and *herbes de Provence*, let everything brown. Finally, add the veal stock and cherry tomatoes. Bake for 15 minutes.

✱WHY TIE THEM UP WITH THEIR FAT WHEN WE'VE JUST TRIMMED IT OFF? *When you trim the fat from a kidney, you also remove a thin film from it. Once the film is removed, you can roll the kidney up again in its fat.*

25 nov — Chicken pot-au-feu

Serves 6

PREPARATION TIME 20 MINUTES

COOKING TIME 40 MINUTES

6 carrots

1 bunch of coriander (cilantro)

3 onions

1 fennel bulb

3 tablespoons olive oil

6 free-range chicken breast fillets

1 tablespoon herbes de Provence *(Provençal herb mix)*

200 ml (7 fl oz) Muscat or sweet wine

salt and pepper

Peel the carrots and cut them into sticks. Pick off the coriander leaves and reserve the stems. Peel and slice the onions and fennel. Sauté the onions in the olive oil in a flameproof casserole dish with the coriander stems for 10 minutes, remove the stems. Add the vegetables, chicken and *herbes de Provence*. Pour in the Muscat and just enough water to cover the meat. Season, cover with a lid and cook over low heat for 30 minutes. Add the coriander leaves just before serving.

26 nov — Frîtas patatas

Serves 6

PREPARATION TIME 20 MINUTES

COOKING TIME: 20 MINUTES

1 kg (2 lb 4 oz) potatoes, peeled

oil, for deep-frying

La frite, every which way: Cut the potatoes into evenly sized chips, immerse them in salted lukewarm water for 10 minutes*, drain well. Heat the oil in a deep frying pan to 140°C (275°F). Plunge the chips into the oil for 6 minutes, drain, plunge them again** into oil heated to 180°C (350°F) for 2–3 minutes, just before eating.

La galette: Grate the potatoes, cook them in a non-stick frying pan to form one large *galette* or several small ones, then deep-fry in oil for 3 minutes on each side.

La pomme Anna: Finely slice the potatoes, rinse them***, dry them, cook them in clarified butter**** until they are well coloured.

La pomme paille (straw potatoes): Grate the potatoes, rinse them very well to remove their starch so they don't stick during cooking. Drain and pat dry. Heat the oil in a deep saucepan to 180°C (350°F) and plunge the potatoes in the oil until nice and golden.

La pomme sautée: Cut the potatoes into small cubes, rinse and cook in a mixture of half-butter and half-oil for about 10 minutes.

✱WHY SALTED LUKEWARM WATER? *They'll lose their starch and soften.*

✱✱ WHY TWO DIPS? *One to cook them, the other for crispness.*

✱✱✱WHAT IS RINSING THEM FOR? *To remove the starch.*

✱✱✱✱ WHAT IS CLARIFIED BUTTER? *When butter is melted and left to rest, the clarified layer of butterfat on top is used. Discard the bottom layer of casein and whey.*

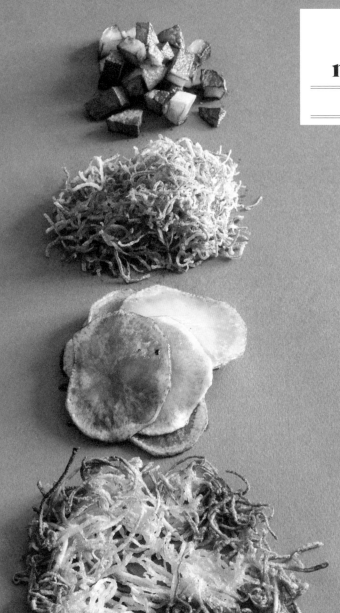

Flürt bluchît rhürt!

27 nov

Gravlax*
Serves 6

PREPARATION TIME 10 MINUTES
MARINATING TIME 48 HOURS

toast, for serving
For the salmon:
800 g (1 lb 12 oz) salmon fillet (the thick part with the skin)
80 g (2¾ oz/¼ cup) coarse salt
2 tablespoons coarsely ground black pepper
2 tablespoons sugar
1 bunch of dill, finely chopped
100 ml (3½ fl oz) gin
For the sauce:
2 tablespoons Savora (honey mustard) sauce
1 tablespoon white vinegar
1 teaspoon sugar
1 bunch of dill, finely chopped
150 ml (5 fl oz) sunflower oil

Remove the bones from the salmon and lay the fillets in a dish. Cover the flesh side with the salt, pepper, sugar, dill and gin. Chill in the refrigerator for 48 hours, regularly draining off the juices released by the salmon. Wipe the salmon dry, cut it into thin slices.
For the sauce, combine the Savora, vinegar, sugar and dill, and gradually whisk in the oil to build up a sauce. Serve the salmon on the toast, topped with the dill sauce.

✱WHAT DOES GRAVLAX MEAN? *A Swedish dish in origin, gravlax means* flürt bluchît rhürt, *which literally translates as: « your salmon marinated with dill and served with this sweet mustard sauce is sooo good ».*

28 nov

Skate with caperberries
Serves 6

PREPARATION TIME 20 MINUTES
COOKING TIME 10 MINUTES

juice of 1 lemon
250 ml (9 fl oz/1 cup) white wine
1 pinch of white pepper
100 g (3½ oz) lightly salted butter, cubed
80 g (2¾ oz) caperberries
6 skate fillets

Put the lemon juice, wine and pepper in a saucepan and cook until the liquid reduces to 2mm (1/16 inch) in the pan. Add the butter, whisking vigorously, then add the caperberries. Poach the skate in boiling water for 5–7 minutes, remove the gelatinous part*, then pour over the caperberry butter. Serve with steamed potatoes on the side.

✱WHAT IS THE GELATINOUS PART? *It's a natural membrane that covers the skate.*

29 nov

Salmon pot-au-feu
Serves 6

PREPARATION TIME 20 MINUTES
COOKING TIME 55 MINUTES

800 g (1 lb 12 oz) fresh salmon
2 garlic cloves
4 onions
3 carrots
6 turnips
3 lemongrass stems, white part only
3 tablespoons olive oil
1 bouquet garni
zest of 1 lemon
salt and pepper

Remove the bones of the salmon, cut the flesh into large cubes. Peel and slice the garlic and onions. Peel the carrots, halve them, and peel and slice the turnips. Slice the lemongrass stem. Sauté the onions and garlic for 10 minutes in the olive oil. Add 1 litre (35 fl oz/4 cups) water, the lemongrass, bouquet garni and lemon zest. Cook for 30 minutes, strain the broth through a chinois (cone-shaped strainer), return to the pan, add the turnips and carrots and cook for 15 minutes. Add the pieces of salmon, season, and serve immediately*.

✱YOU DON'T LET THE SALMON COOK? *Serve it immediately because salmon is best when it's raw in the middle.*

MARIE & LÉON

monday: ravioli, tuesday: ravioli ... saturday ... ravie au lit

In the beginning, Marie Vachecrot, a very ordinary cook married to Léon, a lover of fine food, adored Sunday morning lie-ins beside her virile and always-willing husband.

Lunch often tended to become afternoon tea, to the great despair of Kevin, an always-starving adolescent. A tricky dilemma for Marie — to leave the soft and cosy morning nest to nourish her young or remain clasped to the massive shoulder of her man. She made little snacks ahead of time: pasta, meat, vegetables, all combined together, which she left in the family refrigerator. Kevin thus had a complete meal, thrilled to be able to obtain some balanced nourishment, while Marie, for her part, could remain peacefully recumbent, *ravie au lit* (delighted in bed) with her Léon.

And that is how Marie, destined to the anonymity of her kitchen, became the Marie who went down in history.

30 nov

DIY ravioli

Serves 6

PREPARATION TIME 1 HOUR
COOKING TIME 5 MINUTES

300 g (10½ oz/2 cups) plain (all-purpose) flour + extra
1 egg
4 egg yolks + 1 lightly beaten egg yolk, for brushing
1 tablespoon olive oil
Equipment:
pasta machine or rolling pin + ravioli cutter

Sift the flour, place it on a work bench, place the egg and yolks in the centre with the olive oil, knead until you have a smooth dough. Pass the dough through a pasta machine (or roll out as thinly as possible), then fold the dough. Repeat this process three times, re-flouring the dough each time*. Roll out a strip of pasta, place small mounds of your choice of filling along it, brush around the small mounds with egg yolk, cover with another strip of pasta, press down well, then cut to shape. Cook the ravioli for 2 minutes in boiling water**.

For the filling:

Spinach and ricotta: Combine 200 g (7 oz) spinach, wilted in butter with 100 g (3½ oz) ricotta and 1 finely chopped onion.

Pumpkin and truffle: Combine 100 g (3½ oz) mashed pumpkin (winter squash) with 1 sliver of truffle.

Minced meat and Comté: Combine 100 g (3½ oz) minced (ground) meat with 50 g (1¾ oz) grated Comté cheese and 1 finely chopped onion.

Ham and cheese: Combine 100 g (3½ oz) chopped ham with 50 g (1¾ oz) fresh goat's cheese.

* WHAT WILL THAT DO? *It will give body to the pasta and take away some of its elasticity.*

** HOW SHOULD THEY BE STORED?: *The ravioli will keep for a few days in the refrigerator, lightly floured, in an airtight container (mind the humidity).*

December

01 — Éloi
PARMESAN-CRUSTED FISH

02 — Viviane
CLASSIC LOBSTER

03 — François-Xavier
GRAND MARNIER SOUFFLÉ

08 — Elfi
FOIE GRAS AND TRUFFLE SOUP

09 — Léocadie
FOIE GRAS WITH BLACKCURRANT

10 — Romaric
BLINIS

15 — Nino
SCRAMBLED EGGS WITH TRUFFLES

16 — Adélaïde
BEEF WITH KIDNEY BEANS

17 — Judicaël
BOUDIN BLANC WITH APPLES AND CARROTS

22 — Xavière
BARE-BOTTOM SCAMPI

23 — Armand
SPELT RISOTTO WITH SCALLOPS

24 — Adèle
CHRISTMAS BISCUITS

29 — Abigaëlle
SCALLOP KEBABS

30 — Roger
SEA URCHINS WITH VEGETABLES

31 — Sylvestre
TIME TO DRINK, NOT TO EAT

04
Barbara
POTATO SALAD WITH TRUFFLE

05
Gérald
CHICKEN OVER-STUFFED
WITH FROMAGE BLANC

06
Nicolas
PAIN D'ÉPICES

07
Ambroise
FOIE GRAS AND
TRUFFLE CARPACCIO

11
Daniela
CHILLI LOBSTER

12
Corentin
LOBSTER AND MANGO SALAD

13
Lucie
CHICKEN WITH TRUFFLES

14
Odile
SAUTÉED SCAMPI

18
Gatien
HANGER STEAK WITH
CONFIT POTATOES

19
Urbain
SCALLOPS WITH LEEK
AND CHESTNUT

20
Théophile
SCALLOP AND TRUFFLE
CARPACCIO

21
Hiver
SAUSAGES IN WHITE WINE

25
Noël
BÛCHE DE NOËL

26
Étienne
BOUILLABAISSE

27
Jean
RAY OF SUNSHINE TART

28
Innocent
CITRUS SALAD WITH
COCONUT MILK

01   02   03   04

'It's better to have a crush on a lobster than the reverse.'

01 dec
Parmesan-crusted fish
Serves 6
PREPARATION TIME 30 MINUTES
COOKING TIME 10 MINUTES
100 g (3½ oz) sun-dried black olives
100 g (3½ oz/1 cup) ground almonds
80 g (2¾ oz) butter
50 g (1¾ oz) parmesan cheese
8 onions
2 fennel bulbs
80 ml (2½ fl oz/⅓ cup) olive oil
salt and pepper
6 fillets of sea bass, bream, croaker or snapper

the croaker and the bream

Pit half of the black olives. Process together with the ground almonds, butter and parmesan. Sandwich this mixture between two sheets of baking paper and roll out to a thickness of 5 mm (¼ inch). Peel and slice the onions and fennel and sauté in the olive oil in a non-stick frying pan. Add the rest of the olives and cook for about 10 minutes, then season. Steam the fish for 5 minutes, remove the skin, then cover with the parmesan butter. Cook under a hot grill (broiler) for 3–4 minutes. Serve with the onion-fennel stew.

02 dec
Classic lobster
Serves 6
PREPARATION TIME 5 MINUTES
COOKING TIME 10 MINUTES
3 onions
3 carrots
1 leek
2 tablespoons olive oil + extra for drizzling
3 x 600–800 g (1 lb 5 oz–1 lb 12 oz) live lobsters*
juice of ½ lemon
fleur de sel

Can you put them in the refrigerator? *To keep a lobster or crab that you're not eating straight away, it's better to put them into the freezer alive.*

****What's this for?** *It will stop the lobster from cooking any more.*

Peel and thinly slice the onions, carrots and leek. Sauté them in a saucepan with the olive oil, pour over 3 litres (105 fl oz) water, and bring to the boil. Tie the lobsters to a wooden spoon so they stay straight, plunge them into the boiling water alive, cook for 7–10 minutes, then refresh immediately**. Halve the lobsters and crack the claws. Serve with the strained vegetables, a drizzle of olive oil, a dash of lemon juice and a little *fleur de sel*.

03 dec
Grand Marnier soufflé
Serves 6
PREPARATION TIME 20 MINUTES
COOKING TIME 15 MINUTES
1 vanilla bean
250 ml (9 fl oz/1 cup) full-cream (whole) milk
2 egg yolks
30 g (1 oz) plain (all-purpose) flour
135 g (4¾ oz) sugar
1 tablespoon cornflour (cornstarch)
3 eggs, separated
80 ml (2½ fl oz/⅓ cup) Grand Marnier liqueur*
30 g (1 oz) butter
Equipment:
6 ramekins

Where there's Grand Marnier there's flambéing, isn't there? *The Grand Marnier isn't flambéed in this recipe, it's an ingredient in its own right.*

Preheat the oven to 220°C (425°F/Gas 7). Split the vanilla bean lengthways, scrape out the seeds and add to the milk, then bring to the boil. Combine the egg yolks with the flour, 50 g (1¾ oz/¼ cup) of the sugar and the cornflour. Pour the boiling milk over this mixture, cook for 5 minutes over gentle heat. Whip the 3 egg whites to soft peaks, add the remaining sugar, beat for 5 minutes: the egg whites should have a meringue-like texture. Mix the 3 egg yolks, Grand Marnier and egg whites into the lukewarm custard. Lightly grease the ramekins with butter and fill with the custard mixture to two-thirds full. Cook in the oven for 7–8 minutes. Serve immediately*.

04 dec

Potato salad with truffle

Serves 6

PREPARATION TIME 10 MINUTES

COOKING TIME 20 MINUTES

600 g (1 lb 5 oz) roseval or other waxy potatoes

1 white or black truffle

2 tablespoons sour cream

1 tablespoon olive oil

fleur de sel *and pepper*

Equipment:

truffle shaver

Cook the potatoes in boiling water for about 20 minutes: they need to remain firm. Using a truffle shaver*, make thin slivers of truffle. Season the sour cream with the olive oil, *fleur de sel* and pepper. Halve and arrange the lukewarm potatoes on a plate with the cream, scatter over the truffle slices.

*TRUFFLE SHAVER: *The truffle shaver lets you make very thin slices of truffle. Since truffles are highly perfumed and very expensive, you don't need to use large amounts.*

05 dec

Chicken over-stuffed with fromage blanc

Serves 6

PREPARATION TIME 20 MINUTES

COOKING TIME 50 MINUTES

4 French shallots (eschalots), peeled

1 bunch of dill

200 g (7 oz) fromage blanc or mascarpone

3 tablespoons olive oil

salt and pepper

1 free-range chicken

1 tablespoon juniper berries, crushed

6 garlic cloves

Preheat the oven to 160°C (315°F/Gas 2–3). Finely chop the shallots and half of the dill. Mix these into the fromage blanc, add the olive oil, then season. Stuff the chicken with this *fromage blanc mixture**. Place the chicken in a roasting tin, scatter over the roughly crushed juniper berries, add the garlic cloves and remaining dill, season and cook in the oven for 50 minutes.

*WHAT DOES THIS KIND OF METHOD DO? *The chicken will be nice and crisp on the outside and the fromage blanc will make the flesh moist and tender.*

06 dec

Pain d'épices

Serves 6

PREPARATION TIME 15 MINUTES

COOKING TIME 1 HOUR

1 egg

125 g (4½ oz) sugar

200 ml (7 fl oz) full-cream (whole) milk

350 g (12 oz/1 cup) chestnut honey or your favourite

125 g (4½ oz) butter, softened

500 g (1 lb 2 oz/3⅓ cups) plain (all-purpose) flour, sifted

1 teaspoon bicarbonate of soda (baking soda)*

1 teaspoon ground ginger**

1 teaspoon ground aniseed

zest of 1 lemon

1 tablespoon orange flower water

1 tablespoon sugar

Preheat the oven to 160°C (315°F/Gas 2–3). Whisk the egg with the sugar until the mixture becomes pale and frothy. Heat the milk with the honey, then combine with the egg mixture. Add the butter, flour, bicarbonate of soda, spices lemon zest and orange flower water. Butter and flour a loaf (bar) tin, pour in the mixture, sprinkle over the sugar and bake in the oven for 1 hour.

*WHAT IS THE BICARBONATE OF SODA FOR? *It will play the role of baking powder without the aftertaste, giving a more rustic aspect to the pain d'épices.*

**HOW DO YOU FLAVOUR A PAIN D'ÉPICES? *You can add cinnamon and any spice you like.*

07 dec

Foie gras and truffle carpaccio

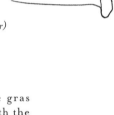

Serves 6

PREPARATION TIME 10 MINUTES

1 truffle
400 g (14 oz) best-quality foie gras
50 g (1¾ oz/⅓ cup) hazelnuts, roughly chopped
1 pinch piment d'Espelette (Basque chilli powder)
     or mild chilli powder
fleur de sel
2 tablespoons olive oil
1 tablespoon white Port

✱How should it be served? *The foie gras is best served chilled.*

Thinly slice the truffle and foie gras and arrange it in a dish. Scatter with the hazelnuts, season with *piment d'Espelette* and *fleur de sel*, drizzle with the olive oil and Port*.

DOWN WITH OFFAL

08 dec

Foie gras and truffle soup

Serves 6

PREPARATION TIME 20 MINUTES

COOKING TIME 45 MINUTES

3 onions
2 carrots
1 celery stalk
50 g (1¾ oz) butter
800 ml (28 fl oz) chicken stock
300 g (10½ oz) foie gras
1 truffle
200 g (7 oz) block store-bought butter puff pastry
1 egg yolk, lightly beaten

✱Who invented soup en croûte? *This soup was created by the master of us all, Paul Bocuse, for the French president Valérie Giscard D'Estaing; it has been nicknamed VGE soup. This is an interpretation of the original.*

Preheat the oven to 180°C (350°F/Gas 4). Peel and cut the onions and carrots into fine dice, and thinly slice the celery. Sauté the vegetables in butter for about 10 minutes, then add the chicken stock and cook for 20 minutes. Cut the foie gras and truffle into small dice. Divide the foie gras and truffle between six individual ramekins. Add the vegetables and broth until two-thirds full. Roll out the pastry, cut out discs 1 cm (½ inch) wider than the ramekins. Moisten the edges of the ramekins, cover with a round of pastry*, brush with egg yolk, then bake for 15 minutes. Serve as is.

VIVE LE FOIE GRAS!

09 dec

Foie gras with blackcurrant

Serves 6

PREPARATION TIME 20 MINUTES

COOKING TIME 10 MINUTES

3 granny smith apples
400–500 g (14 oz–1 lb 2 oz) foie gras*
200 ml (7 fl oz) crème de cassis (blackcurrant liqueur)
1 tablespoon mixed peppercorns, lightly crushed
fleur de sel

✱How do you choose a foie gras? *Duck foie gras is the most common. Choose a top-quality foie gras. It should be a creamy beige colour, without any marks and firm and supple to the touch. These foie gras only lose a very small amount of their fat during cooking.*

Peel the apples, halve them and remove their cores. Slice the foie gras into six escalopes. Place the *crème de cassis* in a frying pan and cook the apples for 10 minutes over gentle heat, turning regularly — they should stay firm. In a non-stick frying pan, brown the foie gras for 1 minute on each side, set them aside on paper towels. To serve, arrange a slice of fois gras on each plate, season with the peppercorns and *fleur de sel*, then add a piece of apple and drizzle over a little of the blackcurrant reduction.

10 dec

Blinis

Serves 6

PREPARATION TIME 20 MINUTES
RESTING TIME 1 HOUR
COOKING TIME 5 MINUTES

250 g (9 oz/1⅔ cups) plain (all-purpose) flour
100 g (3½ oz/¾ cup) buckwheat flour
400 ml (14 fl oz) full-cream (whole) milk
15 g (½ oz) fresh yeast
2 eggs
120 g (4¼ oz) butter, melted
100 ml (3½ fl oz) pouring (whipping) cream
vegetable oil
thick (double cream), lemon wedges, sliced smoked salmon

Sift and combine both of the flours*. Heat the milk to lukewarm, add the yeast and mix together. Combine the eggs with the flours, then add the melted butter, cream and milk. Let the mixture rest for 1 hour at room temperature — it should double in volume. Oil a blini pan and, working in batches, pour in a little of the mixture. Cook for about 2–3 minutes on each side. Serve immediately with a little cream, lemon, smoked salmon … and Champagne.

wheat   buckwheat

✳ WHY TWO TYPES OF FLOUR? *The buckwheat flour complements the traditional flour. It gives the blini a rustic character and adds a sour note.*

12 dec

Lobster and mango salad

Serves 6

PREPARATION TIME 20 MINUTES
COOKING TIME 10 MINUTES

3 live lobsters
1 garlic clove, chopped
3 tablespoons olive oil
1 tablespoon tomato sauce (ketchup)
*1 green mango**
150 g (5½ oz/1⅔ cups) mung bean shoots
3 sprigs of dill

Cook the lobsters alive in boiling water for 7 minutes. Separate the head from the body, scoop out the roe from the head**, shell the rest of the lobster. Peel and chop the garlic, brown it in the olive oil, add the tomato sauce and the roe, cook for 2 minutes and purée. Peel the mango and slice into sticks. In a bowl, arrange the pieces of lobster, the mung bean shoots and mango, dress with the coral dressing and scatter with dill leaves.

✳ WHAT'S A GREEN MANGO? *It's a mango that's not very ripe, with a more sour flavour, perfect for savoury dishes.*

✳✳ IS THAT EASY? WHY? *You use a spoon to scrape the inside of the head to get the roe, which will be used to make the dressing.*

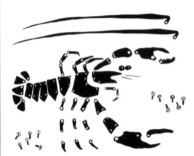

11 dec

Chilli lobster

Serves 6

PREPARATION TIME 30 MINUTES
COOKING TIME 30 MINUTES

2 garlic cloves
2 French shallots (eschalots)
1 celery stalk
1 red bird's eye chilli
30 g (1 oz) fresh ginger
6 tomatoes
3 tablespoons olive oil
100 ml (3½ fl oz) white wine
3 live lobsters
200 ml (7 fl oz) pouring (whipping) cream

Peel and thinly slice the garlic and French shallots. Slice the celery and chilli (remove the seeds*). Peel and chop the ginger. Blanch, peel and seed the tomatoes. Sauté all these ingredients in a saucepan with the olive oil, deglaze with the white wine and cook for 10 minutes. Cook the live lobsters in boiling water for 7 minutes. Separate the head from the body, scoop out the roe from the head, add it to the stewed tomatoes, then add the cream and cook for 5 minutes, purée. Cleave the lobsters at the joints** of the body shell, remove the flesh from the claws. Reheat everything in the chilli sauce.

✳ WHY REMOVE THE CHILLI SEEDS? *So you avoid standing on the table singing* La Bamba *the whole evening.*

✳✳ IS THAT EASY? A TIP? *It's a slightly delicate process — it's important to make the cut at the joints of the shell on the sides.*

13
december

CHICKEN WITH TRUFFLES

13 dec

Chicken with truffles

Serves 6

PREPARATION TIME 20 MINUTES
MARINATING TIME 24 HOURS
COOKING TIME 40 MINUTES

1 truffle
6 free-range chicken breast fillets
salt and pepper
200 ml (7 fl oz) pouring (whipping) cream
3 leeks
olive oil
3 potatoes, peeled
200 ml (7 fl oz) chicken stock

The day before, cut half the truffle into thin slices. Make five incisions in the back of each chicken breast and insert the slivers of truffle. Season, wrap tightly in plastic wrap and refrigerate for 24 hours. Infuse the remaining truffle in the cream. Slice the leeks, sauté them in the olive oil for 10 minutes, then add 3 litres (105 fl oz) water and boil for 30 minutes. Grate the potatoes, season, chop up half of the half-truffle (remove from the cream first!) and add to the potatoes. Cook galettes* of potato in olive oil in a non-stick frying pan. Poach the chicken breasts in their plastic wrap** in the leek broth for 7 minutes. Heat the chicken stock, add the infused truffle cream, season. Serve the chicken with the potato galette and truffle cream.

✳How? Do I SHAPE THEM WITH MY HANDS? *Arrange the potatoes in the frying pan like a small thick pancake.*

✳✳WHY LEAVE THEM IN THE WRAP? *They will keep their shape and cook without becoming waterlogged.*

14 dec

Sautéed scampi

Serves 6

PREPARATION TIME 20 MINUTES
COOKING TIME 5 MINUTES

18 scampi*
1 truffle
3 French shallots (eschalots)
80 ml (2½ fl oz/⅓ cup) olive oil
a few leaves of flat-leaf (Italian) parsley
salt and pepper

✳How SHOULD I CHOOSE SCAMPI? *By smell. It is a highly perishable product and quickly develops an unpleasant ammonia smell. Choose the large ones (3 large rather than 6 small), with a good pink colour and firm shell.*

Carefully extract the scampi flesh from the shells. Cut the truffle into thin slivers. Peel and slice the French shallots. Sauté the shallots for 5 minutes in the olive oil, add the scampi for 1 minute. Off the heat, add the slivers of truffle, the parsley, season and serve immediately.

15 dec

Scrambled eggs with truffles

Serves 6

PREPARATION TIME 20 MINUTES
MARINATING TIME 24 HOURS
COOKING TIME 10 MINUTES

1 truffle
6 eggs
200 ml (7 fl oz) pouring (whipping) cream
2 tablespoons olive oil

The day before, or even the day before that, enclose the truffle with the eggs in an airtight container*. Remove the top of the eggs as carefully as possible, set aside the contents and rinse out the empty shells. Chop up the truffle. Beat the eggs until just combined, add the cream and half the truffle. Heat the olive oil in a heavy-based saucepan and scramble the eggs over gentle heat. At the end of cooking, add the rest of the truffle. Fill the egg shells with this mixture, and serve immediately.

✳WHAT FOR? *The perfume of the truffle will permeate the eggs.*

'**The *boudin blanc* is to *charcuterie* what Michael Jackson is to pop music.**'

16 dec — Beef with kidney beans

Serves 6

PREPARATION TIME 20 MINUTES
SOAKING TIME 24 HOURS
COOKING TIME 1 HOUR 30 MINUTES

300 g (10½ oz/1⅓ cups) dried kidney beans
6 onions, peeled
1 mild green chilli
1 celery stalk
300 g (10½ oz) rump beef steak
1 bouquet garni
olive oil
200 g (7 oz) tomato passata (tomato purée)
3 tablespoons tomato sauce (ketchup)
1 tablespoon dried thyme
1 bay leaf
250 ml (9 fl oz/1 cup) white wine
salt and pepper
Tabasco sauce

The day before, soak the kidney beans in cold water. Drain. Slice the onions, chilli and celery. Cut the meat into small cubes. Cook the beans with the bouquet garni in a large volume of fresh water for 1 hour, then drain. Sauté the onions with the meat, celery and chilli, add the tomato passata and sauce. Put the meat mixture into a flameproof casserole dish with the beans, thyme, bay leaf and wine. Cook over gentle heat for 30 minutes, season, and add the Tabasco, to taste.

17 dec — Boudin blanc with apples and carrots

Serves 6

PREPARATION TIME 10 MINUTES
COOKING TIME 20 MINUTES

2 onions
2 waxy potatoes
2 carrots
2 granny smith apples
80 g (2¾ oz) butter
6 boudin blanc*
1 teaspoon fennel seeds
salt and pepper

❋WHAT IN FACT IS A BOUDIN BLANC? *It's a sausage made from white meats (veal, pork, poultry) cooked with cream and milk. You can buy them at the butcher's and from gourmet food shops.*

Slice the onions. Peel the potatoes and carrots, slice them into rounds, then cook them for 10 minutes in boiling water. Slice the apples into rounds and remove the cores. Melt the butter in a frying pan, gently brown the boudin blanc with the onions and keep warm. Glaze the vegetables and apple in the pan over gentle heat, add the fennel seeds, season.

18 dec — Hanger steak with confit potatoes

Serves 6

PREPARATION TIME 10 MINUTES
COOKING TIME 25 MINUTES

6 good-sized pieces of hanger steak
2 French shallots (eschalots)
6 potatoes
500 g (1 lb 2 oz) duck fat
1 bunch of flat-leaf (Italian) parsley, leaves picked
50 g (1¾ oz) butter
fleur de sel and pepper

❋PEEL THE STEAK: *Remove the membrane covering the hanger steak (if bought whole).*

❋❋A TIP FOR KEEPING THEM WARM? *Put them in a warm oven, covered in foil, with the door ajar.*

Peel the hanger steak*, the shallots and the potatoes. Confit the potatoes in the duck fat over low heat for about 20 minutes (the point of a knife should go through the potato), then cut them into wedges. Finely chop the shallots and parsley. Sauté the steaks in butter for 3 minutes on each side, keep warm**. Brown the potato wedges in the pan the steaks were cooked in, season. Serve the steaks sprinkled with the shallot and parsley. Season with *fleur de sel* and pepper.

20

december

SCALLOP AND
TRUFFLE CARPACCIO

the nut (roe)

19 dec

Scallops with leek and chestnut

Serves 6

PREPARATION TIME 15 MINUTES
COOKING TIME 25 MINUTES

18 scallops
3 bulb spring onions (scallions)
3 garlic cloves
30 g (1 oz) fresh ginger
3 tablespoons olive oil
2 leeks, white part only, rinsed and sliced
200 ml (7 fl oz) white wine
400 g (14 oz) peeled chestnuts
200 ml (7 fl oz) pouring (whipping) cream
salt and pepper

Remove the roe* from the scallops. Slice the spring onions with their green stems. Peel and crush the garlic. Peel and chop the ginger. Brown the garlic in the olive oil in a saucepan, add the leek, spring onion and ginger, lower the heat and stew for 10 minutes. Add the wine and chestnuts, cook for 5 minutes, add the cream and cook for a further 5 minutes, season. Sear the scallops in olive oil in a frying pan over a high heat for 2 minutes each side and serve on the chestnut fondue.

✱AND WHAT DO I DO WITH IT? *You can discard it or use it for another recipe.*

20 dec

Scallop and truffle carpaccio

Serves 6

PREPARATION TIME 10 MINUTES

1 truffle
1 small carrot
1 teaspoon soy sauce
2 tablespoons olive oil
6 large scallops
fleur de sel

Trim* the truffle, finely chop the trimming. Peel the carrot, cut it into a fine dice, then combine with the truffle trimmings. Combine the soy sauce with the olive oil, then add the truffle and carrot mixture. Cut the scallops and the truffle into thin round slices, put the scallop back together, interspersing with slivers of truffle, drizzle with the truffle-carrot dressing, and season with *fleur de sel*.

✱TRIM THE TRUFFLE? *The first slices of truffle will be used in the dressing.*

21 dec

Sausages in white wine (or home from midnight Mass for Papily and mon toutou)

Serves 6

PREPARATION TIME 10 MINUTES
COOKING TIME 20 MINUTES

3 onions
2 silverbeet (swiss chard) leaves
6 large Toulouse sausages
1 bunch of sage
300 ml (10½ fl oz) white wine

Preheat the oven to 180°C (350°F/Gas 4). Peel and slice the onions. Slice the silverbeet leaves. Place the sausages in a baking dish, cover with the onions, sage and silverbeet, then add the white wine (they'll be sozzled before being sizzled!). Bake in the oven for 20 minutes, basting the sausages regularly*.

✱BUT WHAT DO I DO IF I'M AT MASS THEN? *You pray for someone to turn on the oven 20 minutes before the end of Mass, or else you have 20 minutes to enjoy an apéritif before eating.*

22 dec

Bare-bottom scampi (Jacquy's favourite)

Serves 6

PREPARATION TIME 1 HOUR
COOKING TIME 1 HOUR 10 MINUTES

3 onions
3 leeks, white part only
3 tablespoons olive oil
1 bouquet garni
18 scampi
your choice of mayonnaise (a lemony one would be good)

Peel and slice the onions. Roughly chop the leeks. Sauté these ingredients in olive oil in a large saucepan, pour in 3 litres (105 fl oz) water, add the bouquet garni and simmer for 1 hour. Plunge the scampi in the water for 1 minute and remove immediately*. Carefully undress the scampi (it's the bottoms we're interested in, not the tops!), then eat them bare-bottomed with the mayonnaise.

✳ Cooking tip: *Be careful, an overcooked scampi is like cotton wool and completely loses its texture.*

23 dec

Spelt risotto with scallops

Serves 6

PREPARATION TIME 15 MINUTES
COOKING TIME 1 HOUR

1 leek, white part only, rinsed
2 bulb spring onions (scallions)
80 ml (2½ fl oz/⅓ cup) olive oil
200 g (7 oz) spelt
800 ml (28 fl oz) vegetable stock
80 g (2¾ oz) butter
80 g (2¾ oz) shaved
   parmesan cheese
salt and pepper
18 scallops
3 tablespoons soy sauce

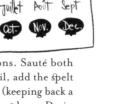

Slice the leek and spring onions. Sauté both in 2 tablespoons of the olive oil, add the spelt and pour in the vegetable stock (keeping back a ladleful). Cook over low heat for 1 hour. Drain the spelt and stir through the butter and half of the parmesan cheese, season. Sear the scallops in the remaining olive oil in a frying pan over high heat for 2 minutes on each side. Remove the scallops from the pan. Add the reserved chicken stock and soy sauce to the pan and reduce. Arrange the scallops in a dish and top with the remaining parmesan cheese, add the spelt, drizzle with the cooking juices.

24 dec

Christmas biscuits

Serves 6

PREPARATION TIME 30 MINUTES
CHILLING TIME 1 HOUR
COOKING TIME 10 MINUTES

The basic recipe:
400 g (14 oz/2⅔ cups) plain (all-purpose) flour, sifted
150 g (5½ oz) sugar
250 g (9 oz) butter, cubed
1 egg
Your choice of flavourings:
100 g (3½ oz/1 cup) ground almonds + 1 tablespoon
   cinnamon + 1 teaspoon ground ginger
100 g (3½ oz/1 cup) ground hazelnuts + 1 tablespoon
   walnuts + 1 tablespoon hazelnuts + 1 tablespoon sultanas
100 g (3½ oz/1 cup) desiccated coconut
   + 2 tablespoons rum

✳ Is there an order for adding the ingredients? *It's however you like!*

✳✳ How long do they keep? *One week in an airtight container.*

Combine all of the ingredients and your choice of flavourings* to make a smooth dough. Divide into three portions and roll up with the flavourings to make a sausage shape; chill for 1 hour. Preheat the oven to 180°C (350°F/ Gas 4). Slice 1 cm (½ inch) thick biscuits, arrange on a baking tray lined with baking paper and bake for 10 minutes.

MARIE & LÉON

the Christmas log trap

$\mathcal{I}$t's Christmas, it's the holidays, we laugh, we have fun, we make jokes. Marie Vachecrot, a very ordinary cook married to Léon, a lover of fine food, was not to be outdone, she was the family's Jean Roucas.

If there's a pun to be made, there's Marie. Dental floss in the fondue? Marie. A *terrine de kinou* on April Fool's Day ... look out, it's Marie again. And what can she do this Christmas to amuse the gathering, already sold on Marie's future mischief-making?

The whoopee cushion has had its hour of glory, the dribble glass has left its mark all over the table, the stink bomb spoiled last Christmas.

This year, it will be a fake log, a good joke for *mon Léon*. A soft *génoise*, a little chocolate, some cream, turn the heating off, and if he goes to light the chimney this Christmas evening, there'll be a good log there for the embers. Léon fell for it like baby Jesus in the manger, he squashed the *bûche* (log) in his hand, laughter rang out on all sides, it was a great joke. Léon couldn't stop himself bringing his fingers to his mouth, he licked them one by one with a great deal of pleasure, turning the amused looks into jealous ones: the log was good. It's Christmas, it's the holidays, there's laughter, they make more *bûches* because they're so good, they enjoy them with a chuckle.

And that is how Marie, destined to the anonymity of her kitchen, became the Marie who went down in history.

25 dec

Bûche de Noël
Serves 6

PREPARATION TIME 45 MINUTES
COOKING TIME 20 MINUTES

For the base:

4 eggs, separated
125 g (4½ oz) caster (superfine) sugar
2 teaspoons vanilla sugar
125 g (4½ oz) plain (all-purpose) flour, sifted

Preheat the oven to 200°C (400°F/Gas 6). For the base, whisk the egg yolks with the caster sugar and vanilla sugar until pale and frothy. Add the flour. Beat the egg whites to very stiff peaks and gently fold them into the yolk mixture. Line a shallow rectangular cake tin with baking paper, pour the mixture into this tin. Bake in the oven for 7–8 minutes, turn the cake out onto a damp cloth*, remove the baking paper, roll up in the cloth straight away.

Two suggestions for filling the *bûche de Noël*:

Chocolate: Melt 200 g (7 oz) dark chocolate with 80 g (2¾ oz) butter in a double-boiler, add 200 ml (7 fl oz) whipped cream, spread over the cooled cake, roll up, cover with grated chocolate, dust with icing (confectioners') sugar and chill.

Sweetened chestnut cream: Combine 200 g (7 oz) sweetened chestnut purée with 100 g (3½ oz) softened butter, add 200 ml (7 fl oz) whipped cream, spread over the cooled cake, roll up, cover with the chestnut cream, dust with icing (confectioners') sugar and chill.

✱WHY A DAMP CLOTH? *It will help to roll up the cake into a log shape.*

MARIE & LÉON

bouillague con!

*I*n the beginning Marie Vachecrot, a very ordinary cook married to Léon, a lover of fine food, spent her time reading magazines which could often be found to the right of the toilet bowl.

This quasi-monastic occupation gave Marie the impression she shared in the superficial and glamorous world of her cherished celebrities, it was big game fishing, heavy stuff *m'sieurs dames*, she almost forgot her Léon.

Léon, *Marseillais* born and bred, hardly left his boat — his refuge, his life. Marie's rusty-coloured moleskin armchair sweated overlooking the harbour, the boat's virgin berth waited for its master's return. Léon made his entrance with a scant kilo of rock fish, his smile worn thin by his meagre catch. Marie, whose smile was undisguisedly mocking, contemptuously threw the fish into a large pot filled with water. She added a few herbs, cooked it for a couple of hours, a whizz with the blender, a few potatoes to give it body ... The mockery caught on, the whole port of Marseille quickly became aware of Léon's Dantesque exploits: a day of fishing for a kilogram rock fish! A few well-intentioned friends, Raoul the crumpled and Baisse the stained, knocked on Léon's door, and surprise, a conger eel; surprise again, a John dory; surprise once more, two *rascasses* (scorpion fish) — the solidarity between fishermen had won the day. By way of thanks, the table grew, the fish took to the broth, the soup was served, the fish as well. The table was overwhelmed, faces transfixed in gastronomic joy (Baisse's look — *la bouille à Baisse* — especially was something to be seen), statues erected in Marie's honour for this magic dish. A legend was born.

And that is how Marie, destined to the anonymity of her kitchen, became the Marie who went down in history.

Rascasse

John dory

Conger

26 dec

Bouillabaisse

Serves 6

PREPARATION TIME 1 HOUR
COOKING TIME 2 HOURS 30 MINUTES

2 John dory
2 rascasses (scorpion fish)
1 kg (2 lb 4 oz) rock fish
6 slices of conger eel
3 weevers (sand perches)
2 onions
1 garlic bulb
3 tomatoes
2 leeks
3 celery stalks
1 fennel bulb
80 ml (2½ fl oz/⅓ cup) olive oil
1 pinch chilli powder
1 pinch saffron threads
6 potatoes
salt and pepper

✳ For an easy rouille: *Process some bread softened in water, roasted red capsicum (pepper), a pinch of smoked hot paprika or cayenne, as much garlic as you can handle with olive oil and a little of the bouillabaisse broth to make a thick sauce.*

Clean and rinse all of the seafood. Peel and slice the onions. Crush the garlic. Dice the tomatoes. Slice the leeks, celery and fennel. In a large saucepan, sauté all of the vegetables in the olive oil for 10 minutes, add the rock fish, chilli and saffron, cover with 3 lîtres (105 fl oz) water and cook for 2 hours. Pass the whole mixture through a chinois, mashing the rockfish well, season. Peel the potatoes, cut them into large cubes and cook them for 10 minutes in the fish broth. Take out the potatoes, then poach the remaining seafood, starting with the thickest and ending with the thinnest. Serve the fish on the side with the potatoes accompanied by a *rouille*✳.

27 dec

Ray of sunshine tart

Serves 6

PREPARATION TIME 20 MINUTES
COOKING TIME 20 MINUTES

For the tart base:
200 g (7 oz/1⅓ cups) plain (all-purpose) flour
50 g (1¾ oz/½ cup) ground almonds
50 g (1¾ oz/¼ cup) sugar
100 g (3½ oz) lightly salted butter
pouring (whipping) cream
For the filling:
2 oranges
150 g (5½ oz) sugar
100 g (3½ oz) butter
1 tablespoon cornflour (cornstarch)
3 eggs

Preheat the oven to 180°C (350°F/Gas 4). Combine the flour, ground almonds, sugar and butter, and work this dough with the palm of your hand against the work bench. Add a little pouring cream to make the dough smooth, wrap in plastic wrap, and chill for 1 hour. Line a tart tin with the pastry, cook in the oven for 15 minutes.

To make the filling, zest and juice both of the oranges. Combine the sugar with the butter, juice and half of the zest, cook for 5 minutes over low heat. Combine the cornflour with the eggs, whisk, add the orange butter off the heat, whisk again. Spread the orange cream over the tart base*. Scatter over the remaining zest.

❋HOW SHOULD IT BE SERVED? *Serve well chilled, the filling will firm up.*

28 dec

Citrus salad with coconut milk

Serves 6

PREPARATION TIME 20 MINUTES
CHILLING TIME 1 HOUR

3 pink grapefruit
4 oranges
200 ml (7 fl oz) coconut milk
*2 tablespoons honey**

❋WHAT HONEY SHOULD I USE? *It depends on tastes, but chestnut honey will work very well.*

Remove the peel and pith from the fruit. Cut into segments. Combine the coconut milk with the honey. Combine the citrus segments, then pour over the coconut milk. Chill for 1 hour before serivng.

29 dec

Scallop kebabs

Serves 6

PREPARATION TIME 10 MINUTES
COOKING TIME 10 MINUTES

18 scallops
18 slices of speck, cartilage removed
80 g (2¾ oz) butter

❋WHY? WE'RE NOT USING IT? *The roe is often tough and doesn't have much flavour, you can always use it to make sauces.*

Remove the roe from the scallops*. Wrap each scallop in a slice of speck, then thread them onto kebab skewers. Cook under a hot grill (broiler) for 5 minutes on each side. Cook the butter until it is a lovely nutty (*noisette*) colour. Pour this butter over the kebabs. The speck should season the scallops.

MARIE & LÉON

eeny, meeny, spiny, mo ...

Brest and the ocean spray, the whole family is here, rounds of tarot cards until who knows what time, it's good to get together again.

Team Vachecrot is passing through, it's a pilgrimage to the cousins. Atmosphere: wood fire, rustic table. Dress code: relaxed cosy. Cider is a member of the party, sea tales are invited to dinner, the storm crashes around them, the waves get bigger. Theatrics are the order of the day, the blue caps come out, the smoking pipes, they let themselves get carried away ... The sea urchins attack in groups of six, their spines, geared to do damage, shine like razor blades in the sun. The tide is rising, the murky depths will soon swallow me up, I can no longer move, HELP ... « *Marie, Marie, are you okay? It looks like you dozed off, there's nothing like this iodine-rich air, you'll have another helping of sea urchins won't you?* »

*How do you cut and prepare sea urchin? *Ask your fishmonger. Otherwise, remove the spines with scissors, insert a pointed knife into the crown of the urchin and carefully cut around its circumference.*

30 dec
Sea urchins with vegetables

Serves 6
PREPARATION TIME 15 MINUTES
COOKING TIME 10 MINUTES

18 sea urchins
1 red capsicum (pepper)
3 celery stalks
3 bulb spring onions (scallions)
100 g (3½ oz) English spinach
3 French shallots (eschalots)
olive oil
100 ml (3½ fl oz) white wine
150 ml (5 fl oz) pouring (whipping) cream
Equipment:
wok

Remove all the spines from the sea urchins*: they're epilated like legs at the beginning of summer. Cut each urchin in half using scissors, collect the roes in a small strainer as well as the juice. Cut all of the vegetables into small cubes, sauté them for 5 minutes in the wok in some olive oil. Add the sea urchin juice and white wine, then reduce for 2 minutes. Strain the vegetables, keeping the cooking juices, add the cream to the juices and reduce for 2 minutes. Place a few vegetables into the sea urchin shells, place a few roes on top, pour over the cream.

MARIE & LÉON

dressing up to the nines on 31st

One more year behind us, another year in front of us. The velvet bow tie is once again brought out of the cupboard, the mothballs have saved its life, the white shirt is waiting for its moment to perfect the point of its collar, it's New Year's Eve. The silk dress with a floral pattern like Provence in June is taken out of its plastic, the strappy heels are highly likely to give blisters, it's New Year's Eve. Marie and Léon are playing it high-class tonight — « *Tonight, we're going out* », tonight it's the restaurant, the kitchen is left behind, the gas is turned off, the saucepans are put away. The kitchen lies dormant, it's a day off. Marie and Léon will be kicking up their heels until who-knows-o'clock — tango, *canapés* ... waltzing, lobster ... rock, *capon* ... slow dancing, *semifreddo* ... It's 3 am, the Champagne bottle's empty, it's time to go home. But what will we eat tomorrow?

31 dec
Time to drink, not to eat

It's been a whole year of cooking, well, today we're released from duties. Now we're going to get ourselves invited out, have a big slap-up meal, make the most of it ... Champagne every step of the way!

Piscine (The Swimming Pool): Champagne, ice-cubes, fresh fruit ... You can easily drown.

Oulalasatape (The Wotanokout): ⅓ Macallan, ⅔ Champagne, 1 dash of grenadine.

Tucroisqcédoux (The Yuthinkitsweet): Juice of 1 lemon, 1 teaspoon soft brown sugar, Champagne.

Jyreviens (The Illbeback): ¼ Cointreau, ¼ Cognac, ½ Champagne.

Indexes
#1 by ingredient
#2 by type of dish

index #01
by ingredient

index #02
by type of dish

index #02
by type of dish

Published in 2010 by Murdoch Books Pty Limited
First published in 2009 by Marabout (Hachette Livre)

Murdoch Books Australia
Pier 8/9,
23 Hickson Road
Millers Point NSW 2000
Phone: +61 (0) 2 8220 2000
Fax: +61 (0) 2 8220 2558
www.murdochbooks.com.au

Murdoch Books UK Limited
Erico House, 6th Floor
93–99 Upper Richmond Road
Putney, London SW15 2TG
Phone: +44 (0) 20 8785 5995
Fax: +44 (0) 20 8785 5985
www.murdochbooks.co.uk

Chief Executive: Juliet Rogers
Publishing Director: Kay Scarlett

Project Manager: Belinda So
Editor: Jacqueline Blanchard
English Translation: Melissa McMahon
Production: Joan Beal

Copyright © Hachette Livre / Marabout 2009

National Library of Australia Cataloguing-in-Publication Data
Author: Reynaud, Stéphane.
Title: Stéphane Reynaud's 365 Reasons to Sit Down to Eat.
ISBN: 978-1-74196-919-1 (hbk.)
Notes: Includes index.
Subjects: Cookery.
Dewey Number: 641.5

Printed and bound by Butler Tanner and Dennis Ltd, Frome and London

IMPORTANT: Those who might be at risk from the effects of salmonella poisoning (the elderly, pregnant women,
young children and those suffering from immune deficiency diseases) should consult their doctor with any concerns
about eating raw eggs.

OVEN GUIDE: You may find cooking times vary depending on the oven you are using. For fan-forced ovens,
as a general rule, set the oven temperature to 20°C (35°F) lower than indicated in the recipe.